HERALDRY

Brudenell tablet at Stonton Wyville church, Leicestershire

HERALDRY

For the Local Historian and Genealogist

S T E P H E N   F R I A R

SUTTON PUBLISHING

First published in the United Kingdom in 1992 by
Alan Sutton Publishing Limited, an imprint of
Sutton Publishing Limited · Phoenix Mill · Thrupp
Stroud · Gloucestershire · GL5 2BU

Paperback edition, with corrections, first published in 1996

Reprinted in 1997

British Library Cataloguing in Publication Data

Friar, Stephen
Heraldry for the local historian and genealogist.
929.6

ISBN 0-7509-1085-2

*Cover illustration: banners in St George's Chapel, Windsor
(reproduced by courtesy of the Dean and Canons of Windsor)*

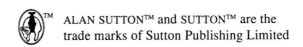 ALAN SUTTON™ and SUTTON™ are the
trade marks of Sutton Publishing Limited

Typeset in 10/12 Times.
Typesetting and origination by
Sutton Publishing Limited.
Printed in Great Britain by
WBC Limited, Bridgend.

. . . of the moldwarp and the ant,
Of the Dreamer Merlin and his prophecies,
And of a dragon and a finless fish,
A clip-wing'd griffin and a moulten raven,
A couching lion and a ramping cat . . .

Shakespeare, *1 Henry IV*, III. i

CONTENTS

LIST OF COLOUR PLATES

ACKNOWLEDGEMENTS

The author acknowledges with grateful thanks the assistance of the following people in the preparation of this book:

John Allen, Jennifer Beaumont, Tony Birks-Hay, Mrs M.E. Burcket, John Campbell-Kease, Peter Clifford, John Coales, Hugh Collinson, Cathy Constant, Dorchester Town Council, Barbara Ferguson, John Ferguson, Dennis E. Gibbs, Brian Gittos, Peter Greenhill, Chris Harrold, James Hervey-Bathurst, the Revd Derek Hillier, Andrew Jamieson, Anthony L. Jones, Louise Kirby, John Lancaster, Joan Langhorne, Alex Law, Brian North Lee, John Mennell, Michael G. Messer, Leslie Milton, David Mounce, Mrs E. Nixon, Malcolm Norris, Tony Seward, A. Silvanus-Davies, Stephen Slater, C.E.J. Smith, Peter Summers, Norman Tait, Nan Taylor, E.N. (Pete) Taylor, Roger Thorp, John Titterton, Anne Watts, Oliver Watts, Geoffrey Wheeler and Lt.-Col. J.L. Yeatman.

The author and publisher would like to thank the following for their permission to reproduce illustrations:

Alphabet & Image/A&C Black 18 (courtesy of D.H.B. Chesshyre and P.B. Spurrier), 63, 75, 87, 107, 134, 164 (photos A. Birks-Hay), plate 1 (photo. Derek Forss), plate 21 (photo. Jim Kershaw); B.T. Batsford Ltd. 71, 84, 85, 91, 92, 94, 108, 115, 122, 133, 136, 137, 162, 173, 213, 244; Bodleian Library, Oxford 54 (Ms. Ashmole 604), 55 (Ms. Ashmole 604), 58 (Ms. Lat. Misc. e. 86); the British Library 56 (Ms. Add 37340, fo. 10 v), 219 (Ms. Add 40742, fo. 6), plate 3 (Ms. Royal 18 A XII, fo. 49), plate 5 (Ms. Add. 48976 no. 17); Mrs Burcket of Isel, Cumbria plate 22c (photo. Barbara Ferguson); The Burrell Collection, Glasgow 98; John Campbell-Kease 52, 230, 241, plate 18; Hugh Collinson iii, 67, 76 (bottom), 77, 95, 101, 131 (bottom), 139, 146, 165 (top), 166, 208, plate 9c, plate 11, plate 13c, plate 19b, c, d, plate 20c; Dorchester Town Council 14; Dorset County Museum, Dorchester 87, 164; Barbara Ferguson plate 22c; John Ferguson v, 170 (drawings), 224, 238; Stephen Friar 73, 97 (top), 80, 89, 116, 141, 145, 153, 165 (bottom), plate 16, plate 22a; The Worshipful Company of Goldsmiths 156; Peter Greenhill plate 7 (painting), plate 8; The Heraldry Society 68, 125 (from *The Colour of*

Heraldry, The Heraldry Society, 1958); James Hervey-Bathurst plate 12, plate 22d (photos Stephen Slater © Eastnor Castle Estates); Horsington House Hotel 145 (photo. Stephen Friar); Andrew Jamieson plate 17; Brian North Lee 60 (photo. Alex Law); John Mennell 65, 69, 72, 103, 111, 172, 240; Michael G. Messer 140 (bottom); L.E. Milton 140 (top), 227, plate 9a; the National Gallery, London plate 4; the National Trust 66, 160, 162, plate 16, plate 22b; Malcolm Norris 119, 126 (top); Stephen Slater 26, 88, 120, 121, 143, 144, 148, 149, 210, 223, plate 9b, plate 10, plate 12, plate 13d, plate 14, plate 15, plate 19a, plate 22; C.E.J. Smith plate 20a; Norman Tait plate 20b; The Worshipful Company of Tallow Chandlers plate 6; West Dorset District Council 170 (drawing: John Ferguson); Oliver Watts 66, 74, 102, 154, plate 22b; the Dean and Chapter of Westminster 50 (Ms. 39, fo. 1), 86, 92; Geoffrey Wheeler 5, 43, 44, 46, 47, 48, 70, 82, 83, 90, 93, 100, 110, 112, 113, 114, 117, 123, 124, 126 (bottom), 127, 128, 129, 130, 131, 132 (top), 142, 160, 167, 168, 220, 222, plate 2, plate 13a; Lt.-Col. J.L. Yeatman plate 22a (photo. Stephen Friar)

All line drawings are by Andrew Jamieson with the exception of those by John Ferguson on pages v and 170. Colour plate 7 is by Peter Greenhill and plate 17 by Andrew Jamieson.

INTRODUCTION

In recent years genealogy and local history have become major leisure activities. But, despite the fact that heraldry occupies a potent place in our historical perspective, many historians and genealogists continue to pay scant regard to a subject which was held in high esteem by the medieval and Tudor establishment. Coats of arms, badges and other armorial devices are ubiquitous in the architecture and decoration of domestic and ecclesiastical buildings, in illuminated manuscripts and official documents and on seals, monuments and memorials. Such devices provide a rich source of genealogical and historical information.

Many students are deterred by the apparent complexity of heraldic language and convention. But these are not difficult to master, and the rewards will fully justify a few hours spent in learning the rudiments of blazon, cadency and marshalling (see Chapters Seven and Eight).

Throughout the text, heraldic terms have been picked out in italic letters and may be found in the Glossary and Index at the back of the book. The colours most commonly used are *Argent* (silver), *Azure* (blue), *Gules* (red), *Purpure* (purple), *Sable* (black) and *Vert* (green). To avoid confusion I have tended to use the term *Gold* instead of *Or*, though the latter is more likely to be encountered in blazons (heraldic descriptions). It should also be noted that, when colours are depicted, white is often substituted for silver and yellow for gold.

Suggestions for further reading are listed in Appendix I and addresses referred to in the text will be found in Appendix II.

Stephen Friar
Caundle Wake, Dorset
December, 1991

One

HERALDRY: AN HISTORICAL PERSPECTIVE

And the children of Israel . . . pitched by their standards,
and so they set forward, every one after their families, according
to the house of their fathers.

Numbers 2:34

Heraldry is concerned with all matters relating to the duties and responsibilities of the kings, heralds and pursuivants of arms – known collectively as the heralds. As such it is frequently (and erroneously) used as a synonym for armory: that aspect of a herald's work which is concerned with the marshalling and regulation of coats of arms and other hereditary devices and insignia according to established conventions, practices and precedents. Confusingly, the word 'heraldry' is also used to describe the depiction of armorial devices in a variety of forms including documents, memorials, stained glass and carved stone.

Origins

The antiquity of what we now call armory is evident in the above passage from the Old Testament in which the children of Israel assembled beneath their household flags, reminiscent of the nobility and their retainers of the high Middle Ages. In ancient Egypt every territorial district had its standard which was used both as a point of muster for its military forces and as a device by which its authority was recognized. Egyptian and Assyrian standards were, in fact, poles with cross-pieces to which were affixed various representational devices, the images of local gods, for example. Early Roman standards similarly carried religious and martial symbols, such as the open hand of military command, and even portraits. Later, devices were adopted to represent both specific units of the Roman army and functional designations. The eagle, for example, became the device of the legion and was accompanied on a legion's standard by its own honours and emblems.

During the so-called Dark Ages the popularity of the modelled or rigid standard declined though the famous Dragon Standard of

ADPRELIVM:CONTRA:ḣAROLD

Examples of lance pennons in
the Bayeux Tapestry

Wessex, which was carried at the Battle of Assingdon in 1016 and
raised on Senlac Ridge in 1066, was probably of the earlier rigid
'vane' type. Harold II is believed to have adopted a personal
banner known as the Fighting Man and the *Anglo Saxon Chronicle*
tells of '. . . the conflict of banners' and how, at the battle of
Brumby, 'the sons of Edward . . . hewed their banners with the
wrecks of their hammers'. Bede also writes of King Edwin of East
Anglia whose banners '. . . were not only borne before him in
battle, but even in time of peace, when he rode about his cities,
towns or provinces . . . the standard bearer was wont to go before
him.'

The majority of flags depicted in the Bayeux Tapestry are of
cloth: small, square or semi-circular and with a number of 'tails'
attached to the fly. That the devices borne on these flags were
territorial or even personal symbols has long been a matter of
dispute, but it is generally acknowledged that the Normans had
not, at that time, adopted the proto-armorial system which is
evident in the lance pennons of their Flemish allies.

It is most likely, therefore, that the origins of English and
Scottish armory are to be found not in Normandy (the Normans
were of mixed Scandinavian and Frankish descent), but in the
system adopted by certain ruling families descended from the
Emperor Charlemagne, the military and political colossus who
ruled the Frankish Empire of northern Europe from 768 to 814.
These families perpetuated much of the administrative organization of the Carolingian Empire, including the use of dynastic
and territorial emblems on seals, coinage, customs stamps and

flags, indeed 'wherever officialdom needed to identify itself both in peace and war' (Beryl Platts). There is evidence to suggest that these devices were common to families or groups linked by blood or feudal tenure, and were of necessity hereditary. With the redistribution of lands following the Norman Conquest, the cadets in England of Flemish families who were of Carolingian descent, and the devices used by them, became integrated in Anglo-Norman society.

During the first Crusade, only thirty years after the Conquest, the mass cavalry charge of mail-clad knights remained the standard tactic of warfare. Order was maintained in the ensuing mêlée by the use of mustering flags bearing the personal devices of commanders and it is clear that these were sufficiently distinctive to be recognized, even in the heat of battle. It is likely that they also possessed a peacetime function – that of marking territory and symbolizing authority – and that the devices used for this purpose also came to be engraved on seals by which documents were authenticated.

Clearly, those English magnates who owed military service to the king, and therefore were required to present themselves from time to time with their armed retinues, found it convenient to display devices by which they and their following could be recognized. But in practice very few of those who held land by military service were obliged to provide more than one or two knights, and during the twelfth century even these fees were progressively subdivided so that, in many cases, land came to be held by the service of one-third, one-quarter or even one-twelfth of a knight. Indeed, not all land was held by military service. Sir William d'Aubigny, Earl of Arundel, held his vast estates by grand serjeanty (specifically, the duty to serve as butler at coronation festivities), for example.

Why then, when so few could demonstrate any military reason for adopting armorial devices, did the practice spread so rapidly throughout Europe in the mid-twelfth century ?

The answer almost certainly lies in what is now known as the Twelfth Century Renaissance, a movement which, between the eleventh and thirteenth centuries, transformed the cultural face of western Europe. The exuberance of spirit inspired by this movement expressed itself in a self-confident delight in personal adornment and visual decoration of which the adoption of armorial symbols and colours was an obvious manifestation. Promoted by the military households (the *familia regis*) of the Angevin kings, popularized by the tournament, communicated throughout Europe by itinerant knights, minstrels and scholars, it was inevitable that the principles of armory should eventually be consolidated as an essential element of the law of arms (see below). The Twelfth Century Renaissance also inspired the notion of chivalry: the code of courage and courtesy which were the ideals of medieval knighthood. It is not without significance that those

English sovereigns who, by example, encouraged the development of heraldry also delighted in the chivalric legends of Arthur and his confraternity of knights – Henry III, who was familiar with Geoffrey of Monmouth's *History of the Kings of Britain*, written in *c.* 1138; Edward I who, in 1278, visited Glastonbury Abbey where a magnificent black marble tomb had been erected over the reputed remains of Arthur and Guinevere and who established the festive pageants and tournaments known as 'Round Tables'; Edward III who, in 1348, founded the Order of the Garter; and Henry VII, whose claim to the English throne included descent from Arthur through the Welsh princes and who ordained that his son, also Arthur, should be born at Winchester.

By the beginning of the thirteenth century, admission to the tournament was established as the prerogative of the knightly class. Heralds were attached to royal or magnatial households as advisers and emissaries and it was they who were responsible for arranging and supervising tournaments: they determined the eligibility of participants and declaimed their prowess, marshalled the contestants and adjudicated at the mêlée. The heralds thereby acquired an expertise which was peculiarly their own. This was concerned, not only with the management of ceremonial and protocol, but also with the ordering and recording of personal devices used on seals, at tournaments and, increasingly, in warfare and because it was they who exercised this expertise, it became known as 'heraldry'. Theirs was the motivating force which enabled armory to develop systematically: it was they who devised its conventions and terminology, and it was they who benefited most from the approbation of the medieval establishment.

Thus far no mention has been made of devices on shields and yet it was the shield that was to become the essential component of the stylized coat of arms and, therefore, the basis of armory.

There is little evidence to support the popular perception that, from the mid-twelfth century, devices were used on shield and surcoat (hence 'coat of arms') in order that heavily armoured knights should be identified more easily in battle. Indeed, common sense suggests that the mud and debris of warfare would quickly obliterate the battered surfaces of shields, rendering them unrecognizable. The earliest recorded seal showing an armorial shield dates from 1136, and thereafter the increasing importance of the shield as a vehicle for armorial display had more to do with the development of armory as a well regulated system than with military expediency. The shield was itself a symbol of the mounted warrior and, while the devices placed upon it were peculiar to the individual, the fact that they were carried on a representation of a shield served to emphasize the status of armiger (Latin *armiger* – an armour-bearer).

Clearly, it was considered both convenient and desirable that an heir, on coming to his estate, should adopt the same device as his

Effigy of William Longespee,
Earl of Salisbury

father as a symbol of familial and feudal continuity. Although
there is evidence to suggest that in northern Europe proto-heraldic
devices were often adopted by succeeding generations of the same
family, the emergence of an hereditary system based on the shield
(in other words, armory as it is now defined) is said to date from
1127 when Henry I of England invested his son-in-law, Geoffrey
Plantagenet, with a blue shield charged with gold lions. The same
shield later appears on the tomb at Salisbury Cathedral of Geoffrey's bastard grandson, William Longespee, Earl of Salisbury
(d. 1226) and the device would, therefore, seem to have acquired
an hereditary significance.

The earliest shields of arms were simple and uncluttered and
consisted for the most part of geometrical shapes derived from the
practice of decorating the raised ribs, bosses and struts of early
wooden shields: simple charges such as stars, scallop shells and
martlets (a small bird, possibly a swift, depicted without legs), or
objects which alluded to a surname or title, often by means of a
visual pun (known as canting arms or *armes parlantes*) such as the
seven winnowing fans depicted in the brass of Sir Robert de Septvans
(d. 1306) at Chartham, Kent (see Chapter Five). Many early shields
of arms were of similar design; the thirteenth-century Herald Roll
identifies 190 shields of which 45 bore lions, for example.

Particular motifs were often adopted to signify feudal relationships. The arms of Luterell (*Gold a Bend between six*

Martlets Sable), for example, were used by the de Furnival, d'Eccleshall, de Wadsley, de Wortley and de Mounteney families, each coat 'differenced', by means of a minor variation of colour and design, to signify seigniorial affiliation. But this was not an invariable practice: the seemingly ubiquitous arms of *three Piles conjoined in base* were used by John le Scot, Earl of Chester (gold with three red *piles*) and by the families of Ridel (gold with three black *piles*), Basset (gold with three red *piles*, all within a black border), de Bryan (gold with three blue *piles*) and Wrottesley (gold with three green *piles*). In such circumstances the researcher has to determine whether a feudal or familial association or dependency actually existed and, if the arms are uncoloured, to ascertain to which armiger they refer. In the example only the Wrottesley and Basset families are known to have been connected. (The foregoing arms are illustrated in colour, plate 7.)

The Age of Chivalry

Throughout the Middle Ages, armory was considered to be an essential element of the *ius militaris*, the law of arms which in western and central Europe prescribed standards of military conduct founded on notions of chivalry and Christian ideals. Contemporary treatises on the law of arms invariably devoted some detail to armory: perhaps the best known being *L'Arbre des Batailles*, which was compiled between 1382 and 1387 by the Benedictine monk and Roman lawyer, Honore Bonet. Chivalry was both the code of courage and courtesy, which were the ideals of medieval knighthood, and the system of knighthood itself.

The terms 'chivalry' and 'cavalry' share the same linguistic root, confirming that knighthood was the prerogative of the mounted warrior. His effectiveness in battle, and thereby his reputation, was greatly enhanced by the development from the eighth century of the stirrup and saddle-bow, which provided both increased manoeuvrability and stability in the saddle.

During the Twelfth Century Renaissance this exclusive class adopted a code of conduct which aspired to the highest ideals though, as history has shown, few of its members succeeded in attaining them. The code comprised three elements:

Belief in the Church and its defence, especially against the heathen as manifested in the Crusades.
Courage, and loyalty towards a knight's companions, his feudal lord and sovereign.
Respect, pity and generosity in the defence of the weak, the poor and women.

To these were added the notion of romantic love which was to inspire much of the literature of chivalry: Roland in France,

Arthur in Britain, El Cid in Spain and the Minnesänger in Germany.

The pageantry of the tournament was the perfect manifestation of the chivalric ethos. Participation, both in the tournament itself and in the attendant festivities, was restricted to those of knightly rank and was enormously expensive. Indeed, throughout the Middle Ages, the cost of maintaining a horse and equipment was such that membership of the warrior élite presupposed a man of some position and estate. It is also clear that the use of hereditary devices on shields was considered to be the exclusive right of this knightly class. Pride in the possession of armorial devices, and of the status of armiger that such a privilege implied, was undoubtedly of greater significance in the development of armory than was its practical application in the field of battle.

The early chivalric orders were fraternities of like-minded men of the appropriate social class bound together in common purpose; that of the Knights Hospitaller, for example, was to succour pilgrims in the Holy Land. Of course, many members of the early crusading orders were simply adventurers, often the younger sons of knights with little prospect of inheritance and, no doubt, motivated as much by opportunism as by religious or chivalric idealism.

Although modelled on the principles of chivalric egalitarianism and humility, the later medieval orders were essentially élitist, membership being the ultimate reward for loyal service to the sovereign or utilized for the purposes of international diplomacy. Of these, the Most Noble Order of the Garter was pre-eminent. The twin strands of the Arthurian chivalric tradition and the exclusive nature of the tournament are evident in the order's foundation, though even today there exists some doubt as to precisely when this was for the original records of the order, up to the year 1416, are lost. The fourteenth-century chronicler Jean Froissart asserts that it was founded in 1344 but it is unlikely that the order would have been established before 1346, the year in which the Black Prince and several of his founder-contemporaries were knighted. The treasury accounts for the prince dating from November 1348 record his gift of 'twenty-four garters to the knights of the Society of the Garter' and it seems likely that the order was quite casually formed, perhaps at a tournament at which twenty-four knights, in two bands of twelve, one under the king, the other under the prince, confronted each other in the tourney. In 1348 the Black Prince was eighteen and several other founder knights were equally youthful: the earls of March and Salisbury were about twenty, Courtney and Burghersh were twenty-two and the king himself no more than thirty-seven. Thus, to begin with, the order was '. . . a Society, Fellowship, College of Knights', a brotherhood of young men in which all were equal 'to represent how they ought to be united in all Chances and various Turns of Fortune, co-partners in both Peace and War, assistant to one another in all serious and dangerous Exploits and through the whole Course of their Lives to show Fidelity and Friendliness towards one another.'

The symbol of the blue garter is said to have been suggested by an incident at a ball at Calais in the autumn of 1347 when the young Countess of Salisbury, Joan of Kent (later to be Princess of Wales), dropped her garter, which the king picked up and tied below his knee with the now famous words, *Honi soit qui mal y pense* – 'Shame on him who thinks evil of it' – and a promise that the garter would become highly honoured. There may be an element of truth in this story, but the garter was not an exclusively female accoutrement and it seems likely that it was adopted because of its suitability as a device (in stylized form) which could also be worn at court or on horseback.

The informal creation of the Round Table after the great tournament at Windsor in 1344 was translated, probably on St George's Day 1348, into the Order of the Garter – twenty-four young men plus the king and his eldest son – founder knights 'foreshadowing a distinguished line of noble successors throughout the history of English chivalry'.

Livery and Maintenance

The practice of maintaining and protecting retainers in return for domestic and military services was common throughout medieval Europe and was a characteristic of fourteenth- and fifteenth-century England, when a magnate's influence was judged by the number of men wearing his heraldic badge and liveries and his ability to protect them when necessary in the courts of law.

Political stability depended on royal patronage and on the support of magnates, such as Richard Nevill, Earl of Warwick, 'The Kingmaker' (1428–71), who had at their disposal huge retinues of mercenaries whose allegiance was bought through the practice of livery and maintenance. More than any other factor, livery and maintenance facilitated the internecine wars of the period, now known as the Wars of the Roses.

The dangers inherent in the system were recognized by successive sovereigns who attempted to legislate against abuses, thereby reducing the effectiveness of the nobles' private armies. But it was not until 1540 that the practice was finally suppressed, the private army effectively abolished and the Middle Ages brought to a close. (See Chapter Nine.)

The Heralds' Visitations

In the high Middle Ages brilliantly emblazoned chantry chapels, memorials, tombs and window glass declared a magnate's magnificence; his retainers mustered at his standards, fought in battle beneath his guidons, and, by their liveries and household badges, proclaimed his authority.

In 1417 the Crown sought to forbid the bearing of arms without its authority and the heralds were given the task of regulating the use of armorial bearings. Nevertheless, 'the bearing of coat armor' was so widely abused that it became necessary to ascertain precisely who was entitled to use arms and the English kings of arms were required to survey and record the devices and pedigrees of those claiming armigerous status and to correct any irregularities. Occasional tours of inquiry were held but it was not until the sixteenth century that heralds' visitations were undertaken in a regular and systematic way.

In 1530, Clarenceux King of Arms was authorized to travel throughout his province (south of the River Trent) and to enter all dwellings and churches to survey and record whatever arms he might find and 'to put down or otherwise deface at his discretion . . . in plate, jewels, paper, parchment, windows, gravestones and monuments or elsewhere wheresoever they may be set or placed' those arms he found to be assumed unlawfully. He was also to denounce by proclamation all those who had usurped arms or titles such as knight, esquire or gentleman.

In practice, it was the heralds and the county sheriffs and their officers who conducted the visitations once the Royal Commission had been presented to the High Sheriff by the King of Arms. The High Sheriff would then obtain from the bailiff of each hundred within his county a list of all persons using titles or arms who would then be summoned to appear before the herald or his deputy at a specified time and place. Each claimant was required to furnish an exemplification of his arms and the authority by which the arms were borne. This might be a pedigree (signifying ancient usage), a document confirming a right to arms, or a grant of arms (by means of letters patent), often on payment of a hefty fine. The herald would then record the pedigree and sketch the arms in sufficient detail for them to be transferred at a later date to the manuscript volumes which now comprise the Library of Visitation Books at the College of Arms. If the arms and pedigree were found to be in order, often by comparison with the records of an earlier visitation, then they were confirmed. If they were lawful but in some way defective, corrections were made and recorded. If the herald was unable to approve the claim, the usurper was required to renounce any right to the title or arms and to sign a disclaimer. His name was then added to the public list of those whose claims had been refused. Those who ignored the directive could be summoned to appear before the Earl Marshal in the Court of Chivalry.

Ancient User was a legal claim based on constant use or custom since 'time immemorial', otherwise known as 'time out of mind'. In common law this is deemed to be 1189, although in the Court of

Chivalry it has been argued that the Norman Conquest of 1066 should be regarded as the limit of legal memory. During the heralds' visitations of the seventeenth century a claim with proof of a prescriptive use of arms from the beginning of the reign of Elizabeth I (1558) was considered to be sufficient.

Encouraged by the visitations, the Tudor period witnessed a proliferation of grants of arms and crests to the new establishment: gentlemen who were concerned more with the administration of the state and the development of commerce than with the tournament or battlefield. The ancient nobility, jealous of their status as armigers, reacted by adding supporters to their arms, often chimerical creatures which had previously been used as badges or on seals and later as crests.

In England major visitations took place throughout the country in 1580, 1620 and 1666, minor visitations being conducted at other times. The practice was discontinued at the accession of William of Orange in 1688 when it was considered inadvisable to draw attention to those who remained loyal to 'the old ways'.

The original heralds' visitation notebooks were used as a basis for manuscript copies, most of which have been published. These are a very useful source of early pedigrees, though it should be borne in mind that they may occasionally contain unauthorized additions or alterations which may not be immediately apparent. Several of these volumes have been published by the Harleian Society and county record societies and many of the manuscripts on which the printed versions are based are held in the British Library in London. There are also good collections of printed visitation records at the Guildhall Library, London, the Society of Genealogists and the Institute of Heraldic and Genealogical Studies in Canterbury.

In Ireland, the social upheavals which followed the plantation schemes of the sixteenth and seventeenth centuries produced many changes in Irish society, not the least of which was an influx of English and Scottish families, many of whom were armigerous. The first Irish visitation took place in 1568 and was conducted by Ulster King of Arms whose office had been created just sixteen years earlier. Not only did the Irish visitations record and confirm arms and titles, they also served to establish the claims of gentry families previously unknown to the Ulster Office. However, the total number of entries of the combined Irish visitations from 1568 to 1649 is less than three hundred.

Of greater value to historians is the series of around three thousand funeral certificates dating from the 1560s to the 1690s. At that time heirs or executors were legally obliged to provide the Ulster Office with a certificate on which were recorded the arms and pedigree of a deceased armiger. The original visitation and funeral certificate manuscripts are held by the Chief Herald of Ireland, and copies of both are deposited with the College of Arms in London.

In Scotland, Lord Lyon King of Arms has generally exercised a greater degree of legal authority over matters armorial than his brother kings of arms in England and Ireland and for this reason visitations have been undertaken for specific purposes and in pursuit of his statutory duties as head of the heraldic executive in Scotland.

Heraldry in Wales

Welsh armory is fundamentally different in that its purpose is to proclaim ancestry. The majority of the Welsh nation consists of a pedigreed population, a distinct caste, descended from the native Welsh aristocracy, warrior farmers and *advenae*, the Norman and English feudal lords who held lands in the Welsh Marches (often described as 'adventurers' in Welsh manuscripts), together with the retainers, officials, merchants and burgesses who accompanied them.

The ancient social system of the Welsh, in which so many rights and obligations were dependent on membership of a tribe, conditioned them to regard a pedigree as of the utmost importance. In Wales there was no such person as an 'armigerous gentleman' as there was in England, for a man was 'gentle' by virtue of his genealogy and gentility followed the blood.

Although the Welsh had been acquainted with medieval armory, it was not until the early Tudor period that they produced a system. Those Welshmen who already bore arms were assumed to have inherited them from tribal ancestors while new arms were attributed to the ancestors of other, non-armigerous families. For example, the numerous descendants of Hywel Dda who lived in the tenth century, those of Cadwaladr who lived in the seventh, of Cunedda who lived in the fifth and of Beli Mawr who probably never lived at all, all received retrospective coats of arms which they hurriedly registered with the English heralds of the new Tudor dynasty.

The Heraldry of the Decadence

During the late and post-Tudor period (now known as the Heraldry of the Decadence), armorial practice degenerated. 'By the sixteenth century the heralds had taught all men that the shield of arms was a symbol and voucher of gentility, and that, without one, wealth was ignoble' (Oswald Barron). The practical application of armory in the battlefield and tournament was replaced by an almost obsessional preoccupation with pomp and panoply, exaggerated ceremonial and 'parchment heraldry'. Coats of arms became stylized, extravagant and often singularly unattractive and it was not until the late twentieth century that there was a revival of heraldic art in the medieval tradition.

In such a climate, purveyors of illegal coats of arms were legion: in 1577 a warrant was issued for the arrest of one William Dawkyns for impersonating a queen's officer, for selling coats of arms and compiling false pedigrees. He was brought before Star Chamber and was sentenced to be whipped and to lose his ears, as well as to be pilloried in every shire where he had transacted his 'noisome business'. Even the heralds were perceived by many to be venal. Ben Jonson, in his *Every Man Out of His Humour* (1599) describes how one Sogliardo procured for himself a coat of arms and the accompanying style of gentleman by paying substantial fees to a herald who devised for him arms depicting a headless (brainless) swine. Jonson was clearly irritated by the prospect of so many counterfeit gentlemen swaggering about and sporting bogus arms to which they were not entitled. In 1616, Garter King of Arms and York Herald were summoned before the Earl Marshal's commissioners and committed to the Marshalsea for facilitating the granting of arms to one 'Gregory Brandon of London, Gentleman' who, it transpired, was the common hangman of the City of London. The felony was further compounded when it was discovered that Garter, the senior officer of arms, had failed to recognize that Brandon's new coat comprised the combined arms of the sovereigns of Aragon and Brabant! The Lord Chamberlain expressed the wish 'that this their Durance might make the one more Wise, and the other more honest.'

Jacobean society was obsessed with the trappings of rank and, therefore, with matters armorial. In the first half of the seventeenth century, notions of medieval chivalry were expressed most dogmatically in numerous widely-read treatises on armory and 'handbooks' for gentlemen. Contemporary literature contains copious references both to the insignia of chivalry and to the metaphysics of honour, and it would appear that these meant far more to the Jacobean reader than is generally acknowledged. Many writers, by using 'lively images', hoped that 'the ruder multitude might, even by their sense, learn to know virtue, and discern what to detest' (Joseph Hall, *Characters of Vertues and Vices*, 1608). These 'character books' were concerned with the Jacobean belief that each class had its own place in the social order and that to abuse this ideal was a sin which required exposure and admonition by ridicule.

In seventeenth-century armory, this preoccupation with form and with the 'correctness' of society, is reflected in a proliferation of armorial 'rules' and an almost obsessional concern for the niceties of blazon (the terminology of armory). It is also evident in the increasing complexity of marshalling and in the stylized funeral heraldry and monuments of the period.

Much has been written on the subject of 'ceremonies of degradation' visited upon disgraced members of the knightly class. But the truth is that in England recorded cases of the formal degradation of knights are few in number and, before 1621, only three instances occur in the records of the College of Arms. In that year Sir Francis Michell was, upon proven charges of corruption, proclaimed '. . . no knight but an arrant knave' and, at a ceremony in Westminster Hall, his spurs were hacked from his heels, his sword belt severed and his weapon broken over his head by the heralds. Earlier traditions, for which there is little evidence, suggest that the ceremony also included the breaking of a knight's shield and the removal of his surcoat which was replaced by a paper version on which his arms were depicted in reverse.

The Eighteenth and Nineteenth Centuries

The last decades of the seventeenth century witnessed the ending of the heralds' visitations in England and Wales and the introduction of a requirement that all new grants of arms should be authorized in writing by the Earl Marshal. After 1676, prospective grantees were required to be holders of public office or able to produce certificates, signed by two gentlemen, confirming that they were themselves of that condition and were well affected to the government. As a result, few grants were made: an average of only eight in each of the years between 1704 and 1707, for example.

The Georgian period (1714–1830) was, of course, notable for the revival of classicism, particularly in architecture. Monuments and ornamentation reflected classical styles and contained minimal armorial references: medievalism sitting uncomfortably alongside classical eloquence. Significantly, a royal warrant of 1747 forbade the use of a commander's personal arms for military purposes, 'No colonel to put his arms, crest, devices or livery on any part of the appointments of the regiment under his command.'

The Industrial Revolution created a new élite, anxious to acquire the trappings of gentility and with a voracious appetite for matters genealogical and armorial. There was a substantial increase in the number of grants of arms made in the late eighteenth and nineteenth centuries, accompanied by a plethora of heraldic 'manuals' and a quite extraordinary level of genealogical activity exemplified by the works of Sir Bernard Burke. The Gothic Revival inspired a return to medieval decorative forms of which heraldry was a significant element, a tradition which was continued into the twentieth century by ecclesiastical architects such as Sir Ninian Comper (1864–1960) whose restored church at Wimborne St Giles in Dorset glows with a profusion of heraldic glass and decoration.

Armory prospered in England because, from the fifteenth century, those who administered the system were encouraged to recognize social change. Unlike their European counterparts, the Lancastrian kings of arms were permitted to grant arms to 'eminent men' and the Tudors adapted the system to mark both status and social change. Grants of arms from the fifteenth century onwards provide strong evidence of social mobility and appear to support the traditional theory that the upper levels of English society were readily accessible to self-made men.

Civic and Ecclesiastical Armory

Civic armory in Britain dates from the late twelfth century when officials of boroughs and towns made use of seals carrying devices. Initially, these were rarely depicted on shields and were simply religious or other emblems of local significance, or sometimes seigniorial devices indicative of feudal allegiance or benefaction, contained within an inscribed border.

With the gradual development of corporate authority in the Middle Ages came a corresponding desire to assert corporate identity in a form which could be equated with that of the feudal magnate, and by the fourteenth century many towns, guilds and corporations had adopted the devices of their seals as coats of arms, simply by depicting them in colour on a shield, and sometimes rearranging charges to conform with armorial conventions.

The seal of Dorchester, Dorset

In the sixteenth and seventeenth centuries several corporations took advantage of the heralds' visitations to record their previously unauthorized arms. Others retained their original emblems, many of which are still used today: the triple-towered castle of Dorchester in Dorset, for example, which is not a coat of arms but, with its royal references, is derived from the town's ancient seal. By 1700 ninety English towns and cities had acquired armorial bearings. Of these, twenty-seven were royal or seigniorial devices; eighteen bore religious emblems; eighteen included castles and seventeen maritime references such as ships. It is clear, therefore, that the majority of these early civic coats of arms derived (in part, at least) from even earlier seals.

The use of unauthorized coats of arms flourished in the nineteenth century, encouraged by the ostentatious excesses of civic pride and corporate rivalry. Crewe, for example, was but a single farmhouse before the arrival of the London and North Western Railway in 1841. To emphasize its newly-acquired civic status after the coming of the railway the council adopted bogus 'arms' which included a canal boat, a stage coach, a packhorse, a pillion and a railway locomotive! Even properly authorized civic arms are generally more complex and contain a greater variety of charges than is usual in personal arms. Such devices are usually intended to represent historical as well as contemporary features of a civic authority and there is very often an understandable desire to include too much information, thereby detracting from the aesthetic quality of the design. This was particularly true when a number of different authorities were combined: during the period of local government reorganization in 1974, for example. The use of supporters is reserved for corporate and civic bodies of particular eminence and distinction: the possession of an ancient charter, for example, which enabled the town council of Sherborne in Dorset to obtain a grant of supporters in 1987, despite its parochial status.

Corporate arms also include those of schools, colleges and universities, public utilities, nationalized industries, public or limited liability companies, professional and sporting associations, guilds and fraternities, and learned and academic societies. The criteria for grants of arms to such bodies now appear to be stability and permanence as well as eminence. Many arms date from the Middle Ages: those of the original livery companies of the City of London, for example, and the fifteenth-century arms of Oxford University (*Azure an open Book proper between three Crowns Gold*) which derive from the arms attributed to Edmund the Martyr, the ninth-century king of East Anglia, by the medieval heralds. (Edmund the Martyr's arms, *Azure three Crowns Gold each pierced by two Arrows Argent*, are still used by the town of Bury St Edmunds.) Similar arms of *Azure three Crowns Gold* were attributed to the ancient kingdom of East Anglia and these have subsequently found their way into the heraldry of the diocese of Ely, the former Isle of Ely County Council, the borough of Colchester and the University of East Anglia. Many institutions adopted the arms of their founders: Exeter College, Oxford (Walter de Stapledon, 1314) and St John's College, Oxford (Sir Thomas White, 1555), for example.

Ecclesiastical heraldry is distinctive, particularly in the manner in which devices frequently reflect religious concepts. But while the symbol of the cross is widely found in ecclesiastical heraldry (though not exclusively so), representations of the Crucifixion were clearly considered inappropriate. References to saints are common; the escallop shell in the arms of Rochester, for example, was the device of St Augustine (who founded the cathedral in 604) and the *saltire* on which it is placed is the familiar cross of St Andrew to whom the church is dedicated. A significant number of diocesan arms contain local allusions. Those of Birmingham (granted in 1906) for instance, are divided *per pale indented* (vertically by a zig-zag line) and refer to the nineteenth-century arms of the City of Birmingham which, in turn, were based on the arms of the medieval de Bermingham family who were once lords of the manor. Similarly, the arms of the diocese of Truro include, on a black border, the fifteen *bezants* (gold roundels) of the Duchy of Cornwall. Several diocesan arms contain references to the personal devices of former abbots or bishops. Those of the See of Hereford, for example, are derived from the arms of Thomas de Cantelope who was bishop from 1275 to 1282: *Gules three Leopard's Faces reversed jessant-de-lis Gold* (upside down and with fleurs-de-lis projecting from their mouths). Composite arms may suggest lines of enquiry: those of Lincoln College, Oxford, for example, provide several references to the college's history. The arms are *tierced in pale* (divided vertically into three) with the arms of the founder, Richard Fleming (1427), to the left and those of Thomas Scott (alias Rotherham), who re-endowed the college in the late fifteenth century, to the right. Both men were bishops of Lincoln and the diocesan arms are depicted between those of the two benefactors.

It should be noted that both dioceses and cathedral chapters have their own arms and, although they may allude one to the other, they are not the same. The arms of the Dean and Chapter of Hereford Cathedral, for example, are *Gold five Chevronels Gules* (five narrow red chevrons on gold) – a reference to the Clare earls of Gloucester before 1313 who bore *Gold three Chevronels Gules*.

The Heralds

As we have seen, from the early Middle Ages heralds were attached to royal and magnatial households.

The heralds and pursuivants (junior heralds) took their titles of office from their masters' names, styles, devices and even mottoes: Blanch Lyon Pursuivant (*c.* 1465) to the Duke of Norfolk, for example, and Il Faut Faire Pursuivant (1443) to Sir John Fastolf.

Kings of arms (the senior heralds) exercised jurisdiction over provinces and were also appointed to the orders of chivalry. The office of Garter Principal King of Arms, the senior English officer of arms, was created in 1415 by Henry V. Garter was both the first king of arms to be appointed to an English order of chivalry and the first permanent 'Roy d'armes d'Angleterre', previous holders of that office being appointed either by seniority or royal favour.

There remains uncertainty as to when the first English royal heralds were appointed. The earliest known reference occurs in 1276 when 'a King of Heralds North of Trent' is mentioned, but the first occasion on which an officer is described by name was in 1327 when Carlisle Herald was created by Edward III – though even then it is not clear whether this was an exclusively royal office. Identification is further complicated by the fact that early officers of arms frequently moved from private to royal service and vice versa, titles of office disappeared and were then revived and some royal and non-royal heralds possessed similar titles. During the reign of Edward III (1327–77) Claroncel (or Clarencell), Norreys, Volant (or Vaillant), Falcon, Aquitaine and Guyenne Kings of Arms were appointed. Clarenceux and Norroy became the titles of the two English provincial kings of arms, but from 1380 to 1419 the king of the southern province of England was Leicester King of Arms and in the reigns of Henry V and Henry VI (1413–66) the 'Roy d'armes de North' (i.e. north of the River Trent) was Lancaster. It is likely, therefore, that prior to 1420 in the south, and 1467 in the north, the governing kings of arms used their own personal titles while the provinces themselves were known as '. . . of the Clarenceux' and '. . . of the Norreys'.

The College of Arms – the Corporation of the Officers of Arms in Ordinary – comprising the thirteen kings, heralds and pursuivants of arms, is part of the royal household and exercises heraldic authority on behalf of the sovereign in England, Wales and Northern Ireland. Royal officers of arms have acted as a corporate body since the early fifteenth century but did not receive a charter until 1484. The college was re-incorporated in 1555 and received Derby House, near St Paul's Cathedral, as a residence. Derby House was destroyed in the Great Fire of 1666 and the present building, with its entrance facing Queen Victoria Street, was constructed on the same site. It is owned and governed by a chapter of the Officers of Arms, presided over by Garter King of Arms, and contains the High Court of Chivalry and a magnificent collection of heraldic and genealogical records and documents.

The Officers of Arms in Ordinary now comprise three kings of arms (Garter, Clarenceux and Norroy and Ulster), six heralds (Chester, Lancaster, Richmond, Somerset, Windsor and York) and four pursuivants (Bluemantle, Portcullis, Rouge Croix and Rouge Dragon). Only a king of arms has authority to grant armorial bearings and in England and Wales this is subject to the formal approval of the Earl Marshal in the form of a warrant. The Officers of Arms in Ordinary act as consultants and charge fees for their advice and services. There are also Officers of Arms Extraordinary who, while not members of the body corporate, assist their brother officers on state and other occasions. They include Arundel, Beaumont, Maltravers, Norfolk, Surrey, Wales and New Zealand Heralds and Fitzalan Pursuivant.

The High Court of Chivalry was established in the early fourteenth century as the Court of the Constable and Marshal, having jurisdiction over matters armorial within England, Wales and Northern Ireland. The Earl Marshal is the great officer of state responsible for state ceremonies (but not 'royal' occasions such as weddings) and hereditary judge of the Court of Chivalry. Since 1521, when the office of Constable became vacant, the Marshal has sat alone, though in practice a surrogate is usually appointed. He has jurisdiction over the officers of arms in matters of heraldry, honour and precedence. The title was originally Marshal but is now Earl Marshal and Hereditary Marshal of England and is vested in the Duke of Norfolk. The Law of Arms is not common law but civil law, and the Court of Chivalry is, therefore, a civil court. There are few records of the court's proceedings before the late seventeenth century when there was a period of considerable activity. After 1737 the court did not sit until a test case was brought in 1954 at which it was established that, despite a lapse of two hundred years, the court's authority was still valid.

In England the prerequisites to a right to bear arms have never

The Garter procession at
Windsor, 1982

been defined but in practice a successful petitioner must be
perceived to be a 'gentleman' and the kings of arms are authorized,
by their letters patent of appointment, to grant arms to 'eminent
men' (which phrase includes, of course, women and corporate
bodies). Armorial bearings are still granted by means of signed
letters patent to which the seals of the granting kings of arms are
appended. In England, arms belong to families and pass down all
male lines, while in Scotland junior male members of a family must
matriculate a variation of the arms which then passes to the heir.

An armiger who has an English coat of arms and a different
Scottish one, is referred to in his Scottish letters patent as 'A noble
of the noblesse of Scotland' and 'a Gentleman of England'. In
Scotland all matters heraldic are the sole responsibility of Lord
Lyon King of Arms and all decisions are in his prerogative, acting
on behalf of the sovereign. In this he is assisted by a number of
officers of arms whose titles vary from time to time but currently
include Marchmont, Albany and Ross Heralds and Dingwall,
Kintyre, Carrick and Unicorn Pursuivants. The office of Lord
Lyon is at New Register House in Edinburgh. In Scotland there
are also several 'private' officers of arms, Slains and Garioch
Heralds, for example, who serve the Earl of Erroll and the
Countess of Mar respectively.

The Chief Herald of Ireland exercises heraldic and genealogical authority within the Republic from his office in Kildare Street, Dublin. He grants arms only to persons of Irish descent who may be considered to have reached 'the port of gentry'. Confirmations of arms are also granted to those who can prove a use of arms for one hundred years or three generations. Heraldic jurisdiction over the province of Northern Ireland is vested in the office of Norroy and Ulster King of Arms in London.

Two

ARMIGERS: NOBILITY AND GENTRY

. . . you have fed upon my signories,
Dispark'd my parks and fell'd my forest woods,
From my own windows torn my household coat,
Raz'd out my impress, leaving me no sign,
Save men's opinions, and my living blood,
To show the world I am a gentleman.

Shakespeare, *Richard II*, III. i

An armiger is one who is entitled to bear arms. Armorial bearings are in the nature of an honour and are deemed, therefore, to emanate from the Crown which is the source of all honour.

Originally, arms were largely self-assumed by members of the knightly class, though there are examples of their being conferred as gifts of feudal superiors or in recognition of military leadership. One of the earliest recorded instances was at the knighting of Geoffrey Plantagenet in 1127 when Henry I (1100–35) hung a shield, painted with golden lions, about his son-in-law's neck.

Implicit in the term armiger is the exclusive right of members of the twelfth-century military élite to possess emblems by which their feudal pre-eminence might be recognized. Terms such as 'armiger', 'noble' and 'gentleman' have constantly been re-defined so that references in documents, memorials and so forth need to be considered in the context of the period to which they relate (see below). Within the feudal system, for example, every man who held land subject to military service was 'known' or 'noted' (in Latin, *nobilis*). While these obligations were frequently commuted to other services, or to the payment of fines, the feudal *nobilis* retained its clearly defined superiority within a two-tier society in which there was an enormous gap between the upper and lower classes: the 'gentle' and the 'simple'. The word 'gentle' is derived from the Latin *gentilis* meaning kinsman referring, in this context, to one related, not by blood, but by feudal tenure. A man was not a gentleman, therefore, because of his personal qualities but because he belonged to the gentle or upper class. It would appear that originally the terms 'nobility' and 'gentility' were synonymous and that, because membership of the class implied an obligation of military service, all those who were noble and gentle were also armigerous. The burgesses of towns (the *communitates civitatum*), who were first admitted to the Commons in 1265, were clearly not considered to be gentle, while the 'Knights of the Shire' (the twelve representatives elected by the gentry of each county) were required, by a statute of Henry VI, to be 'gentlemen born'. Unlike the citizens they were permitted to wear their spurs in the chamber – a distinction which continued into the nineteenth century as a symbol of gentility and knightly pre-eminence.

While the heralds almost certainly advised those who assumed arms, the absence of centralized regulation eventually led to duplication and even to dispute. In 1385 the Court of Chivalry was required to adjudicate in the case of Scrope v. Grosvenor, both of whom bore the arms *Azure a Bend Or*. Significantly, neither side accused the other of having assumed the arms without authority (for this would have impugned the other's dignity), each claiming that their ancestors had used them from 'time immemorial' which, in the Court of Chivalry, was deemed to be 1066.

By the beginning of the fifteenth century the widespread use of assumed arms was evidently causing concern, for in 1417 writs were issued to the sheriffs of Dorset, Hampshire, Sussex and Wiltshire declaring that only those who could prove their armigerous status by right of their ancestors or by grant from a competent authority should use arms in the forthcoming expedition to France. However, an exception was made for those who had fought at Agincourt on St Crispin's Day in 1415 – *exceptis illis qui nobiscum apud bellum de Agincourt arma portabant*.

It was at this time that a middle class began to emerge from the remnants of the feudal system, men who were not of the *noblesse* but who were, nevertheless, rich and powerful and who sought to proclaim their status by acquiring arms. Such men had no hereditary claim to arms and it was necessary, therefore, for the kings of arms to grant and assign new arms on behalf of the Crown. Thus, from the fifteenth century a system which originally related exclusively to the knightly class developed to become a potent instrument of social mobility. Unlike their European counterparts, the English kings of arms were permitted to grant new arms to 'eminent men'. This delegation of royal authority was to have a lasting effect on society, for thereafter no commoner who was perceived to have reached the threshold of gentility was denied the opportunity to apply for armorial bearings, the symbols of that condition.

The Peerage

The term 'lord' is possessed of a number of different meanings and is now defined as the abbreviated style of a peer below the rank of duke, an honorary prefix used by the younger sons of dukes and marquesses and the style of Scottish Lords of Sessions. Originally it was synonymous with 'sire' and implied feudal superiority, as in Sieur de Chambord, 'Lord of Chambord'. The terms 'sieur', 'sire' and 'sir' appear to have a common etymology; 'Sir' being prefixed to the Christian name of a baronet or knight (see below). Marcher lords were the barons who, following the Conquest, were charged with the defence of the English borders with Scotland and Wales under the authority of the palatine earls who exercised jurisdiction over the palatine counties: originally those of the Welsh March, ruled by the Earls of Chester, Shrewsbury and Hereford, and the Scottish borders, ruled by the Prince Bishop of Durham. (The palatinates were necessary for the defence of the Conqueror's new realm but elsewhere holdings were dispersed to prevent the concentration of magnatial power.) It has also been suggested by Robert Gayre in *The Nature of Arms* that the commons of England, the *Communitas Terrae*, consisted of the nobility and their representatives in contradistinction to the lords who formed the sovereign's council, the *Curia Regis*.

The topographical preposition 'de' is commonly found in names such as Robert de Mowbray and Guy de Bryan where it means simply 'of' or 'from'. In the barons' letter to the Pope of 1301 the surnames of forty-one knights are prefixed with 'de' but, according to Cokayne in *The Complete Peerage*, later versions of the prefix were often adopted 'to give an air of antiquity to new creations'. While on the subject of names, it is worth noting that a variety of spellings will be encountered: there are sixteen variants of de Mohun and fifteen of de Bryan, for example.

Inevitably we come to the vexed question of manorial lordships which, in the late twentieth century, have become marketable commodities despite the fact that they bring with them little more than an archaic title and an occasional bundle of documents. Following the Conquest of 1066, England was divided among the followers of William I who remained, in theory, the owner of the kingdom. The smallest holding within these granted estates has subsequently become known as the manor. The highest level of tenancy, held of the king, was the tenancy in chief (lordship in fee) and magnates in this category sometimes let to lesser lords (mesne tenants) who, on occasion, let to their followers who thereby became tenants-in-demesne. The lord of the manor could belong to any of these categories but was always the tenant on whom the actual feudal obligation rested. After 1290, when the statute of *Quia Emptores* forbad further subinfeudation, qualifying clauses were inserted in conveyances to prevent future claims of overlordship. In this context the term 'lord' means landlord and, because he held land within the feudal system, a manorial lord could reasonably claim armigerous status. Today, land and seignioralty are rarely conveyed with manorial titles though those who purchase them often claim armigerous status.

The identity of manorial lords and the service (fees) by which the manors were held, may be obtained from the *Book of Fees*, or

Feudal Aids, and *inquisitions post mortem*. Since 1926 all matters relating to the ownership of manors and the location of manorial records have to be reported to the Master of the Rolls and this information may be obtained from the National Register of Archives.

The term 'peerage' is now used to describe the British degrees of duke, marquess, earl, viscount and baron. Derived from the medieval Latin *paragium*, it means simply 'a company of equals' and was originally applied to those of similar rank within the nobility. But from 1321, the term was used to describe those senior barons of England who normally received writs of summons to Parliament and, later, to the Lords Spiritual. The British peerage now comprises five separate peerages: those of England, Scotland, Ireland, Great Britain and the United Kingdom. The peerages of England and Scotland were combined at the Act of Union in 1707 as the Peerage of Great Britain, and the Peerage of Ireland continued until 1801 when a further Act of Union created the Peerage of the United Kingdom, though occasional creations continued after that date. All peers and peeresses in their own right, except the Irish peers, may sit in the House of Lords and all enjoy certain armorial privileges. In their coats of arms they use a silver helmet with gold bars (facing the sinister, the left when viewed from the front), a coronet appropriate to their rank (see Chapter Seven) and supporters.

Premier peers are those who hold the oldest established title of each rank. The premier royal dukedom is that of Cornwall (created 1337) and the premier dukedom is Norfolk (first creation 1397). The premier marquisate by creation is that of Winchester (1551) and the premier earldom is Shrewsbury (1442), though the distinction is accorded to the (Howard) Dukes of Norfolk by virtue of their descent from Philip Howard, Earl of Surrey who, in 1580, inherited the medieval earldom of Arundel which is deemed to pre-date 1442. The premier viscountcy is Hereford (1549) and the premier barony is De Ros (1264).

In Scotland, the premier peer is the Duke of Hamilton (1599) and Brandon (1711), the premier marquess is Huntley (1599), the premier earl is Mar (1404), the premier 'Earl on the Union Roll' is Crawford and Balcarres (1651), the premier viscountcy is that of Fentoun (1606) which is held by the Earl of Mar and Kellie, and the premier Lord of Scotland is Forbes (1442 or earlier).

In Ireland the Duke of Leinster is premier duke (1766), marquess (1761) and earl (1316), the premier viscountcy is that of Gormanstown and the premier baron is Kinsale (precedence of 1397).

A dukedom is the senior rank of the British peerage. Derived from the Latin *dux*, meaning leader, the rank was introduced into England in 1337 although the style had been known before that date, William the Conqueror being referred to as *Ducis Normannorum et Regis Anglorum*, for example. The first English non-royal dukedom was granted to Henry, Earl of Lancaster, Derby, Lincoln and Leicester in 1351 while in Scotland, David, the eldest son of Robert III, became Duke of Rothesay in 1398. The scarlet robe of a duke is embellished with four bands (guards) of ermine. The wife of a duke is a duchess.

A marquess, or marquis, belongs to the second rank of the British peerage. Although introduced from Europe in 1385, the term *marchiones* had previously been used by lords of the Welsh and Scottish marches. The coronation robe of a marquess has three and a half rows of ermine, and his parliamentary robe has four on the right side and three on the left. The wife of a marquess is a marchioness.

Several of the lords who followed Duke William in his conquest of England held substantial territories, *comtés*, in the Low Countries and France and, although granted English lands and titles by William, they retained the superior title of comté, county or count. The equivalent English rank was that of earl, a title quite different from that of the Saxon *ealdorman*, which originated in Scandinavia and appeared in England in the early eleventh century as *eorl*, an Old English form of *jarl*. The later form *erle* continued in use throughout the Middle Ages. It is the oldest English title and rank, and was the highest until 1337 when the Black Prince was created a duke. The earliest known charter creating an hereditary earl is that of *c.* 1140 by which King Stephen created Geoffrey de Mandeville Erle of Essex. An earldom is now the third rank of the British peerage. An earl's robe is embellished with three rows of ermine and his wife, or a woman who holds an earldom in her own right, is a countess.

A viscount belongs to the fourth rank of the British peerage, the first creation being in 1440, although the title itself is considerably older (in the days of the Carolingian empire the *vice-comtes* were the deputies of the counts and gradually assumed hereditary rights). The coronation robe of a viscount has two and a half rows of ermine and his parliamentary robe two guards of plain white fur. The wife of a viscount is a viscountess.

The word 'baron' is of uncertain origin. It was introduced into England following the Norman Conquest of 1066 to identify the 'man' (vassal) of a great lord, or of the conqueror himself, though prior to the conquest a barony was simply a chief's domain. In Ireland a barony was a medieval division of a county, corresponding to the English hundred. Following the conquest, tenants-in-chief of the king below the rank of earl were often referred to as barons, and from the thirteenth century the title appears to have been reserved for those magnates summoned by writ to parliament, greater barons being those who were summoned by direct writ to the king's council and lesser barons were those summoned through the county sheriffs. During the reign of Edward IV (1461–83) a new and powerful merchant class emerged, principally as a result of Edward's encouragement of trade and commerce, and this was to bring about the eventual dissolution of the feudal baronage. The style itself was introduced by Richard II in 1387 and it is now the fifth and lowest rank of the British peerage. A baron's coronation robe has two rows of ermine and his parliamentary robe two guards of plain white fur. The Life Peerage Act of 1958 enabled the Crown to create non-hereditary peerages with the rank and style of baron. In Scotland, the equivalent rank is that of a Lord in Parliament. (The Baronage of Scotland is a feudal institution entirely different from the English baronage. Of similar status to an English lord of the manor (see above) a Scottish baron enjoys additional nobiliary and armorial rights.)

Courtesy titles are styles conceded by the sovereign to the children of peers. Sons of dukes and marquesses use the style 'Lord' and their daughters, and those of earls, use the style 'Lady' before their Christian names. The sons of earls, and the sons and daughters of viscounts and barons, use 'Honourable' and the eldest sons of dukes, marquesses and earls take their father's second title but are not thereby peers.

Scotland

In the formal organization of Scottish society the Clan, the Family and the Name remain as significant entities. In Scottish armory there is no such thing as family arms. Undifferenced armorial bearings are succeeded to by the heir who may be an heir male, an heir female or an heir of tailzie (an heir nominated within the blood relationship) who then becomes a Head of Clan or a Chief of a Family or Name. Junior members of a family are required to re-matriculate their arms with Lord Lyon who assigns to them a version with congruent differences (see cadency in Chapter Eight). Supporters are granted to peers and, occasionally, to certain minor barons, knights and clan chiefs who may claim them by custom. Unlike English practice, all those of Scots descent (whether armigerous or not) may wear their clan or family crest, displayed within a strap and buckle bearing the chief's motto or 'slogan', as a badge (called a crest badge). The crest badge of a clan chief is distinguished by silver-gilt feathers: three for a clan chief and peer, and two for a chieftain. In Scotland, a chief 'of whole name and arms', i.e 'of that ilk', is also entitled to display a golden coronet in his crest, though not all chiefs do so.

Crest badge of Mackay, Lord Reay

Baronets

A baronetcy is an hereditary rank of the British peerage. Created by James I in 1611, with the objective of raising money to support his troops in Ulster, the first recipients paid £1,095 for the style 'Sir' and 'Lady', or 'Dame', and precedence above knights. In

Hatchment of Sir William Cooper (d. 1837) at Chilton Foliat, Wiltshire, showing the pendant badge of a Scottish baronet

1625 a baronetage of Scotland was established, to provide funds for the colonization of Nova Scotia, and both creations lasted until 1707 when they were replaced by the baronetage of Great Britain. In 1619 the baronetage of Ireland was created and, on 1 January 1801, both the baronetage of Great Britain and that of Ireland were replaced by the baronetage of the United Kingdom which continues to the present day. The premier baronetcy of England is that of Bacon (1611) and that of the United Kingdom is de Saumarez (1801).

Baronets of England, Ireland, Great Britain and the United Kingdom have as their badge 'the bloody hand of Ulster' – a red hand on a white shield which is borne (sometimes on a small square (*canton*) in the top left corner) as an augmentation in their arms. Baronets of Scotland were originally authorized to augment their arms with the shield of arms of Nova Scotia, on a silver field a blue saltire charged at the centre with a shield of the royal arms of Scotland. However, by a grant of Charles I, they were assigned a badge comprising the shield of arms of Nova Scotia within a blue circlet and this is depicted suspended from a tawny coloured ribbon beneath the shield in the arms of a Scottish baronet. All baronets are entitled to use a knight's helmet in their arms, this being of steel, full-faced and with the visor raised.

Knighthood and the Orders of Chivalry

The word 'knighthood' is the modern form of the Old English *cnichthād*, the period between youth and maturity, while the word 'chivalry' is derived from the Old French *chevalerie* meaning armed horsemen. By the mid-twelfth century the two words were virtually synonymous and described both the personal attributes and the code of conduct of the mounted warrior. To begin with, in England, the *cnihthas* were probably the retainers of Anglo-Saxon magnates, young landholders who had pledged themselves to the service of a lord, usually an *ealdorman*, bishop or greater *thegn*. Following the Conquest, the term seems to have been applied to military tenants who, as vassals of *erles*, major barons and bishops, held their estates in return for forty days military service. By that time there seems to have developed some form of ceremonial initiation into the warrior class for young men of noble birth and this almost certainly included the symbolic presentation of a sword or a lance and shield. These customs, and the emergence of paid military service, which replaced service by land tenure, resulted in the creation of an élite of seasoned, professional warriors who were prepared to fight in any cause and from whom the royal military household, the *familia regis*, was formed.

The Crusades of the eleventh and twelfth centuries brought together the *chevalerie* of Europe. Inspired by the climate of holy war, and released from the constraints of feudalism, the warrior class developed a concept of knighthood which found expression in the creation of military and religious orders of chivalry. The military orders, under the command of a sovereign or royal nominee, and often richly endowed, evolved into the great orders of the high Middle Ages, notably in England the Most Noble Order of the Garter, founded in 1348. The religious orders were commanded by grand masters and included the Order of the Poor Knights of Christ and of the Temple of Solomon (the Knights Templar), founded in 1118, and the Military and Hospitaller Order of St John of Jerusalem (the Knights Hospitaller) which was recognized by the Papacy in 1113.

The Grand Priory in the British Realm of the Venerable Order of St John of Jerusalem, a charitable order incorporated by royal charter in 1888, remains active today, its most familiar foundation being the St John Ambulance Service. The senior grades of bailiff, knight, dame and chaplain (who do not claim rank, precedence or title) are permitted to display, behind their shields of arms, the badge of the order, an eight-pointed Maltese cross, while other members may suspend the badge on a ribbon below the shield. Bailiffs and Dames Grand Cross are also entitled to (non hereditary) supporters and may add to their personal arms a *chief* of the arms of the order (*Gules a Cross Argent in the first quarter a representation of the Royal Crest of England*).

The sons of the medieval nobility were schooled in the arts of war and chivalry as members of the households of their fathers' peers. Richard, Duke of Gloucester, later King Richard III, spent three years as a young henchman in the household of his first cousin the Earl of Warwick, for example. They were expected to progress through the degrees of page, squire, knight bachelor and (for some) knight banneret. The conditions of page and squire were

Pendant badges of baronets of the United Kingdom (left) and of Scotland (right)

Augmentations of a Bailiff Grand
Cross of the Grand Priory in the
British Realm of the Venerable
Order of St John of Jerusalem

passed through during boyhood and early teens, and knighthood
was reached at the 'threshold of maturity'. Pages were never
combatant but squires were, and some men remained in the
service of knights all their lives, while others, by means of personal
distinction, progressed beyond the rank of knight bachelor to
become bannerets.

The banneret was originally a chief feudal tenant or lesser baron
and the rank of nobility between knight bachelor and baron. In the
Middle Ages, a knight banneret was permitted to lead troops in
battle under his own banner which, because it was of smaller
dimensions than those of his superiors, was termed a 'banneret'.
(There is a tradition that, when a knight bachelor was promoted to
banneret in the field of battle, the heralds would remove the tails
from his pennon thereby converting it into a small banner.) The
last occasion on which the dignity of banneret was conferred was at
the Battle of Pinkie in 1547 when Lord Protector Somerset
advanced Sir Francis Bryan and two of his companions to the rank
of knight banneret.

Knights Bachelor belong to the lowest degree of knighthood but
also the most ancient. Knights were originally required to perform
military service (knight's fee) in exchange for the lands granted to
them but, as has already been noted, this duty was gradually
commuted to a money payment known as 'shield money' (scu-
tage). In the medieval army the knight bachelor would command
the smallest unit, perhaps consisting of only a few personal
retainers. He was not a member of an order of chivalry and he
displayed his arms on a pennon. In the Middle Ages knights
bachelor received the accolade from their sovereign or from a
superior lord.

Knights of the orders of chivalry were senior to bannerets and knights bachelor and, with the exception of knights of the Order of St John (see above), they remain so.

Mention has already been made in Chapter One of the foundation, in 1348, of the Order of the Garter, the oldest and most prestigious order of chivalry in Britain. The original fellowship consisted of the sovereign and his eldest son together with twenty-four young men of noble birth, but in 1786 the sons of George III and his successors became eligible for membership, even though the chapter might be complete, and in 1805 the lineal descendants of George II were also deemed to be eligible. In 1831 membership was again extended to all the direct descendants of George I. From the late fourteenth century and perhaps earlier, women were received into the order as 'honorary' members with the title 'Dames de la Fraternité de St George', a practice which did not meet with the approval of Henry VIII who was apparently 'altogether un-genial' to the presence of ladies on such occasions. Queens of England were, of course, members as head of the order but it was not until the reign of Edward VII (1901–10) that the king's consort was automatically a Lady of the Garter. (In 1987, on the personal initiative of Queen Elizabeth II, the statutes of the order were amended so that women could be admitted.) Membership was frequently used for diplomatic purposes and foreign royalty have often been appointed as members, 'Stranger Knights and Ladies of the Garter', additional to the twenty-six companion knights.

The arms of the order are a red cross on a white ground (*Argent a Cross Gules*), a device attributed to St George, the order's patron saint, and are usually depicted within a garter, a circular riband with the buckle and strap pendant. The garter itself was worn below the left knee (it was intended that the knights should wear it at all times!) or, by ladies, on the left arm. Originally it was light blue (possibly as a reference to Edward III's claim to the French throne) but was changed to dark blue in 1714 and is edged, buckled and adorned in gold with the enigmatic motto HONI SOIT QUI MAL Y PENSE – 'shame on him who thinks evil of it'. Henry VII introduced the magnificent collar of the order which was composed of twenty-six miniature garters, each encircling a red enamelled rose, originally a Tudor rose, alternating with interlaced knots: '. . . and at the end of the said collar shall be put and fastened The Image of Saint George', mounted and slaying the dragon. The knights wore a dark blue mantle, on the shoulder of which was embroidered the order's arms, and Charles II introduced a broad blue sash, worn over the left shoulder with a small St George device in plain gold (the 'Lesser George') as a clasp on the right hip. For ceremonial purposes the Knights Companion now wear a dark blue velvet mantle lined with white taffeta, with the Star of the order on the left breast. This is an eight-pointed silver star with the arms of the order at the centre. The mantle is worn with a crimson velvet hood lined with white taffeta, and a

Arms of the Most Noble Order of the Garter

black velvet hat with an ostrich feather plume and tuft of black heron's feathers affixed with a diamond-studded band. The officers of the order, Prelate, Chancellor, Registrar, Garter Principal King of Arms, Gentleman Usher of the Black Rod and Secretary, all have their own robes and insignia. The various devices of the Order of the Garter are to be found depicted in documents, monuments, window glass and paintings of all periods from the mid-fourteenth century onwards. Knights are entitled to add supporters to their arms and from the fourteenth century the most common practice has been to encircle the shield of arms (never impaled because membership of the order did not extend to a spouse) with a representation of the blue and gold Garter inscribed with the motto.

The 1522 statutes of the order require that every Knight Companion should display his banner, sword, helm and crest above his stall in the order's chapel of St George in Windsor Castle. The fringed banners are five feet square and the gilded and painted crests are usually carved from limewood or pear. These remain in place during a knight's lifetime and are taken down at his death when they become a perquisite of Garter King of Arms, though they are often returned to a knight's family and displayed in a parish church or private chapel.

A stall plate, depicting a knight's arms, was also affixed to the back of his stall, originally as a memorial but, since the sixteenth century, following appointment. Unlike the crests and banners, these brass and enamelled plates remain in position after a knight's death. They now number nearly 700 and comprise one of the finest and most jealously guarded collections of heraldic art. In stall plates, helms and crests are conventionally depicted as facing the high altar; those to the north of the choir, therefore appear to face in the wrong direction (see plate 2).

Banners, crested helms and stall plates are also to be found in the chapels of the other British orders of chivalry, the oldest of which is the Most Ancient and Most Noble Order of the Thistle. This was revived in 1687 by James VII of Scotland, James II of England, who asserted that the order had been founded by King Achaius in *c*. 800. He designed a sumptuous mantle of green velvet powdered with over two hundred and fifty gold thistles for himself and the twelve knights, a number selected 'in allusion to the Saviour and His Twelve Apostles'. But only eight were appointed before James fled the country in 1688 and the order fell into desuetude. It was revived by Queen Anne in 1703 though the number of member knights remained at eight until a full complement was appointed in 1827. Today the Thistle comprises sixteen Knights Companion in addition to the Sovereign and foreign royalty and the chapel of the order, at St Giles Kirk in Edinburgh, was dedicated in 1911. Knights are entitled to supporters and to encircle their arms with the collar, circlet and motto of the order and to suspend the badge

The arms of John Tiptoft, Earl of Worcester and Knight of the Garter (*c.* 1427–70). Sometime Constable of England, scholar, humanist, patron of Caxton and *avant-courier* of the Renaissance, Tiptoft's ruthlessness and bestial cruelty earned him the sobriquet 'Butcher of England'. The Tiptoft arms *Argent a Saltire engrailed Gules* are quartered with those of his mother, heir of Edward, Lord Chorleton, *Or a Lion rampant Gules*. On an escutcheon of pretence are the arms of his first wife Cecily, daughter of Richard Nevill, Earl of Salisbury (4 *Gules a Saltire Argent and a Label gobony Argent and Azure*), and Alice, daughter and heir of Thomas Montacute, Earl of Salisbury (1 *Argent three Lozenges in fess Gules*) and heir of Monthermer (2 and 3 *Or an Eagle displayed Vert*)

beneath their arms. The badge consists of the figure of St Andrew in gold, his gown green and his surcoat purple, bearing before him a white St Andrew's cross (*saltire*), the whole surrounded by golden rays. The motto of the order is NEMO ME IMPUNE LACESSIT.

The Most Honourable Order of the Bath, the premier meritorious order of the Crown, was established by George IV in 1725.

It was modelled on a 'degree of knighthood, which hath been denominated the Knighthood of the Bath' by Henry IV in 1399, the designation acknowledging the ritualistic purification undertaken by a knight-elect prior to his receiving the accolade. In 1735 this degree of knighthood was restored as a 'regular military order' of thirty-six Knights Companion, called the Most Honorable Military Order of the Bath, and Henry VII's chapel in the abbey of Westminster was appointed the chapel of the order (see illustration, plate 1). In 1815 the order was reorganized with civil and military divisions and three classes, Knight Grand Cross, Knight Commander and Companion. Knights Grand Cross may add supporters to their arms, the shield of which may be depicted within the circlet of the order inscribed with the motto *TRIA JUNCTA IN UNO*. All three classes may suspend the insignia of the order beneath their arms.

The motto of the Most Illustrious Order of St Patrick is *QUIS SEPARABIT*, MDCCLXXXIII – Who will sever us, 1783 – a reference to the political considerations which led to its institution by George III in 1783. Although revised in 1905 no appointments have been made since 1934. The order consisted of the Sovereign, Grand Master, twenty-two knights and an additional number of honorary knights, all of whom were entitled to supporters in their arms, to encircle their shields with the collar, circlet and motto of the order and to suspend the insignia beneath the shield. There was no chapel of the order but, before the disestablishment of the Church of Ireland, investitures were normally held in St Patrick's Cathedral, Dublin and, afterwards, in Dublin Castle. The banners and stall plates of former knights remain on display in both buildings.

The Most Distinguished Order of St Michael and St George was founded in 1818 by George III and has subsequently become an honour for British subjects serving overseas, notably in the diplomatic service. There are three classes of membership, Knight and Dame Grand Cross, Knight and Dame Commander and Companion. All may suspend the insignia of the order beneath their arms and surround the shield with the circlet and motto of the order: AUSPICIUM MELIORIS AEVI – token of a better age – and members of the first class are entitled to supporters. The chapel of the order is in St Paul's Cathedral, London.

The Royal Victorian Order was instituted by Queen Victoria in 1896. There are five classes: Knight and Dame Grand Cross, Knight and Dame Commander, Commander, Lieutenant (formerly Member, Fourth Class) and Member (formerly Member, Fifth Class). Knights and Dames Grand Cross are entitled to supporters and may place the collar of the order around their arms. All classes may suspend the insignia of the order beneath their arms and the first three classes may display their shields within a circlet of the order on which is inscribed the motto VICTORIA. The Chapel of the Savoy is the chapel of the order.

The Most Excellent Order of the British Empire was instituted in 1917, its chapel being in the crypt of St Paul's Cathedral, London. There are military and civil divisions and five classes of membership: Knight Grand Cross, Knight Commander, Commander, Officer and Member. All classes may suspend the appropriate insignia beneath their arms and the first three classes may depict their shields of arms within the circlet of the order on which is inscribed the motto FOR GOD AND THE EMPIRE. Knights Grand Cross are entitled to supporters and may place their shield of arms within the collar of the order.

The Church

The Lords Spiritual are also armigerous as are their sees and the chapters and bodies corporate of cathedrals and major abbeys. In the Middle Ages, archbishops, bishops and royal abbots were tenants in chief and held baronies. They were ecclesiastical magnates, responsible for the administration of vast estates, and held office as privy advisers in the King's Council (*Curia Regis*). Many accomplished clerics were elevated to the great offices of state and their services rewarded with the emoluments of a bishopric, or even an archbishopric, a device by which the Crown was spared the payment of a substantial salary and pension. Bishops were addressed as 'My Lord', as they are today, and many of them were also warriors wielding not the sword, which drew blood, but the mace which apparently did not! Their offices, and those of the senior pre-Reformation abbots, generated huge numbers of documents all of which required seals by which they were authenticated. Ecclesiastical seals are generally oval in shape and by the thirteenth century were predominantly heraldic. Religious motifs from early seals were often incorporated into coats of arms; the elaborate, enthroned figure of Christ in the arms of the See of Chester, for example, first appeared in a seal of Bishop Sigefrid (1180–1204).

The Archbishop of Canterbury, who has precedence immediately after royal princes, and the Archbishop of York are both addressed as 'Your Grace' and, together with the twenty-four bishops of the Church who rank between viscounts and barons, sit as peers of Parliament. All Anglican bishops use a mitre instead of a crest, and sometimes a crozier or crossed croziers are depicted behind the shield. During their terms of office diocesan bishops may impale their personal arms (on the sinister side) with those of their see but on translation to another bishopric the impaled arms of office are changed accordingly. The arms of the Archbishopric of Canterbury, which date from *c.* 1350, are charged with a white *pallium* on which four *crosses fitchy* (pointed at the foot) represent the pins by which it was attached to the vestment. Behind the *pallium* is a gold archiepiscopal staff and the background of the

Arms of the Archbishoprics of Canterbury (top) and York (bottom)

shield is blue. The earliest arms of the Archbishopric of York are of a similar design but with a red field, and these may occasionally be found on monuments. The present arms, which date from *c*. 1398, are red with silver cross keys, as the minster is dedicated to St Peter, and a gold imperial crown which probably evolved from the papal tiara.

Impaled personal and diocesan arms are invaluable when attempting to establish how long a particular incumbent held office, especially when they appear on seals, the use of which can provide precise dating. They will also be found on the tombs of bishops and abbots most of whom were buried in their cathedrals and abbey churches. Although prior to the Reformation most bishops were elected by chapter, it was usual for the Pope to confirm formally the appointment of a king's nominee, a decision which was then ratified by chapter. One effect of this system was that prominent members of the royal household were frequently appointed as bishops and members of the *Curia Regis*. The extraordinary influence of these few families, in matters ecclesiastical and secular, is evident in the ubiquity of their personal arms alongside those of the offices which they held.

Cardinals, who belonged to the highest ecclesiastical rank, and were sometimes referred to as 'old red hat', displayed above their arms a scarlet ecclesiastical hat: a domed hat of felt with a wide brim from which depend cords, interlaced with gold thread, and tassels. These hats, which were worn by cardinals for official engagements, were instituted by Pope Innocent IV in the thirteenth century. Roman Catholic archbishops and bishops normally place a jewelled mitre (*mitre pretiosa*) above their arms but sometimes ecclesiastical hats are used instead. In 1832 the number of tassels to be depicted pendant from these hats was specified according to rank: fifteen on each side for a cardinal, ten for an archbishop and six for a bishop. Similarly, the canons of Roman Catholic cathedrals may use black ecclesiastical hats with three tassels on each side. Individual clergymen bear arms in the same way as other armigerous persons and since 1976 clergymen of the Church of England may choose to ensign their arms with one of a new range of ecclesiastical hats prescribed for that purpose.

Unique among the Lords Spiritual were the prince bishops of Durham who were appointed by the king as counts palatine, head of church and state in a vast territory which included St Cuthbert's seventh-century Bishopric of Lindisfarne. The palatinate was effectively a kingdom within a kingdom and as defenders of the realm in the north the prince bishops were charged with the defence of the Scottish border and maintained a standing army. The circular Great Seal of the prince bishops had, on the obverse, an enthroned figure of a bishop and on the reverse the bishop as an equestrian figure in full armour. By the fourteenth century the palatinate was at the height of its military power and its warrior-bishops are uniquely commemorated in the *ducally-gorged* mitre

Arms and ecclesiastical hat of
Cardinal Newman

Arms of the Bishop of Durham

and crossed sword and crozier in the arms of all subsequent
bishops of Durham. They had their own chancellors, exchequer
and mint; they administered the civil and criminal law; granted
charters for markets and fairs and exercised rights of forfeiture.
Until 1539, most bishops of Durham were appointed by the Crown
(unlike other bishops who were elected by chapter) and, inevitably, their authority was reduced under the Tudor kings. Nevertheless, in 1585 the Bishop of Durham remained the largest
land-holder in the country with eighty manors worth £2,500 in
total annually. The failure of the Northern Rising in 1569 succeeded in suppressing local opposition to the bishops' traditional
domination of local affairs and single-faction politics continued in
County Durham until the mid-nineteenth century. The bishops'
powers were finally vested in the Crown in 1836 and the palatinate
courts abolished by the Courts Act of 1971.

Prelates of the orders of chivalry may use certain insignia with
their personal arms. The bishop of Winchester, for example, as
Prelate to the Order of the Garter, places his shield of arms within
a representation of the blue and gold garter inscribed with the
motto.

The arms of rectors will often be found in churches, but the term
does not necessarily imply an individual. A rector was originally an

incumbent who received the 'Great Tithes', all the customary offerings and dues of his parish. But in many instances benefices were annexed by corporate bodies, such as monastic or collegiate foundations, who then received the Great (or Rectorial) Tithes, the Lesser (or Vicarial) Tithes going to a vicar who was appointed by them to administer the parish. Following the Dissolution of the Monasteries, many monastic estates became the property of laymen who also acquired the right, as lay rectors, to nominate vicars.

Esquires, Gentlemen and Yeomen

In thirteenth-century England, French and Latin terms which had hitherto defined social class, were replaced by English ones, and those which had been founded on tenure and legal status were gradually superseded by terms indicating general social standing or economic function. Some terms were hardly affected by these changes; 'knight', for example was used more often than the French *chevalier* or the Latin *miles* but its meaning remained unchanged. Others such as 'churl' (the Old English *ceorl*) and 'villein' disappeared altogether or retained only a literary usage. New terms were of diverse origin, some originated in the feudal household, 'esquire', for example, which in the fourteenth century came to denote the social rank immediately below that of knight.

This comparatively select number of esquires was but the senior stratum of a substantial group of free land-owners (*valetti*) who, with the knights, represented their counties in Parliament during the first half of the fourteenth century. Those *valetti* below the rank of esquire were in the late fourteenth century described as 'franklins', men of substance and of gentle birth and, therefore, armigerous. But by the early fifteenth century the term 'franklin' had been superseded by two others: gentlemen, who were considered to be men of breeding and armigerous, and yeomen who were not.

By the mid-fifteenth century local society comprised, in descending order: knights, esquires, gentlemen, yeomen and husbandmen, though franklins still made an occasional appearance. Of these, knights, esquires and gentlemen possessed armigerous qualifications and in common usage several of the terms were evidently interchangeable despite the Statute of Additions of 1413 which required that plaintiffs in personal actions should describe precisely the status of their opponents. Fifteenth-century sumptuary legislation similarly propounded a strict hierarchy and in 1445 it was determined that knights of the shire attending Parliament could include 'notable squires' and 'gentlemen of birth' but not those 'of the degree of Yeoman and bynethe'. In the context of local society, a yeoman was therefore a freeholder below the status of gentleman but above that of most other copyhold tenants and was eligible to serve on juries and to vote in county elections.

The term *valetti* was also used in official documents to describe those officers in royal, comital and magnatial households who, although of lower status than knights, were often drawn from 'gentle' families. In the early fourteenth century the *valetti* included esquires, but as the esquires acquired their own distinctive armigerous status, so the term *valetti* came to be translated into English as yeomen. Geoffrey Chaucer (1342–1400), for example, was a yeoman (*valet*) of the king's chamber in 1367 before becoming an esquire. In the sixteenth century the title 'esquire' was also applied to officers of the Crown and was thereby considered superior to that of gentleman, though only by association with a royal office which provided added distinction.

It has already been suggested that to begin with the terms 'nobility' and 'gentility' were effectively synonymous. But in an Act of Parliament of 1429 *les gentiles* was used to describe men holding freehold property of forty shillings a year or more, and from the sixteenth century the term 'gentleman' seems to have been applied to all those who were not required to labour and therefore employed servants. From that time members of professions, military and naval officers, barristers and so on were so described, some of them being entitled also to the designation 'esquire'. The rural 'squire' is generally a lord of the manor or major land-owner, and the term is entirely colloquial.

A steel tilting helm, with closed visor, is used to distinguish the arms of esquires and gentlemen, which terms are now used in letters patent to describe the lowest degrees of armiger (see Chapter Seven). In practice relatively few people are entitled to the designation 'esquire'. They include those who are esquires by inheritance, such as the eldest sons of knights; esquires by patent, such as heralds who are so styled in their letter patent of creation (though pursuivants are described therein as gentlemen); and those who are esquires while holding certain offices, such as justices of the peace. Gentlemen are those who are armigerous and either bear arms, by inheritance or grant, or are considered eligible but have not made application.

Royal and Hereditary Offices

From the time of the Norman Conquest, English sovereigns maintained a number of royal officials responsible for the day to day administration of the royal household which was modelled on that of tenth-century France and consisted of the *domus*, or domestic household, and the *familia regis*, or military household. The most important were the Stewards, the Master Butler, the Master Chamberlain, the Treasurer, the Constables and the Chancellor. Many of these offices still exist, though in modified form, and as the functions of monarchy and government diverged so too did the offices, some became the great offices of state while others remained offices of the royal household. There are eight anciently established state appointments: the Lord High Steward, Lord High Chancellor, Lord High Treasurer, Lord President of the Council, Lord Keeper of the Great Seal, Lord Great Chamberlain, Lord High Constable and Earl Marshal. Today, the sovereign's household in England includes the Lord Chamberlain, the Lord Steward, the Master of the Horse, the Treasurer, the Comptroller, the Vice-Chamberlain, the Mistress of the Robes, Ladies of the Bedchamber and Women of the Bedchamber. The officers of arms are members of the royal household and receive a (meagre) salary from the Crown. The royal household in Scotland includes, at its head, the Hereditary High Constable together with the Hereditary Master of the Household, Lord Lyon King of Arms, the Hereditary Standard Bearer, the hereditary keepers of various palaces and castles and the Captain General of the Royal Company of Archers.

In both countries there were numerous royal foresters, wardens and verderers, and devices allusive to their several offices often appear in the arms of those who held them. These include the heads of stags, woodsmen and foresters, and most commonly hunting horns. As early as 1246 a roll of arms by Matthew Paris depicts a hunting horn beside the arms of John de Nevil, Chief Forester of Henry III, and the hunting horn device of the constables of the Hundred of St Briavels in the Royal Forest of Dean in Gloucestershire may still be seen on the gatehouse tower of St Briavels Castle. In Dorset, the arms of de la Lynde *Gules three Stag's Heads Gold*, commemorate the ancient office of Bailiff of Blackmoor Forest and the Forterishey (Forsey) family bore the arms *Argent three Forester's Heads Sable* in allusion to their duties as foresters of Marshwood.

A characteristic of feudalism was the creation of numerous hereditary, or heritable, offices by which service to the nobility or to the Crown was rewarded. Such offices were not sinecures, however. They were concerned with the administration of those aspects of society which appertained directly to the Crown or to the running of magnatial estates. The earliest recorded offices date from the eleventh and twelfth centuries; in 1119 for example Robert, Earl of Gloucester, was Hereditary Governor of Caen and Hereditary Banner-bearer of Bayeux Cathedral and in the 1190s the Earl of Arundel was Hereditary Chief Butler of England and Hereditary Patron of Wymundham Abbey. Several hereditary offices were often the prerogative of one man; in 1270 for example the Earl of Norfolk and Suffolk was Hereditary Marshal of England, Hereditary Steward of the Household, Hereditary Bearer of the Banner of St Edmund, Hereditary Forester of Farnedale and Hereditary Warden of Romford Forest. Such offices are legion and were by no means confined to the upper echelons of society. Numerous hereditary falconers and farriers, stewards, sewers and sheriffs, constables and chamberlains, warders and keepers of castles, almoners and patrons of religious houses embellish the pedigrees of prince and yeoman alike. Some brought with them arms of office which, for the duration of tenure, could be impaled with the personal arms of the holder. The Kingsley family, former hereditary foresters of Delamere Forest in Cheshire, adopted an 'escutcheon of office' comprising *Argent a Bugle Sable*, for example.

In the late eleventh century the office of shire-reeve (*scīr-gerefa*) superseded that of ealdorman as the Crown's deputy and consequently the most important member of the executive in a county. Prior to the emergence of the justices of the peace in the fourteenth century, the sheriff was the main agent of the courts and was responsible for the Crown revenues of his shire. He was also responsible for the militia until this duty passed to the lieutenant and eventually to the lord lieutenant. In 1170 an inquiry considered malpractices by sheriffs and this resulted in the appointment of coroners.

Since the mid-sixteenth century a lord lieutenant has been appointed as the Crown's representative in each county of the United Kingdom. Before the Tudor period the office was that of the sovereign's 'lieutenant' who was usually a nobleman and in time came to be known as 'lord lieutenant'. A lord lieutenant was custodian of the county records (*Custos Rotulorum*) and was charged with the sheriff's former responsibilities for the county militia and defence.

Magistrates are civil officers responsible for the administration of the law who, in the Middle Ages, were often also members of the executive government. In 1277 and 1287 Keepers of the Peace were appointed by a commission under the Great Seal to keep the peace within a stated jurisdiction, usually a county. These 'inferior magistrates' acquired the name Justices (*Justicers*) and, by a statute of 1361, the power to try minor offences. They gave their services without pay, but, in order to exclude from office those who were considered too poor to be suitable, a statute of Henry VI required that a justice should hold lands worth £20 a year. This was increased to £100 a year in 1744. In the fourteenth century there were usually four or five justices appointed to each county but this number was increased to six in 1388 and to eight in 1390. In 1461 cases previously brought before the Sheriff's Tourn were transferred to the quarter sessions and by 1565 there were between thirty and forty magistrates appointed to each county. The justices tried cases before a jury in quarter sessions and dealt with minor matters in petty sessions.

Serjeanty

In the Middle Ages a serjeant was someone of less than knightly rank in the service of a lord (petty serjeanty), a knight in attendance on a sovereign (grand serjeanty), or an officer of

Parliament charged with enforcing its dictates. By the twelfth century, garrison knights were invariably outnumbered by what contemporary pipe rolls describe as serjeants whose successors appear in later records as owing forty days' military duty in time of war. The importance of this class in feudal society must have been considerable for it undoubtedly included many men of substance who were, in arms and equipment, little inferior to knights. But to a considerable degree they fell outside the process which, in the twelfth century, brought tenure by knight-service under royal control and for the most part the sovereign rarely intervened in the relationship between a lord and the man who held lands of him by military serjeanty. In practice the office of serjeant increasingly came to be associated with the performance of personal rather than military duties, and many serjeants were, for example, gamekeepers or physicians.

Three

DOCUMENTS, SEALS AND MANUSCRIPTS

. . . a seal'd compact,
Well ratified by law and heraldry.

Shakespeare, *Hamlet*, I. i

Documents

Although paper-making was known in Spain and Italy by the twelfth century, parchment and vellum were the chief materials used for writing throughout medieval Europe until the development of printing in the late fifteenth century. Parchment is a writing surface made from the treated skins of sheep or goats. The lighter 'flesh' side was preferred for formal documents but both sides were used in the writing of rolls and books. Vellum is a fine form of parchment prepared, by lime-washing and burnishing, from the skins of calves, kids or lambs. Paper was first used in England as a writing surface from the fourteenth century but it was not manufactured here until the late fifteenth century and even then only in small quantities. In the late seventeenth century Huguenot immigrants specialized in its production.

Watermarks are useful when attempting to date and locate the manufacture of paper and may assist in the detection of a forged document. At first the devices found on both European and British papers were simple shapes, a ram's head on Bordeaux paper of 1330 and a sword in 1351, for example. Armorial watermarks first appeared towards the end of the fifteenth century and in the seventeenth and eighteenth centuries, when watermarks were also used to denote paper quality and sheet size, heraldic devices often indicated royal, noble or civic patronage. More recently manufacturers began to use cyphers, trade marks and logotypes to identify their own brands of paper, though grades of paper used exclusively by sovereigns and departments of government have been marked with royal badges and cyphers for centuries.

Before the eleventh century pens were made from dried reeds. Thereafter, until the nineteenth century, the quill pen was used. This was formed from a goose feather, though feathers of swans, ravens, crows and even turkeys were also used, the hollow quill of which retained a small quantity of ink which was released by gentle downward pressure on the nib while writing. When used as pens, feathers were always stripped down to the quill, the larger end of which was carefully shaped and split with a pen-knife to form the nib. Metal nibs date from the mid-nineteenth century and fountain pens from the end of that century. Most medieval and early modern texts were written in inks made from a mixture of oak-galls, iron sulphate and gum arabic, though a darker but less stable ink was also produced from carbon, gum and water.

Armorial devices are commonly found in documents and in the seals by which they are authenticated. Such documents are almost invariably of a legal nature and often of considerable artistic merit, particularly those dating from the medieval period. A document is said to be engrossed when it is written out in a legal form for signature or copied in a formal hand or in distinct characters. An endorsement is something written on the back (*dorse*) of a document, usually an archival reference or related notes. English letters patent emanating from the College of Arms are endorsed by the registrar, for example. Royal and magnatial signatures on late medieval documents are sometimes accompanied by a motto.

Of the numerous documents on which heraldry is to be found, warrants, charters, letters patent, pedigrees, estate papers and indentures are the most common.

A warrant is an authorization to receive or supply money, goods or services or to carry out an arrest or search and may bear an official seal.

Charters are legal documents providing written entitlement to land or conferring other rights, powers or privileges on a body corporate or on an individual. A royal charter was a formal instrument by which a sovereign granted or confirmed lands, liberties, titles or immunities on his subjects in perpetuity. There are two types of charter roll, the first recording grants and the second confirmations. Both relate to the period 1199 to 1516 after which charters were succeeded by letters patent.

Letters patent are 'open' documents intended for the public to see (Latin *patens* – open). Armorial bearings, for example, are granted by means of signed letters patent to which the seals of the granting kings of arms are appended. They are addressed 'To All and Singular to whom these Presents shall Come . . .'. In Scotland it is an offence to bear arms unless they have been matriculated with Lord Lyon King of Arms and entered into the Public Register of All Arms and Bearings in Scotland. Matriculation is not simply registration, the process requires the correct marshalling of the arms, together with the appropriate marks of difference indicating relationships within an armigerous family, and these are confirmed by means of letters patent. Patent Rolls, which contain copies of letters patent, were begun in 1201 and are still main-

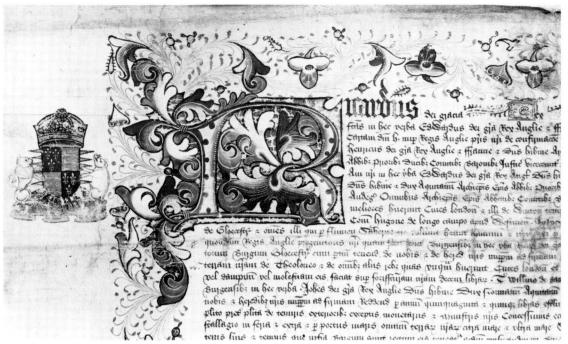

Charter of Incorporation to the City of Gloucester 1483. The arms of Richard III, with the shield set on a Yorkist sunburst, are depicted in the margin

tained today. Private documents may be described as 'letters close' and, unlike letters patent, may only be opened by the breaking of a seal.

A pedigree is a genealogical table illustrating descent through the male line. The term is said to have originated in the practice of writing the names of forebears in groups of circles which, when joined by curved lines, were thought to resemble the imprint of a crane's foot, in French a *pied de gru*. A chart which records all direct line ancestors, both male and female, is termed a birth brief, blood descent or total descent. Many pedigrees include illustrations of the arms of associated families, particularly those which have been accumulated through marriage in the form of quarterings. Pedigrees which emanate from the College of Arms or the office of Lord Lyon are generally definitive, though care should be exercised with regard to English pedigrees from the late sixteenth and seventeenth centuries, some of which compound earlier errors. Many other pedigrees are works of fiction in which a tenuous descent may be claimed, not only from the great magnatial families of the Middle Ages, but also from ancient European dynasties and even characters of legend and prehistory.

Cartularies are monastic or estate register-books containing details of deeds, charters, grants, property and other possessions. Estate papers sometimes carry seals and many (notably estate maps, mostly dating from the eighteenth century or later) include the armorial devices of landowners. Such papers are now lodged with county or local record offices, though some remain in the archives of the major landowners or their representatives. The Royal Commission on Historic Manuscripts and the National Register of Archives collate and publish information from a variety of sources.

An indenture is a formal inventory or agreement; an indenture of retainer, for example, which confirmed the obligations and privileges of livery and maintenance (see Chapter Nine), or that binding an apprentice to a master. The term derives from the practice of repeating the text of an agreement on a single sheet of paper or vellum and separating the two identical texts by cutting in an irregular manner so that the indentations of each party's document complement those of the other, thereby making it impossible to substitute a forged agreement or to alter the original. Medieval indentures were often prepared for a number of parties to an agreement and sometimes the word 'chirograph' was written across the indented line to show that there were several copies of the same text.

Seals

One of the principal functions of armory is on seals which are used to authenticate or protect documents. Seals are found in addition to, or in place of, signatures and are either affixed at the foot of a document or appended to it.

Seal of John de la Pole, Earl of Lincoln (d. 1487)

Seals are most often found singly but may also represent the parties to a contract or those who authorized a particular course of action. The normal practice in such cases was to prepare a document in the form of a chirograph, each copy being sealed by all the parties to the agreement. The *Constitutions of Clarendon* (1164) were prepared in this way but the three identical documents were never sealed. One of the most remarkable medieval documents extant is a letter to the Pope, signed and sealed (but not delivered) by the ninety-six barons summoned to the Lincoln Parliament of Edward I in 1300. The barons' seals appended to this document provide one of the finest contemporary armorial records in England and demonstrate the diversity of armorial practice at that time. But while such magnificent documents are by no means exceptional, the majority of those which will occupy the historian's attention will carry only a single seal or perhaps a pair. These may include statutes, charters, warrants and proclamations, letters patent and letters close, wills and testaments, muniments, title deeds and conveyances, and many manorial, estate, civic and ecclesiastical instruments.

Important documents carried seals before the inception of armory in the mid-twelfth century and these often bore distinctive devices which alluded to the names of their owners: a man called Swinford might use a boar (swine) on his seal, for example. The earliest recorded armorial seal, that is one in which the devices are depicted on a shield, dates from 1136 and this, together with a number of seals dating from the mid-twelfth century, provides evidence of the rapid spread of armory throughout western Europe in a comparatively short period of time. It is also apparent that the use of the same sigillary devices by succeeding generations of the same family served to consolidate the hereditary nature of armory.

A seal or *sigil* is a piece of wax, lead or paper attached to a document as a guarantee of authenticity or affixed to an envelope or other receptacle to ensure that the contents could not be tampered with other than by breaking the seal. The piece of stone or metal upon which the design is engraved, and from which the impression is taken, is called the matrix. Gold, silver, steel or latten (brass or a similar alloy) were widely used for this purpose, while signet rings were made either by engraving the design on gems or agates or in the metal of the ring itself.

The use of red for wax impressions is a relatively recent convention; from the earliest times a variety of other colours has been used including green, dull yellow, white and several shades of brown. Seals were usually circular in shape, pointed ovals being used by ecclesiastics, though not exclusively so. The more important seals were usually impressed on both sides and appended to documents by means of cords which were inserted in the soft wax before the impressions were made (a parchment document from which seals are hung is sometimes referred to as a 'ragman'). The two sides therefore required two matrices, known as the seal and counter seal, to form a single seal with different designs on the obverse and reverse. From the late fourteenth century the wax impression was often covered with a protective layer of paper or encircled with a 'fender' of plaited paper, leaves or rushes.

Many medieval seals have survived, notably in collections at the Public Record Office. But, whereas these may confirm the use of certain arms by individuals, they do not show the colours and it is often necessary to ascertain precisely to which armiger a seal refers, especially where several individuals adopted similar arms. The legend (the surrounding inscription) may include the armiger's name, but not invariably so, and it should be remembered that it was common practice for succeeding generations of eldest sons to inherit both their father's first name and his seal. At a time when documents contained few genealogical references, early seals are often the only source of information regarding the relationships of families of the same surname who possibly held estates in different parts of the country.

In England, the Great Seal of the realm has always been two-sided, like the coinage, with a different device on each side. The first 'great' seal of England was probably that of Edward the Confessor (1003–66) but it is more practicable to trace the development of the Great Seal from the reign of William I (1066–87). The Conqueror's seal was engraved with the majesty, a depiction of the king seated in state, copied from that of Henri II of France, and on the obverse an equestrian figure, also of the king. Subsequently, the faces were reversed: the majesty becoming the obverse and the equestrian figure the reverse. One of the earliest instances of the royal arms in the seal of an English monarch is to be found in the second seal of Richard I (*c.* 1195) which shows an equestrian figure bearing a pointed shield charged with three lions. Typical of the late medieval great seals is that of Edward IV (1461–83) which bears the quartered arms of France and England with fleurs-de-lis and the Yorkist badges of roses and suns interspersed both in the legend and in the diapered background of the majesty.

Great Seal of Henry VIII with equestrian figure and majesty

The legend on the second seal of Richard I refers to the king as *Rex Anglorum*, but thereafter successive English sovereigns were described on their seals as *Rex Anglie* until the legend was changed by James I to *Rex Angliae* (1603) and by Charles I to *Rex Magnae Britanniae* (1627).

Henry VIII (1509–47) also made use of a golden *bulla* on which was depicted the royal arms within a collar of the Order of the Garter. A *bulla* was a disc of metal, orginally lead, which was attached to documents, particularly those emanating from the Pope, hence the expression 'Papal Bull', meaning the actual document.

The Great Seal is still used to authenticate important documents issued in the name of the sovereign and the matrix is held by the

Lord Chancellor who was sometimes also referred to as the Lord Keeper of the Seal. Holders of offices of state, and of the Royal Household, such as the kings of arms, use the seal of their office to authenticate official documents, and when an individual holds several offices he uses a separate seal for each.

The *privatum sigillum* or privy seal was, in England, a twelfth-century innovation and was held by the clerks of the King's Chamber. It was used to authenticate warrants by which documents would be issued under the Great Seal, particularly instructions to the exchequer or chancery. It was also appended to lesser documents which nevertheless required royal approval. By the fourteenth century the authority of the Privy Seal rivalled that of the Great Seal and in the reign of Edward II (1307–27) a *secretum* was introduced for the sovereign's personal use.

Inevitably, from the early thirteenth century, it became fashionable for the lords also to engrave their seals with equestrian figures of themselves in armour, complete with heraldic shields, horsecloths (caparisons) and banners. These seals were often so large, and documents so numerous, that privy seals were required for administrative purposes. These were smaller and therefore less ornate than great seals and usually bore a simple shield within a decorative interstice and legend. A secretum, perhaps a signet ring, was generally used for private matters and, because of their small size, these often bore devices other than coats of arms: the bear and ragged staff badges of Richard Nevill (d. 1471), for example. In magnatial households, as in departments of state, the security of important matrices was the responsibility of an official known as the the Keeper of The Seal.

Shield shapes are a useful guide when dating seals – early shields were elongated but in the thirteenth century the heater shield became fashionable. This was shaped like the base of a flat iron and its use continued into the fourteenth century. In the fifteenth century, shields showing quartered arms (indicative of marital and seigniorial alliances) were popular and, of necessity, these became broader to accommodate the quarterings (see Chapter Seven).

Whereas a simple shield was ideally suited to a circular seal, the elongated fourteenth-century coat of arms, with its helm and crest, created awkward spaces between the central motif and the surrounding legend. These were filled with architectural and decorative patterns (diaper) together with armorial devices and the figures of beasts or chimerical creatures. These were usually personal or household badges which, from the fifteenth century, were often translated into supporters.

Several seals depict stylized sailing ships, that of Thomas Beaufort, Duke of Exeter and Lord High Admiral of England (*c.* 1416), for example, in which the Beaufort arms cover the entire sail.

Regrettably, in recent times, legal documents rarely carry more

Seal of Richard of Gloucester as Admiral

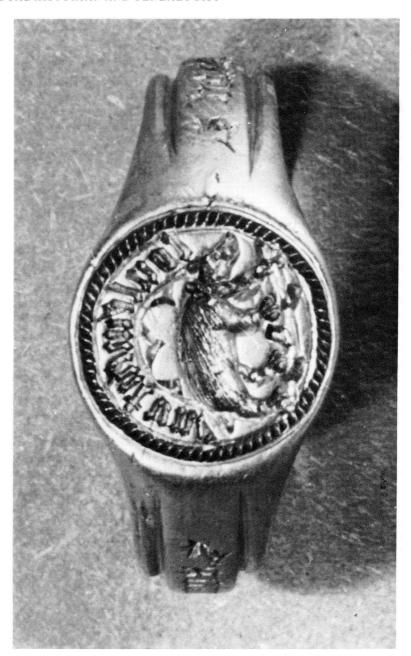

Signet ring said to have been removed from the body of the Earl of Warwick (the Kingmaker) following his death at the battle of Barnet 1471

than a token seal, usually a red adhesive disc of paper, sometimes embossed with the title of the authority by which the document is issued or, occasionally, with the arms of that authority.

Illuminated Manuscripts

Parchment is ideally suited to ornamentation as well as writing, and some of the finest artistic works of the Middle Ages are the illuminated manuscripts produced in the scriptoria of monastic houses and by talented artists who considered calligraphy, illumination and heraldry to be complementary elements of a single craft.

A manuscript which is described as illuminated is one which is decorated in colours and gold. When the page is turned and the gold is caught by the light, it appears to possess a lustrous quality unequalled by other forms of decoration. The gold is applied either in the form of a powder mixed with a suitable water-based medium and used as a pigment or in the form of leaf, either directly to the working surface, or on a plaster ground of *gesso sottile* (deactivated calcium sulphate, lead carbonate, an animal glue and sugar). This raised plaster ground is either applied with a quill pen or painted on and dries hard, flexible and raised. The leaf is then applied and polished or burnished with an agate burnisher.

In Britain, the early medieval school of Ireland and Northumbria produced manuscripts of extraordinary skill and originality in the interlacing and counterpointing of geometrical and animal patterns and subtle variations of colour. The best known of these Celtic manuscripts are the Lindisfarne Gospels and the Book of Kells. In Europe the Byzantine tradition, with its florid use of gold and vermilion, continued into the Carolingian period to produce works in which the emphasis was on illuminated ornamental motifs. In England, the incomplete twelfth-century Winchester Bible contains the work of five different artists and, in its obvious Byzantine influences and its emphasis on naturalistic elements, is one of the finest and most innovative products of the illuminator's art.

From the end of the twelfth century the art of the miniaturist flourished, notably in the production of the great Bibles, and in the later Middle Ages increasing use was made of enlarged and ornamented initial letters in which illustrations of biblical and naturalistic scenes were inserted. Beautifully illuminated breviaries, psalters, missals and books of hours were commissioned by medieval magnatial families as gifts to superiors and as benefactions to religious houses. These contained exquisitely executed illustrations of the agrarian year, biblical scenes, devotional texts and the lives of saints and martyrs, often identified as the patron saints of recipients. Heraldry was eminently suited to illumination and devices included rebuses, badges and the attributed arms of saints and martyrs as well as those of the book's owner or patron.

A missal is a liturgical book containing the words and ceremonial directions for the celebration of the mass and, from the tenth century, combining in one book the devotions which had previously appeared in several. Its development was encouraged by the medieval practice of saying private masses and many missals are exquisitely illuminated, often with the personal armorial devices of their owners.

Psalters, or psalteries, are books containing the Psalms and other matter for recitation at the Divine Office. They were superseded by breviaries: liturgical books containing not only the Psalms but also the hymns, lessons, responsories and canticles used in the Divine Office.

Often the most impressive of all medieval written documents, books of hours, were personal devotional books widely used by the devout laity from the thirteenth century. Most were embellished more-or-less elaborately according to the taste and pocket of the patron for whom they were prepared. Some were presented as gifts by calligraphers and illuminators in hope of patronage. Books of hours provided a series of prayers appropriate to the eight canonical hours into which the day was divided, together with a calendar and various extracts from the Divine Office and Psalms. They were invariably exceedingly beautiful, the illustrations providing also a wealth of information on contemporary social life. An illuminated book of hours commissioned by John, Duke of Bedford (brother of Henry V) as a wedding present for his bride, Anne of Burgundy, was executed in 1423 by a team of artists under Pol de Mimbourg, one of three brothers who were the finest illuminators of their day. The Bedford arms and badges, the silver eagle, the black antelope and the golden tree stump of Woodstock, appear as decorative motifs throughout, as do the arms and devices of Burgundy.

Not all illumination was confined to religious manuscripts. Genealogies, romances and many official documents were also illuminated and almost invariably embellished with heraldry. An illuminated book of French romances presented by John Talbot, Earl of Shrewsbury, to Henry VI's bride, Margaret of Anjou in 1445, contains a magnificent genealogical table showing the French and English royal descents from St Louis. It is filled with heraldic devices, all glittering in burnished gold.

Rolls of Arms

A roll of arms is any collection of heraldry, whether painted, tricked (drawn in outline with colours indicated by abbreviations) or listed in written form using blazon, the language of armory.

The term is most often applied to strips of vellum or parchment, sewn together and rolled up or bound into books, on which rows of shields or heraldic figures have been painted, or tricked, and

OPPOSITE: frontispiece to a book of prayers owned by Margaret Beaufort. Heraldic decoration includes the Beaufort arms and portcullis badge, Margaret's personal device of *margarite* flowers, and (in the initial letter) the eagle foot badge of her husband, Lord Stanley

Tricked arms of Andrew
Forterishey, Member of
Parliament for Bridport, Dorset,
in the reign of Henry V. The
heads are described as those of
foresters – almost certainly a
reference to the name, *forestarias*
being 'forester'

identified. Most of these manuscripts are of medieval origin,
though there are many later copies and compilations and they
illustrate both the development of armory, its terminology and
conventions, and the mobility of the knightly classes throughout
Europe.

The study of rolls of arms dates from the thirteenth century
when heralds exchanged information concerning armorial devices
and compiled their own armorials which are manuscripts or books
concerned with armory. In their simplest form, rolls of arms are

little more than hastily illustrated lists which were compiled on the spot, at a tournament, for example. Others, such as the Rous and Salisbury rolls, are pictorial records of historical characters and events.

There are some 350 surviving European medieval rolls of arms, of which 130 are English. These are usually classified as:

Occasional Rolls, which relate to an event such as an expedition, tournament or siege and are particularly valuable in biographical research and the interpretation of historical events.

Institutional Rolls, associated with foundations and religious and chivalric orders, and often compiled over many generations.

Regional Rolls, which list the arms of armigers in a particular administrative area such as a county.

Illustrative Rolls, which illustrate stories or chronicles and may therefore contain imaginary arms such as those of the Knights of the Round Table.

General Rolls, which are combinations of several collections and sources. Compilers of general rolls would often arranged shields to facilitate reference: in groupings by colour or charges, for example. Such a compilation is known as an ordinary of arms, a term which is also applied to written lists of blazons similarly arranged (see below).

The earliest known roll of arms is that of the thirteenth-century monk and historian Matthew Paris whose, *Liber Additamentorum* (*c.* 1244) includes painted sheets illustrating shields of arms. Some rolls of arms contained paintings of historical characters, together with their armorial devices. The Rous or Warwick Roll, for example, is a vellum manuscript, 28 cm wide (11 in) and 7.5 m in length (25 ft), in which each of the 63 principal characters is described in detail. The roll was compiled between the years 1477 and 1485 by John Rous, a chantry priest and antiquary, as a chronicle of the Earls of Warwick and the accompanying drawings provide a wealth of armorial information. The first version in English included a laudatory passage to Richard III but, following the accession of Henry VII, this was replaced in a second Latin version by a vilification of his former king.

The first ordinary of arms is referred to as Cooke's Ordinary after Robert Cooke, Clarenceux King of Arms, who owned it in 1576. This roll dates to *c.* 1340 and is arranged by reference to armorial charges: shields with crosses, those with lions, eagles and so on. The original is owned by Sir Anthony Wagner but a sixteenth-century copy in trick by Robert Glover (Somerset Herald 1570–88) can be found at Queen's College, Oxford

Pages from Powell's Roll of c. 1345–51. Notice (lower right) how the original Grandison arms (*Paly Argent and Azure*) have been augmented by the addition of a *Bend Gules* variously charged with eagles, escallop shells or cinquefoils to differentiate between different cadet branches of the family

(MS 158 ff 305–346) and includes also the Baliol Roll of *c.* 1332 which is the earliest known roll of Scottish arms.

The standard work on the subject of medieval rolls of arms is Sir Anthony Wagner's *Aspilogia I: A Catalogue of English Medieval Rolls of Arms* (1950) and *Aspilogia II: Rolls of Arms (Additions and Corrections)*, both published by the Society of Antiquaries.

The heralds' visitations of the sixteenth and seventeenth centuries produced numerous records of pedigrees and painted or

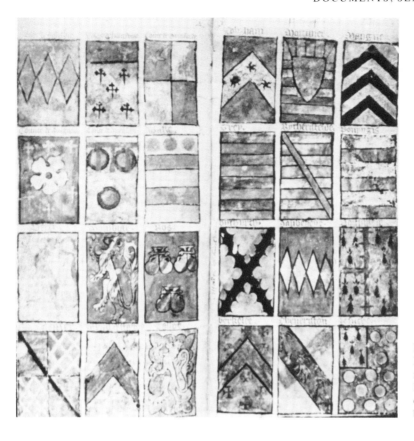

Pages of banners from Powell's Roll of *c.* 1345–51. The roll, named after the antiquarian the Revd D.T. Powell (d. 1848), contains 672 separate shields and banners

tricked sketches of arms which were later transferred to the manuscript volumes which now comprise the library of Visitation Books at the College of Arms and remain the only definitive record. These may be regarded as regional rolls and, being concerned with the aspirations and self-perceptions of society within the counties and hundreds of England at that time, they provide an invaluable source of information for the local historian. Most manuscript copies of the visitation notebooks have now been published, notably by the Harleian Society, though it should be borne in mind that they may contain unauthorized additions and alterations which may not be immediately apparent. Many of the manuscripts on which these printed editions are based are now in the British Library, London. County record offices and reference libraries usually have copies of publications relating to their own areas and there are good collections of printed records of visitations at the Guildhall Library and the Society of Genealogists in London and at the Institute of Heraldic and Genealogical Studies, Canterbury. A comprehensive list of printed manuscript records of visitations is to be found in the author's *A New Dictionary of Heraldry* (1987).

By the sixteenth and seventeenth centuries many editions of earlier medieval rolls of arms were known and to these were added

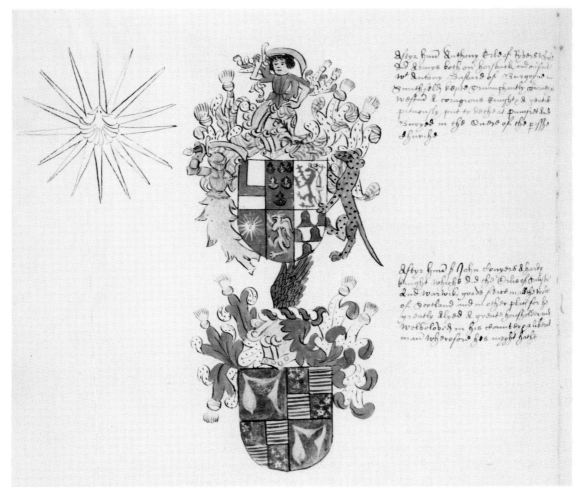

Arms and escallop badge of Earl Rivers and arms of Sir John Conyers. From Writhe's *Garter Book* of *c.* 1480

further listings, compiled by heralds and antiquaries, of collections derived from the Wars of the Roses, the Tudor progresses and heralds' visitations. Notable among these antiquaries was a group led by William Dugdale who, in the early seventeenth century (and fearful of the 'impending conflict'), began transcribing rolls of arms dating from the mid-thirteenth century onwards. The resulting remarkable collection of painted copies is now at the Society of Antiquaries in London.

Rolls of arms in written or printed form include ordinaries of arms and armories. Ordinaries of arms are reference books in which the blazons of shields of arms are arranged alphabetically by the charges they contain. Armories are dictionaries of arms listed alphabetically by surname.

The best known nineteenth-century ordinary of arms is A.W. Morant's edition of J.W. Papworth's *Ordinary of British Armorials* (known simply as 'Papworth' by armorists), published in 1874 and reprinted in 1977. There are also several armories available in reprinted form, notably Sir Bernard Burke's *General Armory of England, Scotland, Ireland and Wales*, published in 1842 and reprinted in 1984. Proficiency in the use of blazon is essential if these works are to be used effectively, and it should be borne in mind that they were compiled at a time when 'research' was often uncritical and dependent on a variety of unverified sources. Both works therefore include many references to arms for which there was no apparent authority.

Treatises and Early Printed Works

Early manuscripts devoted wholly or in part to the subject of armory are difficult to categorize. Many rolls of arms were later cut and bound into book form and a number of well-known medieval treatises containing armorial material were essentially works on kindred subjects such as the arts of war, ceremonial, nobility and so on. Many medieval manuscripts were copied, usually without acknowledgement of the source, and material omitted or added. It is therefore difficult to determine whether a manuscript should be regarded as an original treatise, a copy, or a variant.

Medieval heraldic treatises have, in the past, been dismissed as 'Master Mumblazon' (Oswald Barron) in that they were apparently written by people who were not professional heralds. But it is known that several were considered to be standard works on the subject and were to be found in the libraries of at least two eminent heralds. Copiously illustrated and illuminated books were extremely expensive, as were specially commissioned copies, and it seems unlikely that they should have been acquired by heralds were they not considered of sufficient importance. Indeed, it has been established that some at least were written by heralds and that nearly all were compiled by men who were closely associated with the medieval heraldic establishment.

Possibly the earliest treatise, the Anglo-Norman *De Heraudie* of *c.* 1300, is of unknown authorship and was included in the *St Alban's Formulary* of 1382. It is significant in that it confirms that armorial practice, conventions and grammar were already well established by the end of the thirteenth century.

One of the most important armorial treatises is the *Tractatus de Armis*, written in *c.* 1395 by John de Bado Aureo (possibly Bishop Siôn Trevor). This was compiled in Latin and many copies were made through to the sixteenth century. The treatise begins with a discussion of the origin of arms and the significance of tinctures (colours), beasts and other charges. This is followed by sections on crosses, ordinaries and the royal arms of England.

More typical in the variety of its subject matter, and one of the earliest printed works in England to include armory, is *The Boke of St Albans* of 1486. Authorship was attributed to Dame Juliana

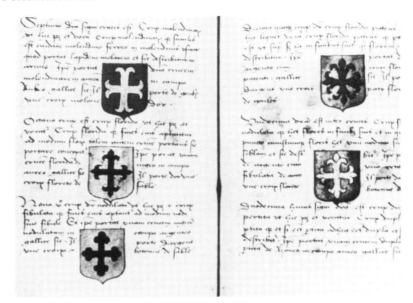

Pages of crosses from *Tractatus de Armis*

Berners by Wynken de Worde who printed the book as *The Treatyse perteyning to Hawkyng, Huntyng and Fyshyng with an Angle; and also a right noble Treatyse which specufyeth of Blasynge of Armys*. Regrettably, the authorship cannot be verified.

Sixteenth-century printed books on armorial and related subjects include Gerard Leigh's *Accendence of Armorie* (1562) and John Ferne's *Blazon of Gentrie* (1586), the former published in a number of editions up to 1612. *A Display of Heraldrie* by John Guillam (1611) ran to six editions by 1724 when it was much augmented by its editor, James Coats. In 1780 another classic, *A Complete Body of Heraldry*, by Joseph Edmonson, Mowbray Herald Extraordinary, was published in two folio volumes, the second of which contains an extensive alphabet of arms.

Details of the best known medieval heraldic treatises, and of other related manuscripts, may be found in Rodney Dennys' *The Heraldic Imagination* (1975). This includes a list of treatises from 1300 to 1500 together with information regarding the location of original manuscripts or copies with references, and of printed texts and commentaries. There are also summaries of the best known heraldic treatises and printed books in the author's *A New Dictionary of Heraldry* (1987).

Bookplates

The eighteenth century was the age of the great country house where large parties of guests were entertained for weeks and even months together. The Hanoverian mansion invariably possessed a library appropriate to its grandeur and to the status of its owner, filled with leather-bound volumes of the classics, illustrated travels, county histories and collections of cartographical plates, engravings and prints. The cover of each book would be stamped with the family arms or crest and the fly-page embellished with an engraved bookplate for *ex libris* identification. Of the many types of decorative bookplate the armorial plate is by far the most valuable to the historian because of the genealogical information it may contain.

Armorial bookplates originated in Germany in the fifteenth century, however, no English plates prior to the sixteenth century have been recorded. One of the earliest, of 1574, was a gift of Sir Nicholas Bacon to the Cambridge University Library and two others, for Joseph Holand and Sir Thomas Tresame (the latter containing no fewer than twenty-five quarterings) both date from 1585.

At least one hundred and fifty seventeenth-century armorial bookplates have been recorded, though it was not until 1690 that they became fashionable, notably those engraved by William Jackson who was responsible for most of the Oxford and Cambridge collegial bookplates of the period. The British Museum collection contains over 630 of Jackson's plates, produced at his workshop near the Inns of Court in London. Designs of this early period are often enclosed within a wreath and are known as the Carolean style.

This was followed by the Early Armorial style, with almost square-sided shields and full mantling (see over, 1).

The Jacobean style (2) appears from the beginning of the eighteenth century and was particularly popular in the 1720s. It is distinguished by ornate floreated scrollwork surrounding the shield and is often further ornamented with brackets, escallops, cherubs' heads and fishscale, diaper or lattice-work. The bookplate of Dr Timothy Goodwyn is in the Jacobean style and his impaled arms of office include also a mitre and the crossed crozier and key of a bishop.

The highly popular Chippendale style (3), dating from *c.* 1740, was both asymmetrical and ornamental, often with intricate sprays of flowers and (in later examples) an excess of cherubs, dragons, fountains, cornucopia, shepherds and shepherdesses. The Chippendale style bookplate of Mr Henry Emmett is quartered and includes a quartered inescutcheon of pretence for his wife who was an heraldic heiress.

In contrast, designs during the period *c.* 1780 to 1810 were often simple shields (known as 'spade shields' because of their shape), symmetrical and elegant and sometimes with festoons or wreaths: exemplified by the bookplate (4) of the playwright, Richard Brinsley Sheridan (1751–1816).

Dated plates occur from 1700 and, although the dates are usually reliable, some may refer back to significant family events such as the creation of a baronetcy.

The use of a crest without the other elements of a coat of arms

1

2

3

4

Armorial bookplates   5

first occurs in the eighteenth century and was common in nineteenth-century bookplates.

A uniquely British style of bookplate, the Bookpile (5), was created by Samuel Pepys for a Dr Charlett in *c.* 1699. This consists of a neatly stacked pile of books so arranged that it completely surrounds the shield or central panel. Interestingly, the plate illustrated leaves a space for different members of the Hall family to add their Christian names.

Many plates of the late eighteenth and early nineteenth centuries were pictorial though some are armorial and may depict a shield leaning against a tree or suspended from an ornamental urn.

In armorial bookplates, the tinctures of the arms may be identified by reference to the Petra Sancta system of hatched lines and dots (see p. 189), but it is necessary to sound a note of caution. During the nineteenth century many meticulously engraved armorial plates were prepared for those who had no right to arms whatsoever. Designs were selected at random from the pages of the numerous heraldic reference books available at the time and used entirely without authority. Similarly, many authentic armorial plates were produced by engravers who had as little heraldic knowledge as their clients, and errors abound.

Many well-known artists turned their hand to bookplate engraving including Hollar, Vertue, Hogarth, Bewick and Millais. The traditional method was copper engraving but etching was also used from the eighteenth century, and some plates were produced by wood engraving in the seventeenth, eighteenth and especially the nineteenth centuries. More recently lithographic methods, line or half-tone blocks and collotype have been used. Bookplates are generally produced in a single colour, though there are coloured plates dating from the Victorian period. Towards the end of the nineteenth century there was a revival in the art of the bookplate, inspired by talented artists such as C.W. Sherborn and G.W. Eve. There are many bookplate collections in libraries and museums, the largest being the Franks Collection at the British Museum.

Maps

Unfortunately, little survives of medieval cartography, but the finest examples from the sixteenth century are brilliant works of art – 'gifts fit for a prince' (R.V. Tooley) – and not simply tools for navigators. These delineate coastlines, as accurately as knowledge allowed, the interstices 'blossoming into a pictorial and heraldic geography', full of fantasy and legend (ibid.).

Christopher Saxton (1542–1611), the 'father of English cartography', produced an entire series of maps of English and Welsh counties during the period 1574–9 by the authority of Thomas Seckford, Master of the Court of Requests and Surveyor of the Court of Wards and Liveries under Elizabeth I. These maps, which were published as *An Atlas of England and Wales* in 1579, were both plain and hand-coloured and the margins contained shields of arms. The most notable of Saxton's later works was a magnificent map of England and Wales on twenty-one sheets and with a scale of eight miles to the inch. One edition of this map was contained within a broad, engraved border comprising eighty-three coats of arms of the nobility and gentry, many of which were amended in a later edition, published by Philip Lea in 1687.

Several heralds of the period were also cartographers: Robert Glover, Somerset Herald, produced a manuscript map of Kent in 1571 and William Smith, Rouge Dragon Pursuivant, compiled *A Description of England* in 1588.

At this time most maps included some heraldry, often the royal arms within a decorative cartouche. Typical of the period is the work of William Camden (1551–1623) whose *Britannia* was published in 1607. This originally included a Latin text and a series of county maps but was reissued in 1610 and 1637 with an English text and the same maps engraved by William Kip and William Hole. These were taken from Saxton's maps of 1579, though reduced in size to 35 × 28 cm (14 × 11 in).

In 1611 John Speed (1542–1629) produced *The Theatre of the Empire of Great Britain*, an atlas of maps for the counties of England and Wales, together with general maps of England, Scotland, Ireland and Wales. These were also based on Saxton's work but included much new material, notably plans or views of principal towns and considerable heraldic embellishment. This work was followed by a 'pocket' atlas which, because of its reduced size, contained less heraldry. Both were particularly popular and ran to many editions. Speed's maps were generally uncoloured, though some contemporary owners commissioned hand-coloured versions.

J. Bleau published his first atlas of the counties of England and Wales in 1645 as part IV of *Theatrum Orbis Terrarum*. His maps included the arms of the principal nobility and gentry of each county, though there are often blank shields, indicative, perhaps, of vanity publishing, the cost of producing the atlas being met in part by the financial contributions of those whose arms appeared in the maps.

Several maps in Richard Blome's *Britannia* of 1673 include civic heraldry.

Early maps are singularly attractive but unfortunately they contain insufficient detail to be of much assistance to the local historian. Hills, forests, rivers and deer parks are shown pictorially and towns and villages are marked with symbols. But roads are rarely shown and while the heraldry and town plans are informative, these too may be depicted inaccurately.

The name of the cartographer is often found inscribed on copies of his maps together with the word or abbreviation *auctore, de., delt., delineavit* or *descipsit*; while the name of an engraver may

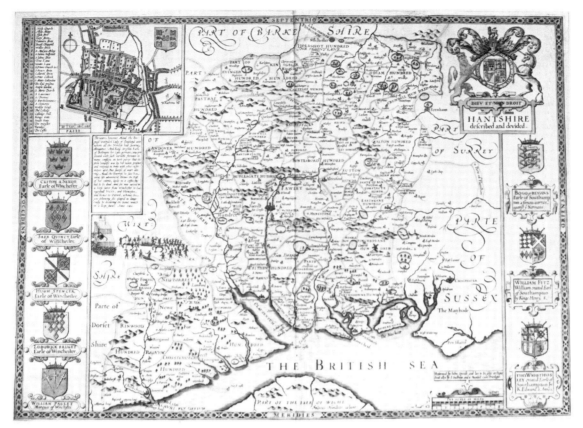

John Speed's *Hantshire*, 1612–14 edition

similarly be denoted by *caelvit, engr., fecit, incidente, sc., sculp* and *sculpsit*.

Cartography improved significantly towards the end of the seventeenth century but heraldry is less in evidence. The works of the prolific Robert Morden (d. 1703) and John Ogilby (1600–76) contain very few armorial references and it was not until Thomas Moule's maps, published during the reign of William IV (1830–7), with further Victorian editions, that armory is again featured, usually the arms of major town and cities, diocesan arms and those of the county nobility.

Four

ARCHITECTURAL AND DECORATIVE FEATURES

A casement high and triple-arch'd there was,
All garlanded with carven imag'ries
Of fruits, and flowers, and bunches of knot-grass,
And diamonded with panes of quaint device,
Innumerable of stains and splendid dyes,
As are the tiger-moth's deep-damask'd wings;
And in the midst, 'mong thousand heraldries,
And twilight saints, and dim emblazonings,
A shielded scutcheon blush'd with blood of queens and kings.

Keats, 'The Eve of Saint Agnes'

It has been suggested that the purely decorative use of armorial devices dates from the mid-thirteenth century. While it is true that many of the earliest known examples of heraldry in carved stone, stained glass and other forms of decoration are of that time, to suggest that heraldry was ever 'purely decorative' is to disregard its function. In medieval society, visual imagery was of great importance in projecting intangible realities. Armorial devices were a means of declaiming feudal authority and knightly pre-eminence: they were outward and visible symbols of a man's position and influence, and of his household's status in society. It was entirely natural, therefore, that heraldry should become decorative, for its function required that it should be seen, and ostentatiously so.

Henry III (R. 1216–72) delighted in 'the boast of heraldry' and it was he who set the fashion in England. In 1237, for example, he presented his queen with a silver platter embellished with the royal arms, and between 1240 and 1266 he ordered that his arms should be painted on the window shutters of his great chamber at the Tower of London and on the doors and shutters of the New Hall and chamber at his castle at Winchester. At the same time, he commissioned armorial glass for the great hall of Rochester Castle and the chapel at Havering and, in 1268, he instructed the Keeper of the Works at Westminster to provide twenty glass windows, containing forty shields of arms, for the queen's chamber at Havering. In 1253 the floor of the chapter house at Westminster Abbey was decorated with heraldic tiles and these include one of the earliest known representations of the royal arms.

Carved coat of arms of Lord
Clive; possibly once an
architectural feature of Styche,
Shropshire, and subsequently
removed to Bishops Castle where
it provided an elegant façade for
the town pump

Encouraged by their sovereign's example, and by the flowering
of the concept of courtly romanticism, the barons and prelates
began embellishing the fabric of their mansions and churches with
heraldry. This was also a reflection of the more secular nature of
late thirteenth-century magnatial society in which the symbols of
feudalism rivalled those of religion.

Stonework

Freestone is an easily wrought building stone which may be
dressed and carved. It should be fine-grained, consistent in both
colour and texture, and capable of taking finely detailed work. A
wide range of stone has been used for decorative purposes, from

The punning Lucy arms at
Charlecote, Warwickshire (a
luce is a pike)

limestones and sandstones to marbles, slates and alabaster, a
translucent, usually white, form of gypsum.

Heraldry was either painted on to the smooth surface of a stone
shield or carved in relief, the design being traced on to the
prepared surface of the stone and the material cut back to a
predetermined background line, leaving the device raised but
unfeatured. The main constituents of the design were then carved,
the overall balance being maintained by working on different
elements at the same time, using steel chisels and gouges, iron
hammers and fruitwood mallets. Individual charges in a shield
were left until last and, being in low relief, these required the most
intricate carving. When the carving was completed, the background was sometimes roughened ('sparrow pecked') with small
chisel marks, to emphasize the three-dimensional appearance of
the work.

Medieval stone carving was often painted and gilded and the
interiors of many stone buildings, both ecclesiastical and secular,
once blazed with colour. But paint and gilt require periodic
refurbishment and today only small areas of colour remain to
remind us of the extraordinary richness of our Gothic buildings.
There are many instances of early stonework having been repainted and gilded several times, not only in the great cathedrals
and abbey churches where such work is more easily identified, but
also in parish churches such as the tiny Norman church at

Heraldic vault of Tom Tower,
Christ Church, Oxford.
Benefactors' arms include Isham,
Berkeley, Spencer and Seymour

Hampnett in Gloucestershire where the sanctuary vaulting was completely refurbished by a Victorian incumbent in *c.* 1871. Original colouring is rarely discernible, for decorative stonework was often obliterated by the iconoclasts of the Reformation. Subsequent work is likely to reflect contemporary tastes and pigments and our present concern for historical accuracy was not always shared by our predecessors. This is particularly true of heraldry, for not every restorer was an armorist and errors abound.

Church monuments provide the most prolific source of armorial devices painted and gilded on carved stone (see Chapter Five), but there are other architectural features which, because of their shape and size, and their conspicuous position within the structure of a building, are also suited to this form of decoration.

The earliest known example of armorial devices carved in stone is a series of shields in the spandrels of the blind arcading in the north aisle of Westminster Abbey. Commissioned by Henry III in 1258, these depict the arms of the king together with those of the royal houses with which he was connected by marriage, and of his principal vassals: Arundel, Bigod, Bohun, Clare, de Lacy, Montford, de Quinci, Warenne and Richard, Earl of Cornwall. The series was inspired by Henry's visit to the French court of Louis IX

Bay twenty-four of the Great
Cloister vault, Canterbury
Cathedral

in 1254 where he was much impressed by the painted wooden
shields, bearing the arms of the nobility of France, which lined the
walls of the Great Hall of the Temple in Paris.

Shields of arms, often contained within carved trefoils or
quatrefoils, are common motifs in the panels and spandrels of
blind arcading, particularly in tombs and chantry chapels of the
fourteenth and fifteenth centuries, where series of shields record
the arms of related and collateral families and other beneficiaries
of a deceased's will for whom chantries were established (see
below). These shields may also contain religious symbols or the
attributed arms of patron saints to whom supplications were
addressed.

Arched roofs of stone (vaults) replaced timber roofs in most
major secular and ecclesiastical buildings, and in those areas of
parish churches where additional strength was required, beneath a
church tower, for example, or as the result of endowments and
bequests, expensive elaboration such as vaulting being indicative
of a benefactor's generosity. This, perhaps, explains the ubiquity

of medieval vaulted porches, many of which have a central shield-shaped boss which would originally have been emblazoned with the arms of the benefactor who paid for the porch's construction. Miniature vaults, often of exquisite workmanship, are commonly found above canopied tombs and chantry chapels, that of the Despencer tomb at Tewkesbury Abbey in Gloucestershire being the earliest example of fan vaulting (*c.* 1378).

Lion gargoyle at Mapperton, Dorset

Bosses, the projecting keystones at the intersection of ribs in a vault, are a rich source of heraldry. The fascinating series of 825 heraldic bosses in the late fourteenth-century vault of the Great Cloister at Canterbury Cathedral in Kent commemorates the benefactors whose gifts paid for the completion of the new cloister following the death of Archbishop William Courtenay in 1396. The shields and other devices, of which the vault is adorned at nearly every intersection, were expertly restored in 1937 and provide a unique record of contemporary magnatial society.

In the fifteenth- and sixteenth-century fan vaults of Sherborne Abbey in Dorset there are no fewer than 800 stone bosses, some of those in the north transept weighing more than half a ton. Each is elaborately carved, painted and gilded with stylized foliage, vernacular and religious motifs, chimerical creatures and heraldry. Devices include the cypher of Henry VII and his queen, Elizabeth of York; clusters of Tudor Roses; the Beaufort portcullis (a Tudor badge); shields of arms, including that of the King (with lion and greyhound supporters); and a rebus of Abbot Ramsam (who commissioned the nave roof) depicting a letter 'P' (for Peter) with an Abbot's crozier through the upright, a ram within the loop and a label with 'SAM' above. In common with many churches, the original painting and gilding was covered with a yellow ochre wash following the Reformation but was refurbished during the Victorian restoration of the Abbey in 1856.

The magnificent chapel of King's College, Cambridge, begun in 1446 and completed in 1515, represents the culmination of heraldic architectural embellishment, the carved stonework devoted exclusively to a triumphant declaration of the supremacy of the Tudor dynasty. Religious imagery is minimal and the entire fabric of the interior of the chapel is encrusted with heavily carved portcullises, roses and other Tudor devices, including immense greyhounds and dragons.

On the outside of buildings, pinnacles were sometimes carved to support armorial weather vanes (see below). At Athelhampton in Dorset, for example, where there is a series of late fifteenth-century pinnacles carved to represent the famous crest of the Martyn family, *a Monkey sejant* (seated) *proper collared Gold looking in a mirror*. The family motto was 'He who looks at Martyn's ape, Martyn's ape shall look at him'! Gargoyles were often carved to depict a grotesque visage, beast or figure but surprisingly few of these are of heraldic significance.

St John's College, Cambridge

So many medieval castles were 'slighted', and the fabric exposed to the elements, that very little remains of decorative stonework. Neglect continued through the eighteenth and nineteenth centuries when 'ivy-mantled towers' and decaying medieval ruins were perceived to be romantic and picturesque. At Raglan Castle in Gwent, a series of finely carved panels above the windows of the state apartments (*c.* 1469) provides evidence of the prominence given to heraldic display at that time. Although they are no longer painted, the late fifteenth-century shields almost certainly bore the arms of Sir William Herbert (*Per pale Gules and Azure three Lions*

OPPOSITE: Herbert *bascule* badge and shields, Raglan Castle, Gwent

Sherborne Abbey, Dorset

rampant Argent) who was created Earl of Pembroke by Edward IV in 1468 as a reward for his capture of Harlech Castle, Gwynedd – the last Lancastrian stronghold of the Wars of the Roses. Alternate panels contain the Herbert badge of a bascule drawbridge, an unusual device which may also be seen above the entrance to one of the fifteenth-century porches of St Mary's church, Usk, and in a seventeenth-century copy of a seal to a Raglan deed dated 1451. In Northumberland, a carved heraldic façade (*c.* 1400) above the entrance to the great hall of Warkworth Castle declares the power and magnificence of the Percy dynasty and inspired many similar Victorian schemes.

Carved heraldic panels may be found above the gatehouses of

OPPOSITE: the High Street gate, Salisbury

Eleanor Cross at Hardingstone,
Northamptonshire

Heraldic *tygers*, 'ducally gorged',
supporting the Digby arms at
Sherborne Castle, Dorset

several medieval walled towns and monastic closes but these are
rarely coloured and many are in poor repair. At Butley Priory in
Suffolk seven closely packed tiers of shields of arms adorn the
gatehouse facade, while the early fourteenth-century gatehouse of
Kirkham Priory in Yorkshire was entirely covered with the arms
of its founders and benefactors. At Glastonbury in Somerset the
panels above the entrance archway to the pilgrims' inn (*c.* 1470
and now the George Hotel) contain the arms of the Abbey and
those of Edward IV. The use of shields to ornament such
panels is a characteristic of Perpendicular architecture – both
ecclesiastical and secular – and provided a model for Pugin's

The Phelips firebasket at Montacute, Somerset

heraldic ornamentation of the Palace of Westminster (begun 1840).

During the Tudor period badges and chimerical beasts were preferred as decorative motifs and coats of arms became more complex. These often included supporters, figures depicted on either side of the shield to 'support' it. Some of the most impressive examples of heraldic stone carving are to be found in the fabric of collegiate gatehouses of the period such as that of St John's College, Cambridge which commemorates the college's founder, Lady Margaret Beaufort, Duchess of Richmond (d. 1509) (see illustration p. 71).

There are numerous examples of carved and gilded representations of the royal arms; above the High Street gate to the Cathedral Close at Salisbury, Wiltshire, for example (see illustration p. 72). At Sherborne, Dorset, a carved (but uncoloured) panel of the royal arms in the south wall of the abbey's medieval lady chapel was replaced in 1660 following the Civil War and again (by a copy) in 1989. From 1560 the lady chapel was used to house the headmaster of the King's School and beneath the panel are the arms of the school's principal benefactors and, in a lower tier, the cyphers of the eighteen founding governors (see illustration p. 73).

Much heraldic ornamentation is commemorative. The Eleanor Crosses erected by Edward I (between 1292 and 1294) to mark the twelve-day funeral progress of his queen, Eleanor of Castile, from Harby in Nottinghamshire to Westminster, were decorated with finely carved shields of England and Castile. The ceremonial which accompanied each stage of the procession established, in England, the elaborate funeral cortèges of the rich and famous, in which heraldry played a major rôle. Eleanor Crosses have survived at Geddington and Hardingstone in Northamptonshire and at Waltham Cross in Essex (see illustration p. 74).

Cavendish with Boyle *in pretence*, Chatsworth, Derbyshire

There are numerous examples of carved heraldic devices on the gate pillars of estates. These are usually supporters or other beasts from a family's arms, or a distinctive charge such as the magnificent fire-basket crest of the Phelips family who built Montacute House in Somerset in the late sixteenth century (*A square Beacon Gold filled with Fire proper*).

In the seventeenth century heraldry rarely featured in the buildings of Inigo Jones, Wren or even Vanburgh, who was himself a herald, and in the eighteenth century armorial devices were usually confined to the embellishment of cartouches within classical pediments, as above the entrance to the magnificent Palladian stables at Chatsworth in Derbyshire (1758) where the Devonshire arms include life-size stag supporters with real antlers.

Montagu arms on the façade of the stable block, Boughton, Northamptonshire

Stained Glass

Comparatively little medieval stained glass has survived in our churches, and in a few secular buildings usually only fragments remain. While that which remains confirms that armorial devices were widely used for decorative and commemorative purposes, medieval man was ever mindful of his transient condition and, in most church windows, heraldry was subsidiary to biblical and allegorical themes. Not so his post-Reformation successors whose window glass declared, not the glory of God, but that of the new Tudor establishment.

The Romans produced slabs of coloured glass, but the idea of holding pieces together within a lead framework to form a patterned window is believed by some to have originated in Byzantium. It is known that in Europe stained glass was used in church windows from the seventh century, however, the earliest surviving examples in England are from the twelfth century. Most medieval coloured glass was manufactured in France and Germany and imported into England where it was made into windows.

Before the sixteenth century, window glass was made from a mixture of wood-ash and river sand which was heated into molten form and either spun on the end of a rod into a circular sheet or, more usually in England, blown into a long cylinder and cut longitudinally to produce a flat sheet. Coloured glasses (pot-metals) were made by adding different metallic oxides to the molten clear glass: cobalt for blue, copper for ruby, manganese for violet, silver salts for yellow, iron for green or yellow, and small quantities of gold for a rose red. The colour depended on the method of firing: different results could be achieved by varying the level of oxidation, for example.

The ruby and blue glasses were very dark and a technique called flashing was used to make them more transparent. Using a blowpipe, a bubble of molten coloured glass was dipped into molten white glass and worked into a panel which was coated on one side with a thin layer of the desired colour.

From the mid-twelfth century most decorative windows comprised a central pictorial motif contained within a medallion and a geometrical border. The design (cartoon) of the window was drawn on a whitewashed table by draughtsmen (tracers) and the pieces of coloured glass cut to the required shape. Before the introduction of the diamond cutter in the sixteenth century, this was done by means of a hot iron which was drawn across the glass and cold water applied, causing the glass to crack along the incision. The pieces were then trimmed with a grozing iron to a more precise shape, and details such as faces, hair, limbs, linen folds and foliage were painted in a mixture of metallic oxide (iron or copper), powdered glass and gum. Finally the glass sections were set out on an iron plate and covered with ash before being fired at a high temperature (using beechwood) in a clay and dung kiln. This fused the paint on to the coloured glass. The pieces were then re-assembled and bound together in a lead framework or armature with putty forced into the crevices between the lead and the glass. Lead was a most suitable material for this purpose, for it was malleable when unheated and, having a low melting point, was easily cast into strips with grooves at the sides to accommodate the glass.

As the craft developed, the lines of the lead framework were incorporated into the design itself and, from the fourteenth century, the flashed surface of coloured glass was often removed (abraided) to leave a pattern of clear glass which, when re-painted with silver oxide and fired, turned to a dark yellow which passed for gold. This was particularly useful in heraldic designs when 'metal' charges, gold or silver, were depicted on a blue or red field, as in the royal arms of England (*Gules three Lions passant guardant Gold*). Many heraldic devices were not of a convenient shape to be confined within strips of lead and while large charges, such as beasts, could be built up of several pieces of glass leaded together, very small or repetitive charges were often difficult to reproduce. This problem was overcome by using small pieces of coloured glass and painting around the outline of the motif with brown enamel to leave only the shape as the unpainted surface. Alternatively, a whole sheet was painted with brown enamel and the appropriate area scraped away to form the desired shape. This technique may be seen in the ancient arms of France (*Azure semy-de-lis Gold*), a blue field scattered with gold fleurs-de-lis, in which the small diamond-shaped panels (quarries or quarrels) bearing fleurs-de-lis alternate with strips of blue glass for the field, producing a pattern of lozenges.

When completed, the window was fitted into the opening by means of lead strips which were attached to iron saddle-bars or, in larger window openings, set within a decorative metal armature. As tracery became more complex in the fourteenth century, so the upper lights of windows were used to accommodate separate sections of an overall design.

Gothic buildings were conceived from the inside, 'the heavenward thrust of glass and stone' culminating in the 'ethereal fragility' of the perpendicular period (Doreen Yarwood: *Encyclopaedia of Architecture*). While window glass in churches of the more austere monastic orders was usually plain, twelfth- and thirteenth-century stained glass (up to *c.* 1260) was predominantly ruby and blue and created a 'homogeneous fabric of light' (ibid.) which induced a sense of almost mystical contemplation. Regrettably, so little early coloured glass remains intact in England that it is difficult for us to appreciate its magnificence without visiting European cathedrals such as Chartres.

The years 1260 to 1325 are notable for grisaille glass (from the French *gris* meaning grey,) large areas of clear quarries surrounded by borders of monochrome foliage decoration and occasional medallions in colour. The unearthly glow of suspended light which characterized earlier windows is rarely found in those of the fourteenth century which inclined more to yellows and greens, and is entirely missing from the wide perpendicular windows of the fifteenth century.

The practice of endowing benefactions and chantries was particularly popular during the fourteenth and fifteenth centuries and for this reason at least half the surviving medieval church glass contains an element of heraldry.

Chantries were bequests which enabled priests to pray for the souls of the departed and of relatives, friends and others, including sometimes the king and influential lords. Shields or other heraldic devices in a chapel window may therefore be those of the people for whom masses were to be said as well as those of the deceased benefactor in whose memory the window was installed. As with brasses and effigies, such windows may have been commissioned before the death of the person they commemorate or, indeed, many years afterwards.

Throughout the medieval and Tudor periods, senior churchmen, magnates, guilds and fraternities endowed money for the repair of churches, and groups of citizens would sometimes combine to pay for the refurbishing of their parish church. Shields of arms may be found in 'donor windows', most often in the upper tracery lights, where they commemorate the generosity of benefactors. At Dorchester Abbey in Oxfordshire, for example, the south window of the chancel contains twenty-one heraldic shields to record those who financed the extension of the sanctuary in *c.* 1340, and at York Minster the nave windows have borders in which are depicted the arms of royal and noble benefactors, and of the great northern families. Occasionally, groups of donors' shields include the devices of non-armigerous benefactors, notably merchants' marks.

The Turberville window (*c.* 1530) at Bere Regis church, Dorset. Typical of numerous memorial windows, the arms of Turberville (*Ermine a Lion rampant Gules crowned Gold*) are impaled with those acquired by marriage with heraldic heiresses. The lapsed lineage of the Turbervilles gave Thomas Hardy inspiration for his novel *Tess of the D'Urbervilles* (1891)

The decoration surrounding the shields may also be significant. At Arkesden, Essex, for example, the shield of Thomas FitzAlan, Archbishop of Canterbury, is set within three crowns, suggesting that the window was erected when he was bishop of Ely (1374–88), the arms of that see being *Gules three Crowns Gold*. Diamond-shaped quarries or small rectangular panels in the border of a window may contain badges, rebuses or cyphers. Donor windows were particularly popular in the late fifteenth century and these often contain full coats of arms (with arms, crests and supporters) or kneeling figures wearing tabards of the benefactor's arms. While some heraldic figures may be immediately apparent, others are more difficult to find. At the church of St Peter Mancroft, Norwich, for example, the fifteenth-century east window comprises forty-two panels of biblical subjects. In one of the panels, however, are two figures kneeling at a prayer desk on which is a quartered coat of arms.

Other windows commemorated events and perhaps the greatest of these is the magnificent fourteenth-century East window in the choir of Gloucester Cathedral. Constructed between 1347 and 1350 it is 11.6 m wide (38 ft) and 22 m high (72 ft) – the size of a tennis court, and is the largest stone traceried window in England. In the lower lights are the shields of the Gloucestershire knights who fought at the battle of Crécy in 1346.

Following the Reformation countless medieval windows were destroyed and replaced with glass in which no religious or allegorical subjects were permitted. The duties of the iconoclast are vividly described by Richard Culmner in *Cathedrall Newes from Canterburie* (1644), '. . . on the top of the citie ladder, near sixty steps high, with a whole pike in the hand, rattling down Becket's glassy bones from the great idolatrous window.' Heraldry was an obvious and politically acceptable alternative and one which appealed particularly to the newly-created Tudor aristocracy. Anxious to prove themselves equal in blood to the old magnatial families, they erected monuments and commemorative windows which positively radiated heraldic splendour, their arms incorporating numerous acquired (or assumed) ancestral quarterings.

From the late sixteenth century, transparent coloured enamels were widely used so that single sheets of glass could be treated as complete pictures and designs were no longer constrained by the need to contain pieces of different coloured glass within lead strips. The Renaissance also brought a change of style, shields were surrounded by wreaths and later by strapwork and cartouches and this practice continued into the seventeenth century.

Armorial glass was less common in the eighteenth century and the first half of the nineteenth, though contemporary donor windows still included some heraldry. The Gothic Revival of the nineteenth century encouraged a return to the use of stained glass. In parish churches many new windows containing heraldic glass were erected by lords of the manor and often these contained series of shields showing the arms of predecessors. This practice seems to have been popular with those who acquired manors by purchase rather than by inheritance, as at Puddletown church in Dorset and at Aldermaston in Berkshire. Also during the nineteenth and twentieth centuries glass may have been installed or refurbished as a memorial to an individual or family and small shields, military insignia and school or university arms were often incorporated in a window design or in the tracery lights. Many such memorials commemorate those who lost their lives in military service. At Cheriton, Hampshire, for example, there are four windows dedicated to the memory of four cousins who were killed in action, and each figure is depicted in armour charged with his arms.

Precisely when, and to what extent, secular buildings were first glazed is uncertain. Chaucer, before 1372, refers to the windows of his chamber which 'with glas were al . . . wel y glazed' with scenes from the Trojan wars. Stained glass in domestic buildings was

Royal arms of Henry VI at
Radley church, Oxfordshire.
Designed by Thomas Willement,
heraldic artist to George IV, and
based on fifteenth-century glass
at Ockwells Manor, Berkshire

intended primarily as a declaration of status, and the heraldry of the owner, and of the families with whom he was associated by marriage or seignorage, were obvious subjects. At Athelhampton in Dorset, for example, there are several superb examples of late fifteenth-century and early sixteenth-century heraldic windows in the Great Hall, though some bays contain Victorian restorations. But stained glass was expensive and, in many cases, heraldry was confined either to a single light or to a glass roundel which was suspended on the inside of the window.

The importance of heraldic display to the Tudor aristocracy is evident in the magnificent library windows at Montacute House in Somerset and at Charlecote Park in Warwickshire. Visits by peripatetic sovereigns were often commemorated by the erection of heraldic glass: at Aldermaston Court in Berkshire, for example, where windows containing the arms of Henry VIII and Elizabeth I recall royal progresses.

Armorial glass rarely featured in the architectural classicism of the eighteenth century but enjoyed increasing popularity during the Gothic Revival, particularly in the grandiose town halls of Victorian England. Much nineteenth-century heraldry is of doubtful validity, however, and at this time there was also a flourishing market in miscellaneous fragments from the windows of restored churches, many of which may still be found illuminating the stair-wells of Victorian houses.

Glass is particularly vulnerable both to the elements and to vandalism and although some stained glass remains in its original location many fragments (or even entire windows) have been moved several times and may now be combined with glass of an entirely different period. Such considerations should be borne in mind when attempting to identify armorial devices in heraldic glass. A series of twelfth-century biblical figures at Canterbury Cathedral, for example, is surmounted by heraldic figures of the fourteenth century. At Salisbury Cathedral there are six thirteenth-century shields at the base of the west window which is composed principally of fifteenth-century glass.

Timber Roofs and Plaster Ceilings

Not all vaults are of stone; that above the presbytery at Winchester Cathedral, Hampshire, for example, is an early sixteenth-century timber imitation with a series of heraldic bosses including the royal arms, crowned thorn bush device and HR monogram of Henry VII.

Many church roofs have been boarded or 'ceiled' between the principal rafters to form ceilings, with carved wooden bosses at the intersections. The ceiling panels may also be carved, as at Shepton Mallet in Somerset where a rounded 'wagon' roof contains 350

Presbytery vault at Winchester Cathedral

Heraldic ceiling of Auckland
Castle, Durham

panels, each of a different design. There are also several fine examples of roof panels which have been gilded and painted, at Cullompton church in Devon, for example, and at St Alban's in Hertfordshire where a series of fourteenth-century ceiling panels in the choir of the cathedral depicts the arms of Edward III, his family and alliances. These were discovered in the nineteenth century and, interestingly, the arms of England are shown in reverse, i.e. *Quarterly England and France Ancient*.

Hammer-beam roofs and double hammer-beam roofs (those with two tiers of projecting beams) evolved in the last decades of the fourteenth century and reached decorative perfection in the fifteenth century, particularly in East Anglian churches. The projections often terminate in carved angels, sometimes exceeding

Top: banners, helms and crests of the senior Knights Grand Cross of the Most Honourable Order of the Bath above their stalls in Henry VII's chapel, Westminster Abbey. *Bottom*: stall plates, at St George's Chapel, Windsor, of knights of the Most Noble Order of the Garter – Walter, Lord Hungerford (d. 1449); Henry Bourchier, Earl of Essex (d. 1483) and Sir John Grey of Ruthin (d. 1439)

2a 2b 2c

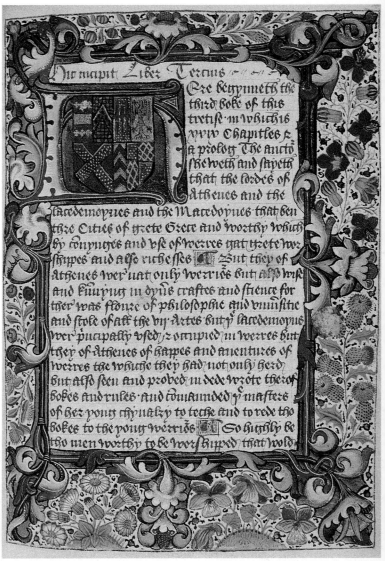

This page, top: a copy of the early fifteenth-century English translation of Vegetius *De Re Militari*, the initial letter of which is decorated with the arms of Anne Nevill, queen to Richard III. *Left*: a detail from the *Wilton Diptych* showing an angel bearing the white hart device of Richard II

Opposite, top: extract from the *Rous Roll* (*c.* 1483) showing the figures and arms of Anne Beauchamp and Richard Nevill, Earl of Warwick – 'the Kingmaker'. *Bottom*: letters patent granting arms (1456) to the Worshipful Company of Tallow Chandlers of the City of London

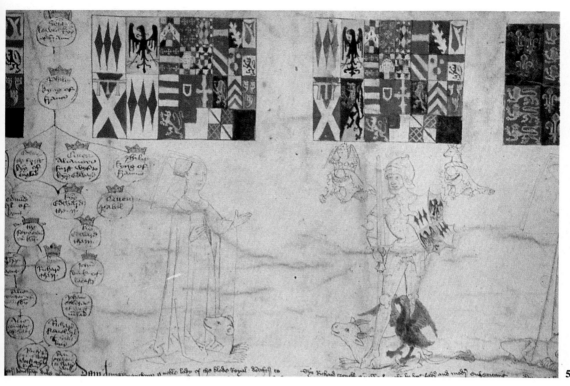

5

6

Lutrell

de Furnival

de Ecclesshall

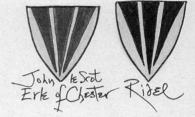
John le Scot
Erle of Chester   Ridel

de Wadsley

de Wortley

de Mounteney

Basset   de Bryen

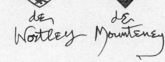
Sir John de Mounteney

Wrottesley

7

8

9a

9b

Opposite, top: seigniorial arms
(see page 5). *Bottom*: the College
of Arms, Queen Victoria Street,
London

This page, top: tomb of Ambrose
Dudley, Earl of Warwick
(d. 1590) at St Mary's church,
Warwick. *Centre*: effigial crests,
at Noseley, Leicestershire, of Sir
Thomas Hesilrige, first Baronet
of Noseley (d. 1629) and
Frances, daughter and heir of Sir
William Gorges of Alderton.
Bottom: heraldry of the Manners
family on the tomb of John,
fourth Earl of Rutland (d. 1588),
at Bottesford, Leicestershire

10

11

12

Opposite, top: one of a series of plates depicting the funeral cortège of John, seventh Earl and first Duke of Rothes (d. 1681), one of the most distinguished statesmen of his time. The procession, which stretched from St Giles Cathedral to the Palace of Holyroodhouse, included trains of artillery, regiments of the army and the Scottish officers of arms. *Bottom*: Cavendish hatchments at Cartmel Priory near the family estate at Holker Hall, Cumbria. The impalement is Lowther and the inescutcheon Compton

This page: magnificent fireplace at Eastnor Castle, Herefordshire. Erected in 1849 for John, second Earl Somers, from a design by Augustus Pugin

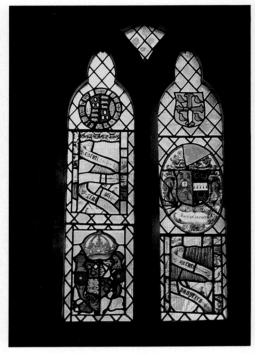

13a

13c

Top left: the figures of John Denston and Dorothy Clopton in medieval glass at Long Melford, Suffolk. *Top right*: Tudor glass, including the royal arms, at Ebrington, Gloucestershire. *Bottom left*: Brownlow heraldry in nineteenth-century heraldic memorial glass at Belton church, Lincolnshire. *Bottom right*: detail from an early twentieth-century memorial window to Major Archibald Leonard Lucas Tooth, second and last baronet (d. 1918) at Holme Lacy, Herefordshire

Heraldic ceiling by William Morris at Jesus College, Cambridge

one hundred in a single roof, and these may bear emblazoned shields or other armorial devices. The wall plate or cornice may also be richly carved with painted and gilded heraldry.

As in window glass, such decoration is not usually devoted exclusively to heraldry. A fine timber roof at Bere Regis church in Dorset, which at first sight appears to be a hammer-beam structure but is not so, was erected in memory of Cardinal Morton (*c.* 1420– 1500) who was born in Dorset but lies in Canterbury Cathedral. The roof is built of carved and painted wood with projecting figures of the twelve Apostles in fifteenth-century costume and great bosses which include a representation of the cardinal himself, his coat of arms and a red rose and cord to symbolize the marriage he arranged between Elizabeth of York and Henry Tudor.

In Scotland, where interior schemes of heraldic decoration, using tempera paint, were popular in the sixteenth and seventeenth centuries, there are several fine painted ceilings. At Earlshall and Collairnie castles in Fife, for example, and at St Machar's Cathedral, Aberdeen, where a series of shields illustrates the political and religious composition of Scottish and European magnatial society in the early sixteenth century.

An early example of an heraldic plaster ceiling from the first half of the sixteenth century is that of the dining room of Haddon Hall,

Derbyshire, which consists of several painted panels containing shields and armorial badges.

Towards the end of the sixteenth-century the painted ceiling was superseded by plaster motifs, armorial subjects being particularly popular, as in the White Room of Broughton Castle, Oxfordshire (1599) and the Great Hall of Kellie Castle, Tayside (1660). Ceilings of moulded plasterwork were also erected in churches and these often include the heraldic devices of local nobles and benefactors, as, for example, at Abbotsbury in Dorset (1638).

Heraldry appears infrequently in the classical ceilings of the eighteenth and nineteenth centuries, but there are fine Gothic Revival examples dating from the mid-nineteenth century; the heraldic painted ceiling in the West Drawing Room of Oxburgh Hall, Norfolk, for example.

Encaustic Tiles

Floor-tiles in the Chapter House, Westminster Abbey, c. 1256

Decorated floor tiles dating from the thirteenth to the sixteenth centuries may be found in many medieval churches. These should not be confused with nineteenth-century Victorian reproduction tiles, manufactured in large numbers for church restorations or re-buildings, and often based on medieval designs but of uniform appearance and texture. Victorian tiles will also be found throughout a church while medieval examples are usually confined to the chancel.

During the thirteenth century several methods were developed for the decoration of plain clay tiles. The pattern could be engraved in outline on the surface of the tile or the design carved in relief or counter-relief on a wood-block which was then pressed into the tile. In both instances the tile was then glazed and fired to produce a patterned tile of one colour. A third method was to fill the matrix of a stamped tile with white pipeclay before it was glazed and fired. This produced the familiar brown and yellow encaustic tile. Occasionally the design was reversed with a dark pattern set into a light coloured tile. Early encaustic tiles are usually $12\frac{1}{2}$–15 cm square (5–6 in) and as much as $2\frac{1}{2}$ cm thick (1 in) with a 2 mm inlay ($\frac{1}{10}$ in).

By the mid-fourteenth century a flourishing English tile manufacturing industry had been established in the Chilterns with its centre at Penn in Buckinghamshire. Penn tiles were smaller than average, only $11\frac{1}{2}$ cm square ($4\frac{1}{2}$ in) and 2 cm thick ($\frac{3}{4}$ in). It seems likely that by this time the various stages of manufacture were combined in a single process: the stamp being dipped into the white slip clay before it was pushed into the malleable tile so that the slip remained in the impression when the stamp was removed. This would explain why the slip is very thin and some edges of the inlay may be smudged or missing. The inlay was usually flush with

Encaustic tiles of the thirteenth and early fourteenth centuries. Although the arms of Fitzpayne (*Gules three Lions passant guardant Argent over all a Bend Azure*) and the lions of Eleanor of Castile, queen of Edward I, have been carved correctly, the resulting impressions are back-to-front

the surface of the tile but a later development in technique resulted in the pattern being slightly concave.

Early tiles were produced to decorate royal and magnatial palaces and important religious houses. During the fourteenth century their use spread to smaller churches and domestic buildings, though in many instances a commonality of design suggests that batches of tiles were 'left-overs' from large monastic commissions and had been donated by a religious house to one or more of its subsidiary churches.

Most designs required four tiles to complete a pattern, some required as many as sixteen, and it is often possible to identify individual tiles from a major monastery which have been laid down inaccurately in a parish church – possibly because insufficient tiles of each type were provided to complete a pattern or the workmen were not familiar with the original. It may be that tilers carried out smaller commissions *in situ*, constructing temporary kilns and carrying a selection of wood-blocks with them. This would explain the occurrence of identical tiles in churches many miles apart.

Many designs were used in encaustic relief and counter-relief tiles including Christian symbols, rebuses and armorial devices associated with royal or monastic foundations or with the bene-

Victorian floor tiles, with the
arms of Prince Albert, at Ham,
Wiltshire

factors of a particular church or chantry. Armorial tiles are a
considerable aid to research but not all lions and fleurs-de-lis are of
heraldic significance. Confusingly, it is not unusual to find that an
armorial design has been carved correctly on the wood-block but
the resultant impression is back-to-front.

Churches

Churches provide the most prolific source of heraldry and that
which most commonly falls within the experience of the local
historian. Monuments, not only of the rich and powerful but also
of the minor gentry, magistrates, squires, merchants and yeomen,
abound (see Chapter Five), and in stained glass and carved and
painted stone and wood, the arms and devices of local families,
benefactors and rectors record the fluctuating fortunes of a
community. However, not all heraldry is as immediately apparent
as the ubiquitous royal arms or that which embellishes tombs and
chantry chapels.

In the Christian church the mass and baptism are considered to be
pre-eminent among the seven Sacraments, baptism emphasizing
entry into the Christian life and the purging of sin. Consequently,
every medieval church possessed its font which was symbolically
located near the entrance. Heraldry was not widely used as
decoration, however, except in the fonts of private chapels and
those which commemorated benefactors. The fourteenth-century
font and cover (now lost) at East Winch in Norfolk, for example,
was embellished with the carved and painted arms of the Howards
and other magnatial families. The lead font at Greatham House,

Fifteenth-century font at
Winterborne Whitechurch,
Dorset

Parham in West Sussex, has the Peveral arms repeated eight times,
and at Winterborne Whitechurch in Dorset one of a series of
fifteenth-century stone fonts, characterized by four supporting
pillars, is richly ornamented with shields and beautifully vigorous
armorial carvings. At St Chad's church at Holt, also in Dorset,
there is a superb fifteenth-century octagonal font carved with
twenty-four coats of arms, badges and other devices, on each of
the faces of the bowl, the shaft and base.

In medieval churches the chancel was a mysterious inner
sanctum in which the mass was celebrated and from which the

Detail of fifteenth-century oak
pulpit at Fotheringhay,
Northamptonshire

congregation in the nave was separated by a chancel screen (see
below). But the popularity of itinerant preachers in the fourteenth
century (notably the Franciscan friars) is reflected in the number
of pulpits erected in that period, usually set against the wall of the
nave or against a pier. The earliest example dates from c. 1340
though most surviving pre-Reformation pulpits are from the
fifteenth and early sixteenth centuries. From the Latin *pulpitum*
meaning platform, pulpits were constructed of stone or of oak with
traceried panels which sometimes contained carved or painted
motifs depicting the likenesses of the four Evangelists or familiar
preceptors such as the four Doctors of the Latin Church:
St Augustine of Hippo, St Gregory, St Ambrose and St Jerome.
Heraldic devices were sometimes incorporated into these decorative panels and may be found on both the sides and tester (a
canopy supported by a screen at the back of the pulpit). At
Croscombe in Somerset, for example, the pulpit was a gift of
Bishop Lake whose personal arms, together with those of his
diocese, are carved on the sides and canopy. A fine fifteenth-
century oak pulpit at Fotheringhay, Northamptonshire, a gift of
Edward IV (1461–83), is richly carved, painted and gilded with
Yorkist heraldry, including the black bull of Clarence and the
white boar of the Duke of Gloucester. Interestingly, but not
exceptionally, in the royal arms the three fleurs-de-lis of France
are carved in reverse. From 1603 all churches were required to
have a pulpit.

Medieval chancel screens of carved wood or stone separated the
chancel of a church from its nave, if surmounted by a rood (a cross
or crucifix), these are known as rood screens; a screen which
separates the open space at the base of a tower from the nave at its
western end is a tower screen. Such screens are generally divided

Chancel screen at Attleborough, Norfolk

into bays, each of which is usually panelled to a third of its height, above which lights terminate in pierced tracery within a pointed arch or arches. Medieval chancel screens were often coloured and gilded but regrettably in most surviving examples little remains to suggest that heraldry was widely used. Conversely, parclose screens, which separated a chapel or tomb from chancel or nave, were of similar appearance and were frequently decorated with the heraldic devices of benefactors or those in whose memory masses were said. The chancel or rood screen should not be confused with the pulpitum which, in major churches, occupied a position between the chancel screen and the choir and was of substantial stone construction, often with heraldic motifs carved in the stonework of the façade and incorporated into the gates or doors of the pulpitum passage. Perhaps the finest armorial doors in England are those to the chapel of Henry VII in Westminster Abbey. Made of bronze in 1509, they are decorated with lions and fleurs-de-lis, portcullis and falcon and fetterlock badges, crowns and roses and HR cyphers. Jacobean screens, usually of unpainted timber, are generally found in collegiate ante-chapels and halls, though there are chancel and parclose screens of this period: at Croscombe in Somerset and at Folke in Dorset, for example. A common feature is a carved representation of the Royal Arms,

mounted above the centre of the screen, and sometimes flanked by the arms of a patron or benefactor and those of a bishop impaling the arms of his diocese. A good example is the screen at Abbey Dore, Herefordshire.

Medieval congregations were rarely provided with seating but as sermons became more popular towards the end of the fifteenth century, and an English liturgy was introduced following the Reformation, so listening became fashionable and benches were introduced. At first these were simply boards supported by trestles but later benches incorporated bench ends which were carved in a variety of sophisticated or vernacular styles, often with allegorical or heraldic subjects. Seventeenth- and eighteenth-century box pews were wainscotted and provided with doors to protect the congregation from drafts. After the Reformation the altar was no longer the focus of attention, but the prayer-desk and pulpit, and it was to these that the congregation was directed when box pews were installed. Certain 'square pews' were reserved for specific families and these were often upholstered and curtained. Others were even more lavishly equipped and furnished, often with a fireplace and private doorway from the churchyard, and with the family's heraldry much in evidence. Such 'parlour pews' were sometimes converted chantry chapels, such as that of the Long family in Draycot Cerne church near Chippenham in Wiltshire and the Hungerford chantry in Salisbury Cathedral which was 'appropriated as a seat for mayor and bishop in sermon time' (Hutchins).

A misericord is a projection beneath a hinged wooden seat on which a person may rest when in a standing position when the seat is turned up. Usually found in the chancel stalls of former monastic and collegiate churches and in chantry chapels, most date from the mid-thirteenth century to the late fifteenth. Their function was to provide support and relief for clergy and choir who were able to rest without sitting as they stood through interminable daily offices (*miserere* – 'have pity'). Where misericords have survived, every stall seems originally to have been provided with one, suggesting that it was not only the elderly and infirm who had need of them. Most misericords were vigorously carved but while many designs are unique, others, or variations of them, were widely used by carvers who appear to have worked from design books. These would be submitted to the patron or chapter who would then select those designs which were considered appropriate to a particular church, at the same time commissioning others which were entirely new. Each collection, therefore, has its own unique flavour and reflects the tastes of a period as well as local influences and contemporary political allegiances. Fifteenth-century Ludlow in Shropshire, for example, was thrust into the forefront of national politics as one of the principal strongholds of Richard, Duke of York, and in Ludlow church Yorkist badges are much in evidence, both in the misericords and in the splendid bosses of the chancel roof immediately above the stalls. There is evidence to

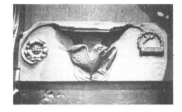

Misericords at Tansor, Northamptonshire (above), with Yorkist badges of falcon, fetterlock and white rose and at Ludlow, Shropshire (below) with antelope of Henry VI between two pagan 'Green Men'

OPPOSITE: centre gate, Henry VII's Chapel, Westminster Abbey

Dole cupboard at church of
St Martin, Ruislip

suggest that in some instances both stalls and misericords may
once have been painted and gilded and heraldic symbolism was
ideally suited to such carvings, as were images culled from the
medieval bestiaries and from folklore and legend, moral allegories
and cautionary tales. Misericords have often been removed from
their original stalls and re-arranged during restoration. In some
instances they have been moved elsewhere: at Tansor in
Northamptonshire, for example, where the mid-fifteenth century
misericords originated in the collegiate chancel at nearby Fother-
ingay.

Dole cupboards may still be found in some churches. These
once contained loaves of bread for distribution to the poor and
most date from the sixteenth century or later. Charitable 'doles'
(hence 'on the dole' etc.) were rarely provided anonymously and

Heraldry in the west doors of Bath Abbey commemorates James Montagu, Bishop of Bath and Wells 1608–16

the arms of a benefactor are almost invariably carved on the front of the cupboard.

Commanderies and Preceptories

Commanderies were manorial estates and hospices belonging to the Military and Hospitaller Order of the Knights Hospitaller of St John of Jerusalem (known as the Knights Hospitaller, founded before 1113). They were usually staffed by a small complement of knights with a chaplain and servants and enjoyed certain privileges. The parish of the commandery at Dinmore in Herefordshire, for example, remained entirely free of tithe, the owners of the estate benefiting from immunities granted to the Hospitallers by Pope Paschal II in 1113. Dinmore ranked as third or fourth in importance among the fifty or so similar Hospitaller commanderies established in England and Wales in the twelfth and thirteenth centuries, though recent additions (1936) are redolent more of twentieth-century romanticism than of medieval altruism. Each commandery was the responsibility of a senior knight of the order, the gift of a commandery being the usual reward for outstanding service in the Crusades. In addition to providing income for the order by the management of the estates, commanderies were regional military training centres and hospices or places of rest for those who returned injured or invalided from the Holy Land. They also afforded shelter and refreshment to travellers and sustenance to the sick and needy. Commanderies accumulated extensive tracts of land, acquired both from the Templars, following their suppression in 1312, and from the endowments of corrodians: those who were not members of the order but enjoyed residential benefits in return for their generosity. It is the heraldry of the knights commander and of corrodians which is most often in evidence, together with the arms of the order (*Gules a Cross Argent*) and its badge, the familiar white Maltese cross of eight points which is always associated with black livery.

The parallel Order of the Poor Knights of Christ and of the Temple of Solomon (the Knights Templar, founded in 1118) possessed similar establishments called preceptories though, following the suppression of the Templars in 1312, these were transferred to the Knights Hospitaller who also adopted the term to describe some of their later commanderies. Typically, the preceptory at Chibburn in Northumberland was built around a central courtyard approached through an arched gateway in a northern two-storey range of domestic buildings, and with a chapel to the south and dwelling house to the west. The banner of the Templars was the famous Beau Seant (*Per fess Sable and Argent*) and its habit was white with a red cross of eight points on the shoulder. Templar badges included the *Angus Dei* (a Paschal Lamb with a banner and halo charged with a cross) and a strange device consisting of two knights riding a single horse was later translated into a pegasus in the arms of the Inner Temple in London.

Agnus Dei

Secular Buildings

Armorial devices, used for decoration and identification, will be found as architectural features in a wide range of secular buildings from medieval fortresses and manor houses to the ironmasters' mansions of the Industrial Revolution. Some buildings may be of a single architectural style while others incorporate features of many periods. Most have much to tell of the aspirations and fluctuating fortunes of their various owners and many have developed as the result of changing political circumstances. Heraldic references are usually contemporaneous with the period in which the work was carried out and may include the arms and other devices of the owner who commissioned the work, and of his family's ancestors. Others may include the arms of previous owners or of lords of the manor, notably during the nineteenth century when many houses were refurbished by industrial magnates and entrepreneurs who were not themselves armigerous.

Medieval heraldry, like contemporary architecture, was essentially functional. Armorial devices displayed on flags and incorporated into the fabric and furnishings of a residence were a necessary, though attractive, adjunct of feudal lordship for they declaimed status and confirmed authority. But the Dissolution of the Monasteries (1536/39) was to have a significant effect on the application of heraldry in England. Firstly, the sale of monastic buildings and lands encouraged a new class of property-owning gentlemen, eager to emulate the nobility and, often, joining its ranks. Secondly, the Reformation and the desecration of church interiors, combined with legislation which encouraged ecclesiastical austerity, resulted in the diversion of resources from endowments to the church to expenditure on the home. This is reflected in the magnificent armorial window glass, fabrics, furnishings and architectural features of the period.

Heraldic decoration was generally consistent with the artistic and architectural fashions of a particular period and was at its height during the sixteenth and early seventeenth centuries, and again during the Gothic Revival. Architectural decoration of the nineteenth century reflected, not only a renewal of interest in matters medieval, but also a reaction to the French Revolution and victory at Waterloo (1815). The British aristocracy celebrated its seigniorial supremacy by the medievalizing of titles and surnames and by incorporating armorial devices into the buildings and accoutrements of its vast estates. Cottages belonging to the Wingfield-Digby estates in Somerset and Dorset, for example, still have small enamelled plaques, bearing the Digby ostrich crest and a reference number, affixed to their doors which are painted in a rather unpleasant dark pink livery. At Arundel, in Sussex, the cast-iron bollards in the town streets bear the ducal lion of the Norfolks, and at Tatton in Cheshire, it was proposed that all the milestones on the public roads within the estate should be embellished with the Egerton arms. A.W.N. Pugin's exemplary use of heraldry in the new Palace of Westminster (begun 1840) set the standard for Victorian heraldic decoration, including magnificent and scholarly schemes in the 1870s by Charles Buckler, Surrey Herald Extraordinary, at Arundel Castle in Sussex and General de Havilland, York Herald, at Carlton Towers in Yorkshire.

In Scotland, heraldry remained a predominant element of architectural decoration from the fourteenth to the seventeenth century, for it was a prestigious and yet economical form of embellishment, well suited to a proud country which rarely enjoyed the prosperity of its southern neighbour. Castellated domestic architecture, characterized by turrets and crow-stepped gables, lent itself to the lavish use of heraldry and there is hardly an ancient building in Scotland which does not have some heraldic

Doorplate with ostrich crest of Digby

Early sixteenth-century gateway
to Hornby Castle, now in the
Burrell Collection, Glasgow

carving. Notable are the façade of Glamis and the staircase towers at Huntly and Druminnor.

In the Middle Ages, the great halls of castles and important houses were usually separated from kitchens and domestic quarters by a screens passage, the space above forming a platform, sometimes referred to as a minstrels' gallery. Such screens, which were usually of timber, were eminently suited to heraldic display, and continued in use for more than five centuries, one of the last examples being that at Montacute House in Somerset which was completed in 1601. A number of Scottish galleries, such as those at Pinkie and at Earlshall in Fife, have survived, but in England few medieval domestic screens remain. Their secondary functions, the conservation of heat and the prevention of draughts, were transferred to the screened porch and hallway of the Jacobean period and, eventually, to the similar arrangement found in most large Victorian and Edwardian houses. The highly patterned and coloured glass lights of the Victorian hall screen are often composed of armorial devices, fleurs-de-lis being particularly popular. It is most unlikely that these designs possess any armorial significance, however, and many contemporary stained-glass coats of arms and crests are entirely bogus or may consist of fragments salvaged from church restorations of the period.

With the entrance hall, the stairwell of a large house is a principal thoroughfare and, as such, is ideally suited to heraldic decoration. Walls are often embellished with paintings, hangings, tapestries and frescoes which may contain armorial devices; and newel posts, of wood or stone, are sometimes surmounted with carved beasts, often bearing shields of arms. At Boughton in Northamptonshire, each tread of the mid-eighteenth-century chinoiserie staircase displays a shield of the arms of the Dukes of Montague, referred to by Horace Walpole as 'the descent of the Montagues'. Some of the finest heraldic window glass will be found illuminating stairwells as, for example, at Godiston Park in Kent.

By the early fourteenth century stone hoods were provided to direct smoke from hearths into long, vertical chimney flues, set within the thickness of walls. This development had a significant effect on the social history of western Europe for it resulted in a previously unknown luxury – privacy. Domestic rooms became smaller and, therefore, greater in number, and allowed for a variety of functions which the old communal hall had not. Excessive draughts were no longer necessary to sustain a large central fire and consequently corridors and stairways were enclosed, external doors provided with porches and windows more extensively glazed. Fireplaces were invariably the focal point of any room and heraldry was the dominant theme in the decoration of medieval and Tudor chimneypieces. Regrettably few medieval examples remain but those of later times are legion, many of them

Fireplace in the Great Tower of Tattershall Castle, Lincolnshire, built by Ralph, Third Baron Cromwell (d. 1456), Treasurer to Henry VI

splendidly flamboyant references in gilded plaster, wood or stone, to the status and gentility of the owner and his ancestors. At Audley End in Essex, for example, Sir John Griffin Griffin, proud of his maternal Howard descent, celebrated his elevation to the peerage as Lord Howard de Walden, and an impending visit by George III and Queen Charlotte, by creating a suite of state apartments of which the saloon or Great Chamber remains (1784–6). The ornate overmantel above the fireplace, 'a historicist confection of carved wood of different dates and styles', includes an ornate representation of the quartered Howard arms.

In many large houses, the Gothic Revival inspired fine heraldic chimney pieces and stimulated a ready market for 'medieval' glazed tiles. In the drawing room of Arundel Castle in Sussex, for example, a magnificent carved and gilded representation of the arms of the fifteenth Duke of Norfolk (impaling those of his wife, Flora Abney-Hastings) is set into the chimney piece above a series of seven shields depicting the principal medieval quarterings inherited by the Duke. Minton tiles in the fireplace bear the arms of Howard, Fitzalan and Warrenne (see also plate 12).

Universities and colleges, especially those of Oxford and Cambridge, possess an impressive number of heraldic architectural features; even the lead drainpipes of Magdalen College, Oxford, are charged with the college arms. Much of the heraldry is that of

Heraldic chimneypiece at
Boughton House,
Northamptonshire, showing
Montagu lineage

benefactors and several Oxbridge colleges continue to use the arms of their founders, or of the alumni which gave them lustre. Many collegiate porches are embellished with heraldry; that at St John's College, Cambridge, for example, contains a wonderful display of late medieval carving, carefully restored in its original colours. The college was founded by Lady Margaret Beaufort (d. 1509) and the panel is dominated by her arms, *Quarterly France and England within a Bordure Argent and Azure* (the Beaufort liveries), and magnificent supporters, *two Yales Argent bezanty armed unguled and tufted Or*, together with Beaufort portcullis and Tudor Rose badges and punning marguerites (see illustration p. 71). Heraldry is not confined to college buildings, however. In Cambridgeshire, a series of milestones, dated 1728, bears the arms of Trinity Hall, Cambridge (*Sable a Crescent and a Bordure engrailed Ermine*), together with the impaled arms of former Masters of the College. Unfortunately, the colours have been reversed during subsequent repainting.

Many schools are armigerous or have adopted the arms of their founders. At Steeple Aston in Oxfordshire, for example, Dr Radcliffe's Church of England Primary School uses the arms of its sixteenth-century founder, Dr Samuel Radcliffe (*Argent a Bend engrailed Sable with a Mullet charged with a Martlet for difference*). A boldly carved stone panel of the arms was removed from the

Heraldic panel at Dr Radcliffe's
School, Steeple Aston,
Oxfordshire

school's original site and incorporated into its new buildings in
1972. This is a particularly interesting feature, not only for the
unusual academic cap which surmounts the shield in place of
a helmet and crest, but also for the detailed depiction of
cadency marks signifying that Dr Samuel Radcliffe was the
fourth son of a third son (see Chapter Eight). More typical, at
Woburn in Bedfordshire, a carved tablet of the arms of the
Sixth Duke of Bedford is set above the porch of the nineteenth-
century school as a memorial to the duke's philanthropy. Such
heraldic tablets are a common feature of model estate buildings
of the period.

Hospices and almshouses, endowed for the support and lodging
of the poor and infirm, usually possess some form of commemorative plaque erected in a prominent position to record for posterity
the benevolence of a patron or group of benefactors, often a guild
or fraternity, together with their arms and other devices such as
merchants' marks. In the façade of the Seamen's Almhouses in
King Street, Bristol, for example, is a panel of the arms of the
Merchant Venturers who built the almshouses in 1696. Many
hospices are of an early foundation: the Almshouse of Noble
Poverty at St Cross, Winchester, for example, was re-founded by
Cardinal Henry Beaufort in *c.* 1440 as a retirement home for his
elderly retainers. The large quadrangle comprising an entrance
tower, hall and chambers has survived and still houses brethren
who wear the cardinal's scarlet livery. An almshouse would be
administered by a warden, master or prior and would usually
comprise an infirmary hall and chapel, similar in plan to a monastic
infirmary. Known as hospitals, bede houses or *maisons dieu*, some
were devoted to the care of lepers or lazars (such as the lazar
houses of the Order of St Lazarus) and these would be divided into
small cells or separate cottages instead of a corporate infirmary. In
the later Middle Ages many spitals became permanent homes for
the poor and elderly but in 1547 most were dissolved as places of
worship. The Elizabethans, however, re-established many old
hospitals as almshouses and, encouraged by their example, the
wealthy and charitable of the seventeenth and eighteenth centuries
founded new establishments, the inmates of which were carefully
selected for their unquestionable virtue. Typical of a number of
medieval foundations which continue to operate today are the
almshouses at Sherborne in Dorset, built in 1437 under royal
licence at a cost of £80 raised (unusually) by public subscription.
They were intended for 'twelve pore feeble and ympotent old men
and four old women', cared for by a housewife who was required
to share in the meals of the residents, presumably to ensure that
they were properly fed. Several of our great hospitals, such as
those of St Bartholomew and St Thomas in London, have medieval foundations and continue to use arms which recall their
origins: the Cornish choughs or 'Becket birds' in the arms of
St Thomas, for example, and the beautiful *Per pale Argent and*

Arms and wyvern crest of the Herberts at Powis Castle near Welshpool, Powys

Sable a Chevron counterchanged of St Bartholomew's Hospital, the earliest representation of which was in a seal of 1423.

The lodge, or pair of lodges, of a country estate was often built in a style similar to that of the main residence – an architectural hors-d'oeuvre. While ostensibly its purpose was to house the gatekeeper, the lodge and its ornate gates also served to impress the visitor and to remind the estate community of its dependence on the 'great house'. Most gates and lodges will contain an element of heraldry in their design, usually on the gate pillars (see above), in the fabric of the lodge, within the ornamental ironwork of the gate itself or on an enamelled plaque above. Large country houses, surrounded by parkland, invariably possessed a number of entrances and at each would be a lodge or gateway suitably embellished in a manner appropriate to its use. Today, many estate gates are no longer in use though, somewhat incongruously at times, the heraldic finery remains to remind us of a former owner's professed gentility.

Of course, heraldry is not confined to ecclesiastical, collegiate and domestic buildings. In Norwich, Norfolk, the splendid sixteenth-century doorway to the Guildhall is embellished with the arms of Henry VIII, the city corporation and one Thomas Bassingham who commissioned the original doorway for his house in London Street from where it was later removed. In Broad Street, Bristol, the entrance to the former hall of the Merchant Taylors' Company has a fine mid-eighteenth-century shell hood decorated with the guild's arms. Civic heraldry will be found in the porticoes of many shire and county halls, especially those built in the nineteenth century when civic pride and corporate rivalry often attracted vulgarity and ostentation. Nevertheless, there is much exemplary heraldry: terracotta shields on the red brick façade of the Bute Dock Office at Cardiff (1896), for instance, declaim the 'triumph of enlightened paternalism' and record the arms of the third Marquess of Bute (who owned the docks) and of the City of Cardiff. At Glossop in Derbyshire, the lion crest of the Howards stands guard over the entrance to the railway station, constructed in 1847 by the Thirteenth Duke of Norfolk as part of the town's ambitious urban development scheme. His predecessor, the Twelfth Duke, also commissioned life-size models of the Howard lion crest and Fitzalan horse to embellish the towers of the Norfolk Bridge over the Adur at Shoreham in Sussex. (The suspension bridge, constructed in 1833, was rebuilt in 1933 and the figures removed to Arundel Castle.) Undoubtedly the worst heraldry of the period is to be found in the devices adopted by many of the railway and steamship companies which, although ostensibly coats of arms, were invariably bogus or clumsily combined the heraldry of the towns they served.

Weathercocks and Vanes

A weathercock is a three-dimensional, hollow metal sculpture mounted on a spire, or above a tower, and revolving easily to indicate the direction of the wind. Not all weathercocks are cockerels, which symbolize vigilance, some are the emblems of patron saints, such as the gridiron of St Lawrence on the churches of St Lawrence, Jewry in the City of London, Ramsgate in Kent, and Tidmarsh in Berkshire. On the church of St Mary-le-Bow, Cheapside, a huge 2.7 m (9 ft) dragon, weighing over 2 cwt, is probably a representation of the mythical Thames dragon which appears in the coat of arms of the City of London. There are other dragons at Ottery St Mary in Devon, Sittingbourne in Kent, and Upton in Norfolk, and a magnificent golden galleon on the tower of Henstridge church in Somerset was the gift of Royal Navy airmen stationed at the nearby aerodrome during the Second World War. Without documentary evidence weathercocks are often very difficult to date. One of the earliest references, a riddle in the *Exeter Book* of *c.* 750, describes a weathercock as a hollow belly pierced by a rod. Many are of medieval appearance but are likely to have been replaced several times, though the original design may have been copied on each occasion.

Unlike weathercocks, weather vanes were intended to show both the direction of the wind and to display heraldic devices. They are effectively rigid metal flags and it has been argued by Col. R. Gayre in his *Heraldic Standard and Other Ensigns* that, in the medieval period, the shape of a vane was dictated by the rank of its owner. The use of vanes, which probably originated in France, is evident in England from the thirteenth century and it is likely that the word is a corruption of *fane*, derived from *fannion* meaning banner. Heraldic vanes are generally found on the gables and pinnacles of major domestic buildings, particularly those of the late medieval and Tudor periods. There are excellent examples of vanes, shaped like swallow-tailed pennons, at Lambeth Palace in London and at Charlecote in Warwickshire. Typically, the Charlecote vanes are painted with the allusive arms of Lucy (whom Shakespeare caricatured as Justice Shallow, the 'Old Pike'), *Gules semy of Cross-crosslets three Luces* (pike-fish) *haurient Argent*. The Lucy crest, decorative fleurs-de-lis and 'tails' are gilded to catch the sun. Unfortunately, most weather vanes have lost their original heraldic decoration and Victorian examples are often Gothic Revival imitations and were never painted (see plate 22).

Five

MONUMENTS, EFFIGIES, BRASSES AND HATCHMENTS

And yet time hath its revolution:
there must be a period and an end
to all temporal things.
Finis rerum, an end of names and
dignities, and whatsoever is terrene.
Where is Bohun, where's Mowbray,
where's Mortimer?
Nay, which is more and most of all,
where is Plantagenet?
They are all entombed in
the urns and sepulchres of mortality.

Sir Ranulph Crew, '*Memento Mori*', 1625

Incised Slabs

Memorials in churches, erected to perpetuate the memory of an individual, developed from the practice of carving designs on stone coffin lids and on slabs which were exposed in a church floor. It should always be borne in mind that a memorial does not necessarily mark the place of interment.

Among the earliest examples in Britain of engraved stone memorials, known as incised slabs, is a collection of over two hundred, dating from the eighth to the tenth centuries, at Clonmacnois in Ireland. These are carved in shallow relief with simple decorative designs, usually foliage or Christian symbols. Slabs were usually of hard sandstone, though there were regional variations: Purbeck and other marbles in the south of England, gritstone in Derbyshire and Northumberland, and Bath and Ham stone in the south-west, for example. By the Reformation alabaster was widely used for this purpose in the English Midlands.

It is likely that depiction of the human form was reserved, in the twelfth century, for eminent ecclesiastics, the earliest known example in England being that of Abbot Gilbert Crispin (d. 1117) at Westminster Abbey. Military figures, such as a twelfth-century knight at Sollers Hope in Herefordshire, were comparatively rare at that time.

HERE RESTETH Ŷ BODYES OF Ṣ IOHN FITZ IAMES
OF LEWESTON IN Ŷ COVNTY OF DORSETT KT·d
OF MARGARET HIS WIFE DAVGHTER OF
NATHANEEL STEPHENS ESQ OF EASTINGTON
IN Ŷ COVNTY OF GLOCESTER HEE DYED
Ŷ 21 OF IVNE 1670

Seventeenth-century ledger stone at Long Burton, Dorset, to the memory of Sir John Fitzjames, showing the elaborate mantling of the period and the unusual crest of *A Dolphin Argent devouring the top of an Antique Cap Azure lined Ermine*

Unlike monumental brasses and effigies (see below), incised slabs rarely depict heraldic figures, armorial devices generally being confined to small shields. Unusual examples of heraldic figures include those of Sir Johan de Botiler (*c.* 1285) at St Brides Major in West Glamorgan and of John Foljambe (d. 1499 monument *c.* 1515) at Sutton Scarsdale, Derbyshire. The latter is depicted in full armour and emblazoned tabard, with his head resting on a crested helmet and his feet on a *chatloup*, a chimerical creature with a wolf's body, cat's face and goat's horns, granted to the Foljambe family as a badge in 1513.

Incised slabs, which were almost invariably laid in the church floor, were clearly liable to excessive wear and many were eventually lifted and set upright against a wall or raised on to a plinth. An even greater number have been lost or their detail defaced.

Some incised slabs were embellished with inlaid materials, especially those imported from the Low Countries, and these would almost certainly have included richly emblazoned heraldic devices. Regrettably, little remains of the pitch and painted lead (and occasionally copper or enamel) with which the figures were coloured.

During the seventeenth century incised slabs were replaced by ledger stones and these remained popular until the nineteenth century. Ledger stones were usually set in the floor above an interment though they may also be found on tomb chests and table tombs. They were usually of black marble or local stone, such as slate, and bore a simple inscription and a deeply incised roundel containing a coat of arms or other device.

Effigies

Unlike brasses (see below), the recumbent figures depicted in effigies were modelled in three dimensions. There is an extraordinary diversity of character evident in the faces of effigial figures and it is sometimes hard to accept the expert view that, despite their often life-like appearance, effigies are essentially stylized representations of a deceased person and not portraits, which were rare before the Restoration period.

Among the earliest lay effigies are those of Robert Curthose, Duke of Normandy (d. 1134, monument early thirteenth-century) at Gloucester Cathedral; King John (d. 1216, monument dated 1230) at Worcester Cathedral and William Longespee, Earl of Salisbury (d. 1226) at Salisbury Cathedral. Through the thirteenth to the fifteenth century most monuments were carved in stone, often Caen stone or alabaster, a form of gypsum found in certain strata of rocks in the North Midlands, the Isle of Purbeck in Dorset and elsewhere. Dressed alabaster is easily worked, is exceptionally smooth to the touch and is white with occasional flecks of red, though most tombs were originally coloured and gilded. The effigy of Henry III (d. 1272) at Westminster Abbey was the first of a series of gilt bronze effigies created for members of the English royal family, a fashion later emulated by the nobility, notably Richard Beauchamp, Earl of Warwick (d. 1439), in his effigy at the collegiate church of St Mary, Warwick. This magnificent tomb still retains its gilded hearse or barrel-shaped metal cage, originally intended to support mass candles and a pall cover which was removed only on special occasions. The earl's head rests on a helm with a swan crest and at his feet are the bear of Warwick and the griffin of Salisbury. Niches in the sides of the Purbeck marble tomb chest contain bronze angels and weepers representing the great magnatial families with whom the Beauchamps were connected, each identified by a shield of arms.

The medieval practice of interring a man's heart, the 'seat of love and piety', in a place other than that in which his body was buried was particularly common during the thirteenth and fourteenth centuries. Frequently, such heart burials took place in monastic churches, notably the sequestered abbeys of the Cistercian order such as Sweetheart Abbey (*Dulce Cor*) in the county of Dumfries and Galloway where the heart of its founder John Baliol was buried. Similarly, the heart of a thirteenth-century Bishop of Hereford was interred at the Cistercian abbey at Dore in Herefordshire, the spot being marked with a miniature effigy of the bishop. In many localities, tradition links these miniature effigies with the heart burial of a local crusading knight; a not unreasonable assumption when the difficulties of transporting a rapidly deteriorating corpse from the Holy Land are considered. In Mappowder church, Dorset, the miniature effigy of a recumbent knight, complete with hauberk, surcoat, sword and heater-shaped

OPPOSITE: effigy, at Ickenham, Middlesex, of Robert Clayton, who died 'within a few howres after his birth'

Gilded bronze effigy of Richard Beauchamp, Fifth Earl of Warwick (d. 1439) at the collegiate church of St Mary, Warwick

shield, set within a recess of the chancel wall, measures just 45 cm (18 in) in length and clasps what appears to be a casket, presumably that in which his heart was buried. There are other good examples at Horsted Keynes in Sussex (probably the work of the same artist), at Bottesford in Leicestershire, Halesowen in the West Midlands, and Tenbury Wells in Worcestershire.

Medieval effigies provide invaluable evidence for the development of costume and armour, though it should be remembered that effigies and brasses were often commissioned in anticipation of death or erected some considerable time after interment and therefore reflect the fashion of the time in which they were made rather than that of the person they commemorate.

Armorial display was particularly important and, until the middle of the fourteenth century, a knight's effigy usually bore a shield and was clothed in an embroidered surcoat, cyclas or jupon, on which the arms were often carved and painted. Dating from the

Heart burial at Mappowder,
Dorset

Crusades of the twelfth century, the long linen surcoat, which was
split at the sides to facilitate movement on horseback, was
originally intended to protect mail from heat or rain. It also
provided an obvious means of displaying armorial devices – hence
'coat of arms'. A variation of the surcoat was the cyclas which was
cut short at the front and long at the back. During the Camail
Period (defined as such from the introduction into England from
c. 1360 of the *camail*, a form of mail cape suspended from beneath
the helmet) the surcoat was succeeded by the jupon, a short,
sleeveless, tight-fitting coat worn over armour and emblazoned
with the arms.

The detail of arms carved on shield and tunic may still be visible,
depending on the depth of the original carving and the effects of
defacement and erosion. Effigies were often painted but surviving
contemporary medieval paintwork and gilding is rare, a number
having been refurbished at a later date. For example, the early
thirteenth-century carved oak effigy of Robert of Normandy at
Gloucester is coloured, but in fact the original tomb chest was
replaced and the effigy refurbished in the fifteenth century, and
again following the Civil War. A sketch of the tomb, made by

Effigy of Sir Rhys ap Thomas, in
Garter robes, at Carmarthen,
Dyfed

Effigy of Sir Robert Whitingham (d. 1471) at Aldbury, Hertfordshire

Robert Cooke, Clarenceux King of Arms, in *c.* 1569 shows the duke wearing an emblazoned surcoat and a tomb chest decorated on the sides with ten shields of arms.

From the mid-fourteenth century, shields of arms are more often incorporated into the fabric of the tomb chest or canopy and often display multiple quarterings. The importation into Britain of magnificent German and Italian armour during the fifteenth century encouraged a fashion among the nobility for discarding any form of heraldic over-mantle and effigies of the period often reflect this. There was a brief period during the late fifteenth and early sixteenth century when the tabard became popular. This was a dress coat worn over armour, similar to the jupon, but reaching below the thigh and with broad sleeves to the elbow. Tabards were emblazoned front and back and on the sleeves and served a purely

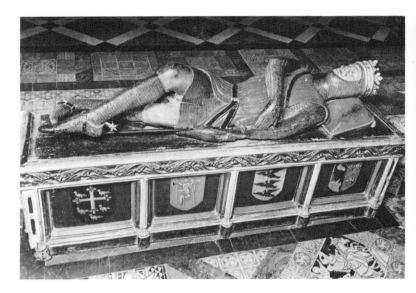

Effigy of Robert Curthose,
Duke of Normandy, at
Gloucester Cathedral

armorial purpose. Today, tabards of the royal arms are worn by
the heralds on ceremonial occasions.

The use of heraldry in medieval and Tudor effigies was not
merely decorative; armorial devices were outward and visible
symbols of authority and power and accumulated quarterings and
badges conveyed details of ancestry more proudly than any
inscription.

Women sometimes embroidered their marital arms on a *kirtle*
(gown or outer petticoat) or *mantle* (cloak) and these appear in
effigies as they would have been worn in life. The earliest example
is the effigy of Matilda, Countess of Salisbury (d. 1281) in
Worcester Cathedral. She was daughter and heiress of Walter
de Clifford and her cloak is powdered with small shields bearing
her paternal arms. Between 1280 and 1330 it was usual for women
to display their arms on a mantle which was worn on ceremonial
occasions. In effigies and brasses the sides of the garment fall
forward from the shoulders and the quartered or impaled arms are
emblazoned with the husband's arms on the dexter (the left when
viewed from the front) and the woman's paternal arms on the
sinister (the right) – though when the garment was actually worn it
was intended to be viewed from the back and the arms would
therefore have been the other way round. Sometimes there are
'missing' quarterings and one may reasonably assume that these
are simply not visible (see Lady Howard p. 125). Thereafter, for
the remainder of the fourteenth century, a close-fitting kirtle was
worn beneath a sleeveless *cote-hardie*, the female equivalent of the
jupon, and this was often emblazoned with the impaled marital
arms. There are also instances of both mantle and kirtle being used
for armorial display and in such cases it is always the mantle which
bears the husband's arms 'in dominion' over the woman's paternal

Effigy of Matilda de Clifford, Countess of Salisbury, at Worcester Cathedral (from a drawing by George Hollis of 1840)

Ape crest in the effigy of
Sir William Martyn, Puddletown,
Dorset

arms which were embroidered on her kirtle. In the Tudor period heraldic kirtles and over-mantles continued to be depicted in monuments, though kirtles were now loose-fitting and without a waist. But it seems unlikely that such garments were worn after the mid-sixteenth century, even for ceremonial purposes, and their use in effigies and brasses is seen to decline rapidly from this time. Of course, it should be remembered that heraldic costume, as depicted in effigies and brasses, was intended primarily as a vehicle for armorial display and does not necessarily illustrate a contemporary fashion.

The shield and heraldic garment were not the only means of armorial display; recumbent effigies, both male and female, often have their heads resting on cushions which may incorporate heraldic devices in the embroidery. From the fourteenth century a knight's head normally rested on a helm to which was attached his crest with wreath and mantling.

The figures in most effigies (and many brasses) are depicted with their feet resting on a beast: most often a lion for a man and a pet

Wodehouse and ragged staff devices in the effigy of Sir Robert Whitingham at Aldbury, Hertfordshire

dog for a woman. The use of other animals is almost certainly of heraldic significance: the Martyn ape crest in effigies at Puddletown in Dorset, for example; a wodehouse (or wild man of the woods) in the effigy of Sir Robert Whittingham at Aldbury, Hertfordshire, and the fine male griffin in the brass of Sir Thomas Boleyn KG at Hever, Kent (1538). (This last depicts Sir Thomas in his Garter robes and collar – see p. 127.)

The Gothic Revival of the nineteenth century resulted in a return to the 'medieval' tomb chest and effigy, sometimes surmounted by a canopy, and to the figured monumental brass. But most Victorian effigial tombs combine a variety of medieval influences and rarely reproduce accurately the style of a particular period.

Monumental Brasses

A monumental brass is a flat metal plate engraved with a figure, and sometimes an inscription, and affixed as a memorial to the floor or wall of a church or to a tomb chest.

Medieval brasses were, in fact, made of an alloy of copper (75–80 per cent), with 15-20 per cent zinc and small elements of lead and tin. In the Middle Ages this material was known as *latten*, and later *cuivre blanc* (white copper). Those who worked on monumental brasses were described as 'marblers', a possible reference to the craft of engraving incised slabs from which the monumental brass developed. Indeed, it seems likely that workshops which had traditionally produced lavishly expensive effigies turned also to the production of brasses as an alternative form of memorial which could be afforded by the average cleric, merchant or gentleman.

Brasses originated in the Low Countries in the thirteenth century. The earliest surviving figure brass is that of Bishop Yso von Wilpe (d. 1231) at Verden in Germany. Flemish brasses were imported into England, no doubt at considerable expense, the most important of the fourteenth-century manufacturing centres being at Tournai on the river Scheldt. These brasses were large rectangular sheets of metal set into a slab, the background between the figures being engraved with diaper-work, heraldic devices or other smaller figures. Typical of these large, elaborate, imported brasses is that of Abbot Thomas de la Mare at St Alban's, Hertfordshire which measures 2.8 m by 1.5 m (9 ft 3 in x 4 ft 4 in).

English brasses comprised a number of separate pieces, cut from a single sheet of metal, each of which was engraved and set within an indentation (matrix) carved out of the stone slab so that the brass was flush with the surface. Each section was secured within its matrix in a bed of black pitch, which also protected the metal from corrosion, though later brasses were often fixed by means of brass rivets driven into lead plugs. In many instances coloured enamels were let into the concave surfaces of the brass to provide heraldic decoration and this practice continued well into the sixteenth century. Slabs were generally of local stone or Purbeck marble.

The segmented nature of medieval brasses made them particularly vulnerable to vandalism and effacement and few complete examples have survived. Nevertheless, there are some 7,500 brasses in England, more than in any other European country.

The majority of surviving English brasses originated from workshops, established in the early fourteenth century at Norwich, York and (notably) London. Each workshop developed a series of templates from which the client would select the most appropriate 'off the peg' design to which personal devices and inscriptions were added. Others were specially commissioned and engraved to a client's specification. It is possible to identify the products of a particular workshop by comparing the style and method of manufacture of surviving brasses but, as with effigies, brasses of this period portray only a stylized representation of a deceased person, not an accurate portrait.

The earliest figures were usually life-size or slightly smaller but there are examples of demi-figures and miniatures. Figures are generally accompanied by an inscription, Christian symbols and heraldic devices, all set within a decorative engraved canopy.

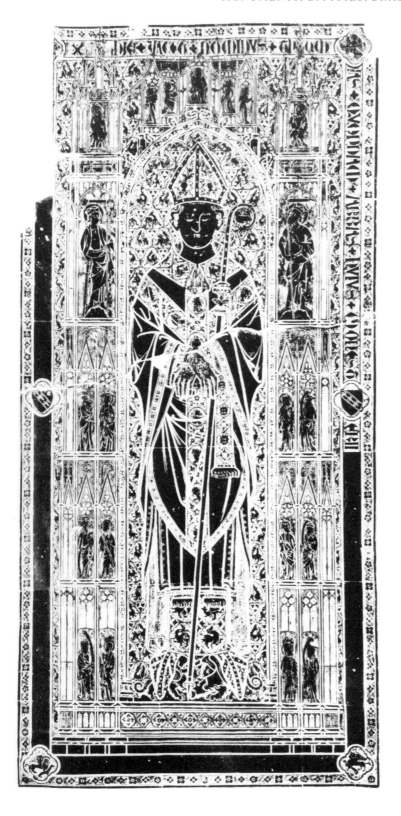

Brass to Abbot Thomas de la
Mare at St Alban's

Brass to Sir John d'Abernon at
Stoke D'Abernon, Surrey and
(opposite) Sir Robert de
Septvans at Chartham, Kent

The first English brasses are those of bishops or abbots, the earliest of which date from the late thirteenth century, but by far the most interesting category is the 'military brass', so called because figures are depicted in armour. Almost invariably these brasses contain heraldic devices which facilitate dating and identification and often provide genealogical and personal information not included in the inscription. Indeed, it was for this reason that armory was considered to be such a necessary component in memorials and of course it also declared the authority and status of the deceased.

The earliest military brass, now only a collection of gaping matrices, is at Aston Rowan in Oxfordshire and dates from *c.* 1314. A series of military brasses, dated from between 1320 and 1330, illustrates the early use of armorial devices on memorials. The brass of Sir John d'Abernon at Stoke D'Abernon in Surrey shows a knight bearing a shield and pennon on which there are traces of blue enamel from his arms *Azure a Chevron Or*. This was once considered to be the oldest English military brass but has recently been re-dated to 1327. Three other splendid figures of this period are those of Roger de Trumpington at Trumpington in Cambridgeshire, Sir William de Septvans at Chartham, Kent, and Sir Robert de Bures at Acton, Suffolk. All three hold shields of their arms – trumpets for de Trumpington and seven winnowing fans (*sept vans*) for de Septvans, and these are repeated on the ailettes (shoulder-guards) of the Trumpington and Septvans brasses, and the surcoat of the Septvans figure. With the revised dating of these brasses, the earliest heraldic example may be that of Margaret, Lady Camoys (*c.* 1310), at Trotton in Sussex. Regrettably, all nine enamelled shields which were once set into Lady Margaret's gown are now missing.

Most early fourteenth-century military brasses are of figures wearing heraldic surcoats, but inexplicably the majority of brasses from the later Camail period depict armorial devices, not on the jupon which is plain, but on separate shields above or surrounding the figure. Between 1360 and 1460 only one tenth of military brasses have figures wearing heraldic garments and it is strange that contemporary workshops should have continued to produce designs which included the jupon when clients clearly were not interested in using it in their brasses for heraldic display. Perhaps the cost of enamelling was excessive or it may be that the jupons were emblazoned in a medium of which no trace remains, though this seems unlikely. This fashion, if such it was, anticipated that of the fifteenth century when many figures, in both brasses and effigies, were depicted wearing the plate armour of the period, uncovered and without embellishment. This reflected the current popularity, among the nobility at least, of the magnificent and expensive products of German and Italian armourers. However, from the 1460s an increasing number of brasses and effigies show figures dressed in heraldic tabards and these continued well into

Brass to Margaret de Camoys at Trotton, Sussex

Harsyk brass (1384) at
Southacre, Norfolk

Willoughby brass at Wollaton, Nottinghamshire

the sixteenth century; the complexity of quarterings increasing significantly in the Tudor period when descent from (or association with) an 'ancient' family (i.e., pre-Bosworth) was highly prized by the newly created Tudor aristocracy.

Crests and helmets are also represented in military brasses, particularly in those of the fifteenth and sixteenth centuries, when the helm is usually placed beneath or near the head of the figure, though there are examples from the late fourteenth century such as the hunting horn crest of Sir William de Bryene at Seal in Kent (1385) and the panache of feathers in the crest of Sir John Harsyk at Southacre, Norfolk (1384).

Occasionally, badges, rebuses and other devices may also be found, incorporated within the overall design of the brass, as at Wollaton, Nottinghamshire, where the slab of Richard Willoughby and his wife, Anne, is inset with brass whelk shells (1471).

There are also numerous examples of female figures in armorial kirtles, cotes-hardie and mantles throughout the medieval and Tudor periods, notably in the late fourteenth-century brass of Matilda, Lady Foxley, at Bray in Berkshire (Foxley impaling Brocas) and that of Catherine, Lady Howard, at Stoke by Nayland, Suffolk. This is a good example of a retrospective memorial (see below). Lady Howard died in 1452 but her brass was not laid down until *c.* 1535 to commemorate descent from a singularly distinguished medieval family. Her family arms (de Moleyns) are on the left side of her mantle and three Howard quarterings (Brotherton, Howard and Segrave) on the right. No doubt we are to assume that the family's other equally prestigious quarterings (Mowbray, Warenne and Braose) are out of sight on the back of the mantle. The brass of Elizabeth Goringe (1558), at Burton in Sussex, is believed to be unique for she is depicted wearing a man's tabard.

Attempting to trace the development of armour or costume through the study of monuments is not as straightforward as may at first appear. Many brasses (and effigies) were not contemporary with the death of those they commemorate; some were prepared in anticipation of death while others were often retrospective, or their erection was delayed because of unreliable executors or contested wills. Conversely, the dating of brasses by reference to costume and armour is equally complex. For example, the famous Trumpington brass (see above) was for many years attributed to the first Roger de Trumpington (d. 1289). However, it was later noted that the small shields on the sword scabbard, and the arms on the ailettes, were crudely engraved with a five-pointed label. These, it was concluded, had been added after the original brass had been engraved and the question of dating was re-examined. It is now believed that the brass was commissioned in anticipation of death by the son of Roger I, Sir Giles de Trumpington (d. 1332), and that it was appropriated, and the arms hastily changed, for the tomb of his son, Roger II, who predeceased his father in *c.* 1326

OPPOSITE: (left) Lady Foxley at Bray, Berkshire, and (right) Lady Howard at Stoke-by-Nayland, Suffolk

and whose arms were distinguished by the addition of a silver label.

Brasses do not always mark the place of interment. At Felbrigg in Norfolk the brass of Sir Simon Felbrigg (1416) was engraved in anticipation of his death and placed over the tomb of his first wife Margaret, but when Sir Simon died in 1442 he was buried at Norwich.

From about 1570 the use of figures declined in popularity and heraldic designs generally comprised a central, multi-quartered coat of arms surrounded by separate shields representing hereditary and marital connections.

In the sixteenth century brass plates were incorporated into wall monuments (see below) and these were usually single sheets engraved with figures, inscriptions and other devices including shields of arms.

Few monumental brasses were commissioned from the mid-seventeenth century until the Gothic revival of the nineteenth, when the brass figure, set into a slab, and the brass wall monument with ornate Gothic inscriptions and elaborate heraldry of the period, enjoyed a revival.

Livery Collars

Insignia of office and of the principal orders of chivalry are commonly found in effigies and monumental brasses, together with livery collars.

There are many effigies and brasses in which the figure wears the Garter on his left leg and may also be robed in the mantle of the

The Trumpington brass at Trumpington, Cambridgeshire

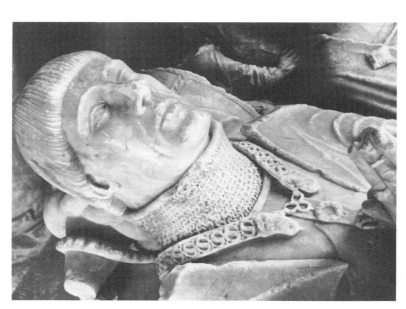

Collar of SS in the effigy of Walter Fitzwalter at Little Dunmow, Essex

order. The brass of Thomas Boleyn (father of Anne Boleyn) at Hever in Kent, for example, shows him in his full Garter robes.

From the late fourteenth century, collars incorporating armorial devices, and sometimes with pendant livery badges, were worn to indicate adherence to a royal or noble house, and (by implication) to a political cause. It seems likely that collars were originally granted as marks of favour and that some became insignia of office. The collar of SS is still worn by certain officers of the Crown, for example, including the Kings of Arms.

This famous collar is of obscure origin. It is composed of, or studded with, 'S's and was probably worn and given as livery by 'time-honoured Lancaster', John of Gaunt, and later by Henry IV, with the swan of de Bohun as a pendant. Between Henry's return from exile and his seizure of the throne he distributed 192 collars of SS to his retainers and later ordained that '. . . all the sons of the king, dukes, earls, barons and baronets, might use the livery of our Lord the King of his collar as well in his absence as in his presence; and all other knights and esquires should use it only in the presence of the King'. Generally the collar comprised a strip of leather, silk or velvet set with 'S's in silver gilt, silver or latten, and terminating in two buckles linked by an ornamental trefoil from which a badge could be suspended. The S letters were of several different shapes, sizes and styles, sometimes reversed or horizontal, and were set at varying distances from each other. In earlier versions the 'S's appear to have been attached to the material, possibly by rivets, and the collar fitted tightly over the camail when worn with armour. Later collars were made entirely of metal with the 'S's elaborately strung or linked together. The collar of SS remained the cognizance of the House of Lancaster for fifty years and the Tudors adapted the device, alternating the Lancastrian SS with Beaufort portcullises and with a Tudor Rose or portcullis as a pendant. There are over one hundred late medieval brasses and effigies in which the SS collar shows that those they commemorate owed allegiance to the House of Lancaster, and yet the meaning of the SS badge itself remains a mystery.

The corresponding Yorkist collars are composed of alternate suns and roses with a white lion pendant (for Mortimer) or, under Richard III, a white boar. There are nearly one hundred examples of effigies and brasses with Yorkist collars but, of these, only two have boar pendants: a remnant in a Nevill effigy at Brancepeth, Durham, and that of Sir Ralph Fitzherbert at Norbury in Derbyshire.

These fifteenth-century Yorkist and Lancastrian collars are of particular interest to historians for they are indicative of preferment and allegiance, though their depiction in an effigy or brass does not necessarily mean that they were actually presented and may imply simply long service to a particular royal house. The

Brass to Sir Thomas Boleyn (d. 1538) at Hever, Kent

Yorkist collar and white boar
pendant on the effigy of Ralph
Fitzherbert (d. 1483) at Norbury,
Derbyshire

Massyngberd brass at Gunby in Lincolnshire is interesting in that it
is possible to discern that the brass was made without a collar and
was later cut for its insertion. Tudor SS collars were generally
more substantial and were essentially chains of office rather than
symbols of allegiance.

A pair of effigies, apparently husband and wife, at Broughton,
Oxfordshire, provides the local historian with a fascinating
instance of mistaken identity. The 'husband' wears a Yorkist collar
of suns and roses while his 'wife' has a Lancastrian SS collar –

Effigies of Elizabeth Wykeham and Lord Saye and Sele at Broughton, Oxfordshire

hardly a recipe for matrimonial bliss! However, research will reveal that the effigies have been moved and are of Elizabeth Wykeham and the second Lord Saye and Sele who was killed at Barnet in 1471 and was probably the husband of Elizabeth's granddaughter.

Plain collars may also be found on several fifteenth-century effigies and (more often) on brasses. These are likely to be erased Lancastrian or Yorkist collars, while others were never completed, suggesting that a family may have been 'hedging its bets' when commissioning a memorial at a time of political uncertainty.

It seems likely that magnates also had their own collars and pendants but very few of these have survived in effigies or brasses. The brass of Thomas, Lord Berkeley, at Wotton-under-Edge in Gloucestershire (*c.* 1417), for example, shows him wearing a collar of mermaids and it is known that this device was used by the Berkeleys from at least 1322. But 'Mermaids of the Sea' are also referred to in the Black Prince's will and it is possible that the Berkeley collar may therefore be indicative of Thomas's attachment to the Black Prince. It has also been suggested that some plain collars represent strips of leather or cloth on which livery colours were enamelled or painted; that on the brass of John Leventhorp at Sawbridgeworth, Hertfordshire, for example.

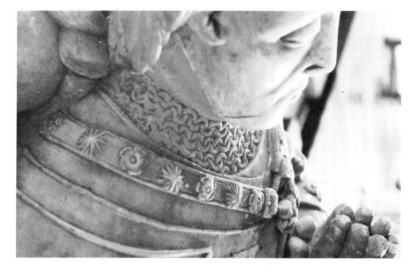

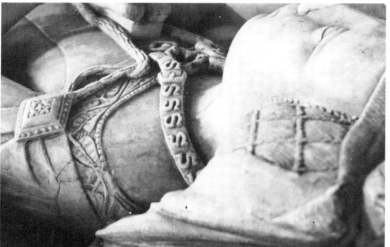

Lord Saye and Sele (above) and
Elizabeth Wykham (below)

Tomb Chests, Canopies and Chantry Chapels

Tomb chests first appeared in the thirteenth century, though the
term is misleading, for they do not contain mortal remains and are
simply a form of monument. Early tomb chests had a coped top
but these were superseded by incised slabs, brasses and effigies.
Most tomb chests were free-standing but many have been moved
to a side wall and, where this has occurred, the decorative carving
may be seen to continue to what is now the back of the chest.
Where tomb chests were originally set against a wall they were
usually placed within a low arch which provided a canopy.
Alternatively, the tomb chest, together with its canopy, pillars and
arch, may be combined to form a screen between two parts of a
church – the chancel and an adjacent chapel, for example. In the
thirteenth and fourteenth centuries the decoration of the sides and

Alabaster tomb and effigies of Ralph Fitzherbert (d. 1483) and his wife, Elizabeth, at Norbury, Derbyshire

ends of a chest reflected contemporary architectural styles: panels containing carved quatrefoils (or, more rarely, trefoils, sexafoils or octofoils), for example, or miniature blind arcading, often with weepers (stone or bronze figures symbolizing perpetual mourning) placed within the recesses. From the mid-thirteenth century painted and gilded shields of arms were added, either within the quatrefoils or the recesses of the arcading, or on the spandrels on either side of the figures. These shields were usually of carved and painted stone or were enamelled metal plaques which were affixed by lead plugs set into holes in the stone surface. Inevitably, the fractured plugs are all that remain of many examples.

Weepers first appeared on tombs towards the end of the

Late sixteenth-century tomb of the Knightley family at Fawsley, Northamptonshire

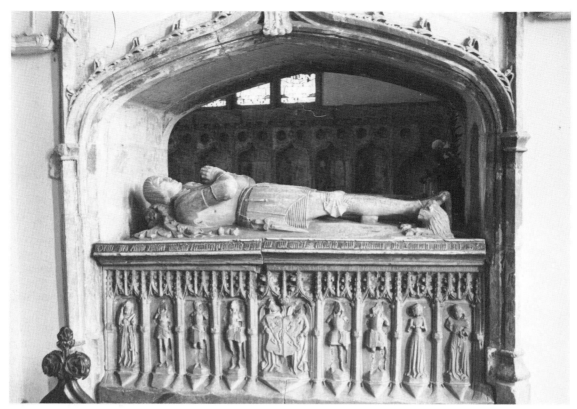

Tomb and effigy of
Sir Christopher Matthew
(d. 1526) at Llandaff Cathedral

thirteenth century and remained popular throughout the medieval, Tudor and Jacobean periods. The figures usually represent a dead man's family and on medieval tombs may include members of eminent and magnatial families with whom the deceased was related by inheritance or marriage. Individuals may sometimes be identified by small shields of arms placed beneath the niches in which they stand. Medieval weepers were finely-carved, dignified figures, sometimes cloaked and hooded, their heads bowed and their hands clasped in supplication or supporting a shield. Elizabethan and Jacobean weepers are often crude by comparison and usually comprise two graduated groups of kneeling figures – one of sons and the other of daughters, and occasionally a babe in chrisom cloths bringing up the rear. Angel 'weepers' were fashionable in the fifteenth century and again during the Gothic Revival of the nineteenth century.

In the sixteenth century, Renaissance influences are evident in the gradual introduction of classical forms, both in the decoration and in the structure of the tomb chest itself. The sides of the chests were often divided into panels using balusters, pilasters and colonettes, and heraldry, on both the tomb chest and its integral canopy, became increasingly elaborate. From the end of the sixteenth century, many tomb chests were constructed on two

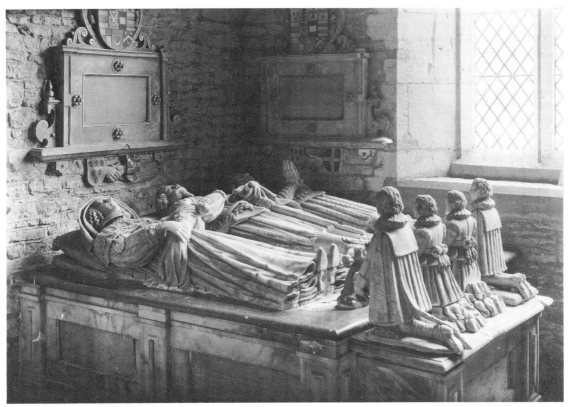

Monument (1631) to the Savage family at Elmley Castle, Worcestershire

levels to accommodate two or even three effigies. From the mid-seventeenth century, the tomb chest was superseded by the hanging wall monument (see below), though for a time both might be found together. A finely carved monument, dating from this transitional period, is that of the Savage family at Elmley Castle in Worcestershire. On a tomb chest, beneath a simple heraldic wall monument, lie the effigies of William Savage (d. 1616), his son Giles, and the latter's wife, cradling an infant in her arms. At their feet are the kneeling figures of William's four surviving grandchildren.

Tomb chests should not be confused with table tombs which are chest-like memorials of stone erected in many churchyards over the graves of the more prosperous members of seventeenth- and eighteenth-century society. The wonderful collection of Cotswold clothiers' tombs at Painswick in Gloucestershire provides many of the best examples. Confusingly, such memorials are also described as 'chest tombs'. It was not until the Gothic Revival of the nineteenth century that tomb chests became fashionable once again.

Canopies developed in the thirteenth century, principally over the tomb chests of prelates, and may have originated in the roof-like structures which were sometimes placed above shrines. The overall design of a canopy followed contemporary architectural

Canopied monuments to Thomas Winston (d. 1609) and Sir John Fitzjames (d. 1625) at Long Burton, Dorset

style and decoration, indeed that above the Despencer tomb at Tewkesbury Abbey in Gloucestershire contains the earliest example of fan vaulting (1378). Heraldry was a common theme, both in the miniature bosses and spandrels of the vaulting and in the ornamentation of the moulding. The canopy of Edmund Crouchback's tomb at Westminster Abbey, for example, contains no fewer than 150 shields of arms. Canopies above recessed tombs, those which were set within a church wall, are usually less ornate, the spandrels formed on either side of the arch containing simple shields of arms, though the canopies of late perpendicular recessed tombs often have decorative cornices with carved and gilded shields of arms and other devices such as badges, cyphers and rebuses.

During the sixteenth century classical columns, pediments and entablatures gradually replaced Gothic pillars and arches. The Renaissance was also a time when families were eager to to display all, or at least the most significant, of the heraldic quarterings to which they laid claim, and the canopy was ideally suited to such a display. There are various combinations, but usually a central achievement containing all the principal quarterings was flanked by two smaller ones above the pediment, usually of impaled arms with the various arms acquired by marriage depicted individually in shields on the columns and pediments. (For the marshalling of quarterings see Chapter Eight.) Supporters were often modelled, not necessarily in stone, on either side of the central achievement or were incorporated into the overall design of the monument, flanking an obelisk, for example. Arches provided spandrels for further shields and the underside of the arch was often decorated with shields, badges and other devices. Smaller shields in a frieze along the base of the pediment, or on the back plate of a wall monument (see below), were used to display the marriage alliances of children and ancestors and, where a monument was erected to the memory of two or more generations, the alliances of each generation would be shown.

Highly emblazoned canopies and tomb chests were often surrounded by ironwork which sometimes included heraldic pennants, as in the tomb of Elizabeth, Lady Hoby (d. 1609) at Bisham, Berkshire, which is set against a wall, and that of Bishop Montague (d. 1618) in Bath Abbey, Avon.

From *c*. 1630 classical forms predominated and heraldry was, for the most part, confined to segmental pediments while the shield was gradually replaced by the cartouche. From the end of the seventeenth century, a single shield or armorial cartouche was incorporated within the canopy and, during the eighteenth century, the canopy itself became an ornamental feature, eventually being replaced by the wall monument.

A chantry was a private mass celebrated regularly for the repose of the soul of a testator and others nominated by him in his will. It was the conviction that a regular offering of the Eucharist was the most effective means of redemption that encouraged medieval man to make provision in his will for a chantry or chantries. Some chantries were endowed during the lifetime of the founder and the mass priest would be obliged to celebrate masses for his well-being on earth and for his soul after death. Others were endowed by guilds and fraternities for the benefit of their members. Chantries could be a very cheap form of endowment, for even the most humble testator could provide for one or two masses to be said for his soul. But it was those with the largest purses and, one suspects, the heaviest consciences who were responsible for the erection of

Monument to Robert Dudley, Earl of Leicester (d. 1588), at St Mary's church, Warwick

OPPOSITE: the Beauchamp Chantry Chapel at Tewkesbury Abbey, Gloucestershire

the ornate chantry chapels of the late Middle Ages. Cardinal Beaufort (d. 1447), for example, provided for 3,000 masses to be said at the altar of his magnificent chapel at Winchester and, in 1478, Richard of Gloucester obtained licences to establish collegiate churches at Barnard Castle and Middleham as perpetual chantries at which masses were to be celebrated in perpetuity for himself, his duchess and his family. A further scheme, for a college of 100 priests at York, was begun in 1483 but was never completed. Was this to have been Richard's mausoleum?

The essential difference between an ornate, canopied tomb

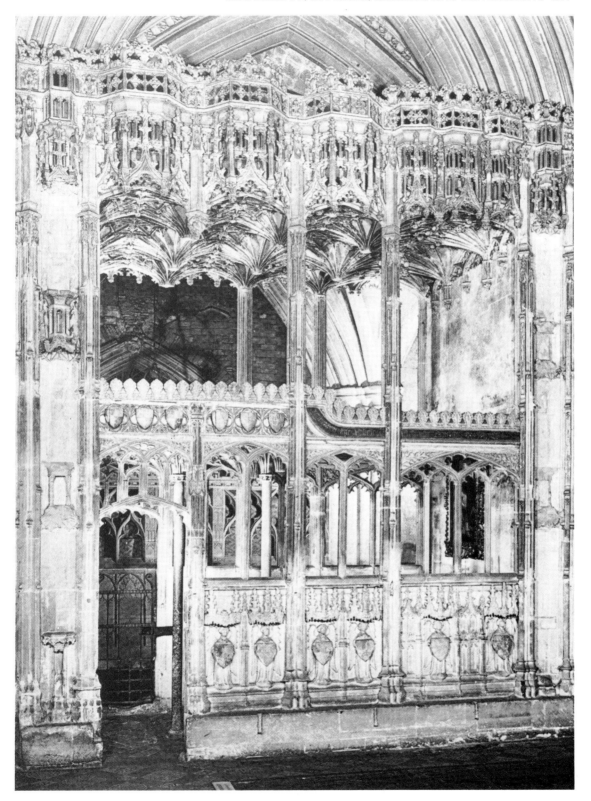

chest and a small chantry chapel is the presence in the latter of an altar at which masses were celebrated. Some were large additional chapels, built on to the main body of the church, such as those at Ely and the glorious Beauchamp Chapel at St Mary's, Warwick, but the majority are very much smaller and usually comprise a gilded and painted rectangular 'cage' of ornate stone or metal and a delicately vaulted canopy. It is significant that the chantry chapels of the high Middle Ages should coincide with the flowering of the perpendicular style of architecture in England. Heraldic embellishment is often sumptuous and will almost invariably include badges, cyphers and rebuses, as well as arms and crests, incorporated into mouldings, bosses and panels. These devices often allude to those for whom masses were to be said, as well as to the deceased and his family, and may also include religious symbols, such as the Instruments of the Passion, and the attributed arms of patron saints. Such chapels are generally found bridging the piers of the chancel arcade or adjacent to the presbytery. At several churches an additional aisle was constructed to accommodate chantry chapels: those at Devizes in Wiltshire and Tiverton in Devon, for example. With the termination of chantries, following the dissolution of the monasteries (1536–9), many chantry chapels were used for other purposes. The superb Hungerford Chantry at Salisbury Cathedral, for example, was converted into an exceptionally ornate civic pew.

It has been estimated that 90 per cent of medieval monuments have been destroyed or lost through neglect. But the magnificence of those that remain, many encrusted with richly gilded armorial devices, provides evidence of both the potency and the ubiquity of heraldry at that time.

Wall Monuments and Tablets

A late sixteenth-century development of the canopied tomb chest, the wall monument was either secured to the wall (hanging wall monument) or supported at ground level (standing wall monument).

The style and decoration followed that of the canopied tomb chest with figures shown kneeling or as demi-effigies. Heraldry proliferated, often ostentatiously so, reflecting the changing nature of armory itself. Armorial devices were usually concentrated in the canopy during the sixteenth and seventeenth centuries but, in the eighteenth century, the canopy was abandoned or reduced to an ornamental form rather than an architectural structure.

During the eighteenth century wall monuments varied considerably, both in size and style, and heraldry remained an important though subdued element of design with a small shield or cartouche of the arms often being the only element of colour in the monument. When the deceased had enjoyed a military or naval

Seventeenth-century Bedingfeld
monument at Oxburgh, Norfolk

career, or had been a prominent churchman, the monument may
be flanked by guns, flags, a crozier or other appropriate devices.

During the late eighteenth and early nineteenth centuries heraldry was often restricted to an inconspicuous crest or was omitted
entirely. It was almost as if the armigerous status of the deceased
(and of his relatives) was taken for granted and yet this fashion
coincided with a marked increase in the popularity of funeral
hatchments (see below). At Pangbourne in Berkshire, for
example, there are hatchments to seven members of the Breedon
family but none of their monuments includes heraldry.

Monument to John Alleyne
(d. 1792) at North Cerney,
Gloucestershire

Wall tablets in the north aisle of
Bath Abbey

Modest versions of the wall monument are often described as wall tablets. In the seventeenth century, these were of stone and usually consisted of a central plaque, sometimes of engraved brass, bearing an inscription and set within a frame surmounted by a coat of arms and decorated with the shields of families related by marriage through heraldic heiresses.

Elegant neo-classical black-and-white tablets characterized the period 1780 to 1840 and were a reaction against the flamboyance of earlier Baroque monuments which recited the virtues of the deceased both in their architectural and sculptural ostentation and in the banality of their inscriptions. In these tablets a panel of white marble, usually a scroll or sarcophagus bearing a dignified inscription, is set against a background of black marble with sculpture in shallow relief. The tablet may be oval, rectangular, or shield-shaped and surmounted by a draped urn, a broken column, tree of life, or a figure of grief with a bowed head.

Wall tablets were comparatively inexpensive and enabled all and sundry to elbow their way into posterity, often at the expense of architectural good taste. At Bath Abbey in Avon, for example, the aisle walls are encrusted with tablets dating from the eighteenth and nineteenth centuries: 'These walls, so full of

monument and bust / Shew how Bath waters serve to lay the dust' (Sir John Harrington d. 1816). Indeed, prior to restoration in 1834, even the pillars of the nave arcade were covered with memorial tablets, and the floor is entirely composed of ledger stones, though most are now concealed by seating which was installed in 1871. A survey of 1915 recorded no fewer than 614 visible monuments in the abbey but, unfortunately, a number of heraldic plaques were muddled during restoration and anomolies will be found, such as the military gentleman who acquired the arms of a woman!

Brass wall plaques were popular during the Victorian period, with their now familiar Gothic lettering, decorative capital letters and occasional armorial devices which were usually engraved or enamelled.

Victorian brass wall tablet to the Ninth Baron Digby (d. 1889) at Minterne Magna, Dorset

From the end of the nineteenth century, large funeral monuments became unfashionable and, in most cases, impracticable. Memorials took the form of modest but finely executed commemorative wall tablets, plaques or window glass (often containing, as minor elements, coats of arms and the devices of colleges, schools and regiments), or bequests of church furnishings 'In Memoriam'.

Unfortunately, many monuments of all periods have been re-painted and gilded by artists who had little knowledge of, or regard for, heraldry, and the historian should always be alert to the possibility of inaccuracies. One of the most telling clues is often to be found in the treatment of a crest wreath which should be of six 'twists' of alternate colours, that to the dexter, the left when viewed from the front, being gold or silver. When this is not so, it is safe to assume that the heraldry has been re-painted by one who is not familiar with the conventions of armory and other details should, therefore, be viewed with suspicion.

Funeral Heraldry

Funerary helm above the tomb of Henry VI in St George's Chapel, Windsor

Funerals of the late medieval and Tudor royalty and nobility were often magnificent spectacles, not least the processions which preceded the committal in which the deceased's accoutrements were paraded in the cortège. These included his spurs, gauntlets, crested helm, shield (*targe*), sword, tabard and banner. After the service these symbols of chivalry were retained for display in the church but regrettably very few early examples remain, the best known being the helm, scabbard, gauntlets, shield and surcoat of Edward, the Black Prince (d. 1376) at Canterbury Cathedral. (These are kept near his tomb: those which are on display being replicas.)

Of Thomas Howard, the Second Duke of Norfolk, it was stated that '. . . no nobleman was ever to be buried in such style again.' Following his death in May 1524, the duke's body lay in state for a month in the chapel of Framlingham Castle, Suffolk, in which were hung funereal drapes and numerous shields of arms. The duke's coffin, drawn on a chariot and embellished with gold shields, was accompanied on its twenty-four mile progress to Thetford Priory in Norfolk by nine hundred mourners including heralds, gentlemen of his household and numerous black-robed torch-bearers. At Thetford the coffin was placed on an enormous black and gold catafalque, adorned with 700 lights, black-robed wax effigies holding eight 'bannerols', and 100 richly emblazoned shields of arms. The service included a procession of heralds carrying achievements of the duke's arms and the dramatic entry of a mounted knight, wearing the dead duke's armour and carrying his inverted battleaxe (see also plate 10).

Several less grandiose examples of funeral accoutrements have

survived from the sixteenth century and from these may be traced
the gradual evolution of funeral heraldry from the practical
equipment of medieval warfare and tournament through the
stylized artificial helms, crests and tabards of the late Tudor period
to the armorial substitute, the funeral hatchment, of the seventeenth, eighteenth and nineteenth centuries (see below). At
St Mary Redcliffe, Bristol, the monument of Admiral Sir William
Penn (d. 1670), whose son founded Pennsylvania, is surmounted
and flanked by his breastplate, crested helm, gauntlet, spurs, shield
banner and pennons. But for the most part only odd items remain.
At Swinbrook, Oxfordshire, for example, there are two imitation
helms with the griffin crests of the Fettiplace family and at
Aldershot, Hampshire stylized funeral helms bear the crests of Sir
John White (d. 1573) and his son Richard (d. 1599).

Banners of members of the various orders of knighthood will be
found in many churches. These are invariably 1.5 m square (5 ft),
embroidered with the knight's arms and fringed in two or more
colours. The banner of a deceased knight is the perquisite of the
king of arms of the order to which he belonged but, in practice, it
is normally conveyed to the family and displayed in their parish
church.

Funerary accoutrements above
the monument to Admiral,
Sir William Penn (d. 1670) in
St Mary Redcliffe, Bristol

Memorial Boards

Panels of wood or canvas, erected on a church wall for the purpose
of displaying armorial devices, are of three types: hatchments (see
below), boards on which the Royal Arms are depicted (see
Chapter Ten) and memorial boards.

Dating mostly from the sixteenth and seventeenth centuries,
memorial boards were an inexpensive form of wall monument,
erected to commemorate individuals and usually bearing the
words 'Near here lies buried . . .' or 'In loving memory of . . .'.
Unlike hatchments they almost invariably include a biographical
inscription and often a biblical quotation or verse praising the
character of the deceased. Memorial boards are generally square
or oblong and vary in width from 60 to 200 cm (2 to 6 ft).
Diamond-shaped memorial boards will also be found, which may
be mistaken for hatchments, while several early hatchments were
painted on rectangular boards.

Of course, there are many armorial panels which fit none none
of these categories. At Avington in Berkshire, for example, a
hexagonal panel bears the arms of Lord Howard de Walden. It is
known that this was placed in the church by de Walden's wife
during his lifetime and it cannot, therefore, be a hatchment or
memorial board. An even more unusual example, at Upper Dean
in Bedfordshire, is a black diamond-shaped board with a coat of
arms in the base and, in the centre, an inscription recording the
charitable donations of one Joseph Neal (d. 1710).

Seventeenth-century armorial boards at Lydiard Tregoze, Wiltshire. These examples demonstrate the transition from true memorial board to hatchment: Ayliffe impaling St John (above) and St John with numerous quarterings (below)

Hatchments

A hatchment is a diamond-shaped armorial panel usually found in a church where it may be affixed to a wall (often above the arcade) or removed to a ringing chamber, vestry or some other equally inaccessible quarter. The word itself is a corruption of 'achievement' and suggests that it originated in the funeral heraldry of the medieval nobility (see above).

Hatchments were certainly associated with funeral practices but their precise function seems to have varied according to a particular location or period. If, as seems likely, the hatchment is descended from the medieval funeral achievement – the shield, spurs, sword etc. carried in the funeral procession and retained in the church as 'honours' above the tomb – then it is not unreasonable to assume that it was carried in procession to the church in which it remained following interment. However, there is ample evidence to suggest that, immediately following the service, it was returned to the deceased's house where it was hung above the door during a period of mourning before being returned to the church. It is uncertain how long a hatchment remained outside a house; exposure to the weather would have caused rapid deterioration of the flimsy fabric.

In Scotland two hatchments were painted, one for the house and the other for the church, while in England there are several examples of hatchments for the same individual being erected in the churches of his various estates.

A hatchment comprises a shield of arms (often with helm, crest and mantling and, where appropriate, a peer's coronet and supporters) painted on a wooden panel or on canvas within a wooden frame. Occasionally a frame will carry a brief inscription and some hatchments include initials and a date. The earliest hatchments date from c. 1627, though the rectangular memorial board, erected to the memory of an individual and bearing both his arms and, unlike hatchments, a more detailed inscription, is usually of sixteenth-century origin (see above).

Early hatchments are generally small, 1 m square (3 ft) with narrow frames decorated with symbols of mortality such as hourglasses, mortheads and crossbones. They were painted in a vigorous style unlike those of the nineteenth century which, for the most part, are of poor artistic quality. Late eighteenth- and nineteenth-century hatchments are larger, their wider frames often covered with black cloth and decorated in the corners with rosettes. Many hatchments were painted for minor gentry, usually by local craftsmen who rarely appreciated the niceties of armory, and errors of interpretation are therefore not uncommon.

The use of hatchments was at its peak in the mid-nineteenth century but declined rapidly during Victoria's reign. Of the 4,500 hatchments recently recorded in England, only 120 are of the present century. The *Hatchments of Britain* series, edited by

Hatchment above the entrance to
Horsington House, Somerset
c. 1880

Summers and Titterton, in ten volumes lists all 4,500 hatchments
recorded since Peter Summers and his colleagues began their
survey in 1952.

It is the treatment of the background which makes the hatchment
unique: essentially, this is coloured black beneath those parts of a
coat of arms which relate to the deceased (see illustration p. 147).

The system was well established by 1700 but there are numerous
traps for the unwary, especially in early hatchments. At Marnhull
in Dorset, for example, the death of a nine-year-old girl is
commemorated in a hatchment of the arms of her living parents
together with the child's intitals, MAS, and date of death, 1663.

When a wife is an heraldic heiress her arms are correctly shown
on a small shield at the centre of her husband's (*in pretence*). But
because this cannot be reflected in the colour of the background,
the arms are sometimes placed side by side (*impaled*) or both
impaled and in pretence, and the appropriate background used.
This demonstrates the need for caution when interpreting
hatchments, for the conventions of marshalling are not always
applicable (see Chapter Eight).

The impalement of a blank half-shield indicates that a wife was
not armigerous, or alternatively no impalement is shown, but the
background of the hatchment is divided as though there were. It is
therefore possible to interpret a hatchment as being that of a
bachelor when, in fact, it commemorates a man whose death

Punning arms of Rabbet in a hatchment at Bramfield, Suffolk. In this example the widow's arms are depicted on a white background though the crest is clearly that of her late husband

followed that of his non-armigerous wife: both would show a single shield and an all-black background.

Several methods are used to indicate two or more wives (see illustration), and again these usually defy the normal conventions of marshalling. The sinister half of the shield may be divided with the arms of the first wife at the top and those of the second wife below. Alternatively, the shield may be divided vertically into three with the husband's arms in the centre between those of his first wife to the dexter and his second wife's to the sinister. This may be confused with another method in which the husband's arms appear in the dexter and those of his former wives successively to the sinister. A further and less confusing method was to depict the husband's personal arms in the centre and the impaled arms of his various wives on small shields set in panels on either side. The backgrounds of each panel would be appropriately coloured to indicate which of the marital partners had died. In a hatchment at Moulton in Lincolnshire, the impaled arms of Henry Bolton (d. 1828) and his fifth wife are surrounded by shields of the impaled arms of her four predecessors. Similar practices were occasionally adopted by ladies who had two or more husbands.

Hatchments erected to commemorate knights of the orders of chivalry will usually contain two shields side by side and slightly overlapping (known as *accollé*). The knight's personal arms, together with the insignia of his order to which his wife is not entitled, are to the dexter and the impaled marital arms to the

Funeral Hatchments

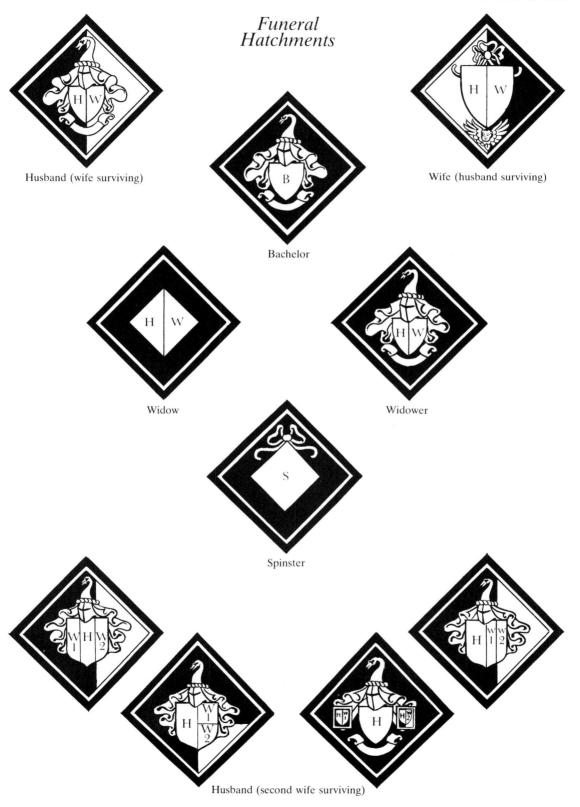

Husband (wife surviving)

Bachelor

Wife (husband surviving)

Widow

Widower

Spinster

Husband (second wife surviving)

Hatchment, at Farley, Wiltshire, for Georgina Lennox, eldest daughter of Charles, second duke of Richmond and Lennox, who was created Baroness Holland of Holland, Lincolnshire, in 1762. Her husband, Henry Fox, was created Baron Holland of Foxley, Wiltshire in 1763. Husband and wife therefore each held titles in their own right – hence the two baronial coronets and the arms *accollé*

sinister, with the appropriate black and white background. Where an archbishop, bishop, college warden, etc. impales his personal arms with those of his office, the background behind the arms of office, to the dexter, will be white to indicate the continuation of the office after his death or, when married, the shields may again be depicted *accollé*. In a number of hatchments, usually later ones, a peer's arms will be found depicted in front of a manteau, a ceremonial robe which may also be surmounted by a coronet of rank. While in England the manteau has no heraldic significance, it is used by the baronage of Scotland.

Non-armorial devices appear in hatchments of all periods – cherubs' heads are frequently found above the lozenges in women's hatchments; skulls fill the vacant corners beneath motto scrolls; and flags, sometimes bearing battle honours, embellish the hatchments of many military or naval men.

Mottoes in hatchments are most unreliable. Many refer to mortality (e.g. *Resurgam* or *In Coela Quies*) and should not be confused with family mottoes which may also appear in a hatchment, but rarely so.

Eighteenth- and nineteenth-century illustrations and engravings and the records of antiquarian county histories indicate that there were once many more hatchments in our parish churches than there are today. Canvas and wood or, in one known case, carpet fabric, are unlikely to survive centuries of damp and neglect or the over-enthusiastic 'restorations' of the nineteenth century. At Shrewsbury in Shropshire two churches contain twenty and twenty-one hatchments respectively, but in Britain this is exceptional. Most churches, if they have any, have one or two.

Miniature (45 cm square) hatchment for the Revd Richard Huntley (d. 1831) at Boxwell, Gloucestershire

In Scotland, there are few hatchments remaining and these tend to follow the European practice of surrounding the central coat of arms with small shields representing probative branches of the deceased.

As in most aspects of heraldry there is room for the vernacular. At Stourton Caundle church in Dorset a 'hatchment' of the arms of the Worshipful Company of Blacksmiths of the City of London, surmounted by a winged hourglass and what appears to be a golden goose sitting on a nest (clearly a misinterpretation of the company's phoenix crest), commemorates one John Biddlecombe. village blacksmith and clock-maker, who died in 1741.

Six

HERALDIC ARTEFACTS

This age did exceedingly abound with impresses, mottoes and devices, and particularly King Edward III was so excessively given up to them that his apparel, plate, bed, household furniture, shields, and even the harness of his horses and the like, were not without them.

Ashmole, *The Institution, Laws and Ceremonies of the Most Noble Order of the Garter*

Heraldry has always been used to distinguish an armiger's possessions not only in the fabric of his buildings and memorials but also in his servants' liveries (see Chapter Nine) and on artefacts as diverse as books and wine bottles, ceramics, crystal and silverwear, furnishings and fabrics, carriages and horse trappings, cast-iron door-stops, playing cards and gaming counters. Even the broad leather collar of the Sixth Duke of Devonshire's mastiff, Hector, was embellished with the Cavendish crest and ducal coronet in silver (1832). From 1793 to 1882 the use of armorial bearings was taxed, indeed a requirement that a licence should be obtained in order to display arms remained in force until as recently as 1945.

Paintings

Heraldry is much in evidence in the portraits and family groups which line the walls of stately homes. Armorial paintings usually contain a simple, often quartered, shield of arms, sometimes a coronet of rank and, where appropriate, insignia of office or of the Order of the Garter. Many have been purchased or borrowed from collections and do not relate to the history of the house in which they are located. Not all are as informative as *The Great Picture* of the Clifford family, at Appleby Castle in Cumbria, which contains nearly fifty individual shields of arms, several of which are depicted in separate portraits painted within *The Great Picture* itself.

Armorial triptychs and diptychs, though rare, are often of particular interest. A triptych is a set of three painted panels which are hinged so that they may be folded together. These probably originated in the portable altars of the medieval nobility and are usually placed against a wall or are free-standing. Like the two-panelled diptych, a triptych usually depicts religious themes, though a number include genealogical and armorial information: the St John triptych at Lydiard Tregoze in Wiltshire, for example, which was erected *c.* 1615 for Sir John St John (d. 1594) by his son, also Sir John, Bart. In this, the front is painted with a number of genealogical trees together with the arms associated with each generation. When opened, the panels reveal paintings of Sir John and his wife kneeling on a sarcophagus and flanked by their daughters and their son and daughter-in-law. Not all heraldic references are immediately apparent. In the magnificent Wilton Diptych of *c.* 1380–90, Richard II is depicted, in the company of his patron saints, venerating the Virgin and Child and surrounded by angels, each of whom wears the king's white hart device in the manner of medieval retainers (see plate 4). (The term 'diptych' is also used to describe lists of names of living and departed Christians for whom prayers were offered.)

Coach Panels and Horse Harness

Painted heraldic panels for coaches were particularly popular in the eighteenth and nineteenth centuries. Many have survived, for they were often removed and stored when a coach was dismantled. Several examples include a feature which is rarely found elsewhere in English heraldry, other than in hatchments and a small number of coins. This is the mantle, or manteau, a robe worn by members of the nobility, the baronage of Scotland and certain orders of chivalry. It is widely depicted in European and Scottish armory as a constituent part of a coat of arms, forming a background for the shield, crest and other components, and may be surmounted by a coronet. When painted, the mantle is shown in the 'open' position, retained by coloured cords and tassels like the entrance flaps of a tent, and, because of its canopy-like appearance, it is sometimes described incorrectly as a pavilion. Mantles were not used in England until the eighteenth century when the arms of peers were sometimes painted in hatchments and on coach panels on a background of a red and ermine mantle with gold cords and tassels. But, unlike their Scottish and European counterparts, English mantles are entirely decorative.

Metal pendants for enhancing horse harness appear to have been used since the late Bronze Age. Most early examples are extremely plain but medieval pendants were cast to a high quality and richly decorated using heraldic devices in coloured enamels (see below). Several good examples have survived, including a fourteenth-century pendant of the Stoke arms, now in the Dorset County Museum (*Vair a Chief Gules*), and two, in the Salisbury and South Wiltshire Museum, of the arms of Sir Robert Fitzpaine, Governor of Corfe Castle, Dorset, in 1304, and of St Maur and Lovell, presumably commemorating the union of the two families in 1351.

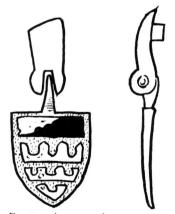

Fourteenth-century horse pendant, front and side view, bearing the Stoke arms

By the eighteenth century it was the fashion to decorate carriage-horse harness with finely wrought silver crests and other armorial devices on the brow bands, blinkers, side-straps, martingales and saddles. In imitation of these, nineteenth-century harness ornaments (horse brasses) were bought in large numbers to embellish the harness of plough and wagon teams, dray horses and carriers' and roundsmens' cobs in an age when the appearance of a team reflected the status of the owner as well as the self-esteem of the employee. Such ornaments were not entirely decorative. Like the ancient protective amulets from which they derived, they were considered to bring good luck and to safeguard a horse from evil. Early nineteenth-century brasses were manufactured from sheets of latten (an alloy of copper, zinc, lead and tin) with a hammer and punch and are of simple design and inferior quality. But from the mid-nineteenth century, when the prosperity of a farm or estate was invariably equated with the number of working horses it employed, the production of harness ornaments increased significantly. Victorian horse brasses, although mass-produced by casting and lacquered to reduce corrosion, were often superbly designed and executed. Designs (usually pseudo-heraldic beasts, eagles, crosses, crescents etc.) were skilfully carved in a close-grained wood, usually pear, which was applied to a mould of damp sand. These traditional horse brasses are known as 'Walsalls' because of a near-monopoly of manufacture in that area in the nineteenth century. In the early years of the twentieth century, ceramic enamels were applied to provide areas of solid colour in horse brasses, many of which were made by hand using a repouseé technique rather than by sand casting.

One of the first representations of a horse bell is in Caxton's *Game and Playe of Chesse* (1476) in which an illustration of a mounted knight, fully armed and his horse caparisoned and 'coveryd with hys armes', shows a large bell on the horse's crupper. By the early seventeenth century horse bells were offered as prizes at the races. In 1610, for example, a magnificent set of three engraved silver gilt bells was presented for this purpose by the Sheriff of Chester. The first bore the arms of 'the Kynge' (James I) and one of the others the arms of 'the Princes'.

Metalwork and Enamelling

The furniture of doors and chests was often both functional and decorative, and sometimes incorporated armorial devices. These were not normally of a personal nature until the fifteenth century when cyphers and badges became popular forms of ornamentation, particularly in lock plates and the bows of keys. Moulded armorial doorplates and brass or cast-iron door-stops, often in the form of heraldic beasts, may have been acquired during Victorian or Edwardian refurbishing, though there are earlier examples.

Over three thousand medieval bells are still rung in English belfries and many are inscribed with dedications to saints, with foundry marks and other devices, some of which are heraldic, including the arms of lay rectors, such as Oxford and Cambridge colleges, and benefactors.

Wrought-iron circlets suspended by chains, on the rim of which are candle-holders and drip-pans (*corona lucis*), are often decorated with heraldic devices, usually enamelled shields and crests. Most examples are of Victorian origin and reflect the Gothic Revival style.

Medieval effigies (see Chapter Five) were often enclosed in an ornamental metal framework (hearse), such as that on the tomb chest of Richard Beauchamp (d. 1349) at St Mary's church, Warwick (see page 110), and these may have been covered with a shroud which was removed only on ceremonial occasions. Many of the more grandiose late sixteenth- and early seventeenth-century monuments were provided with ornate railings which sometimes incorporated painted or enamelled devices, including heraldic pennants. There are also numerous examples of eighteenth- and nineteenth-century churchyard monuments, the protective railings of which often include heraldry.

The gradual introduction of the enclosed chimney flue and fireplace from the late thirteenth century resulted in a number of innovations including the cast-iron fire-back which both protected the stone wall at the back of the hearth and reflected heat into the room. It was also found that because the metal absorbed and conserved heat (effectively an early storage radiator) the up-draught in the chimney flue could be maintained, thereby improving the efficiency of the grate. Many fire-backs incorporated traditional designs such as religious symbols, floral motifs and scroll-work. Others were made for specific fireplaces and may include armorial devices appropriate to the family who commis-

Graveyard tomb of Thomas Guest (d. 1904) at Henstridge, Somerset

sioned them. Care should be exercised, however, for it may not be assumed that a fire-back has remained in its original location and the heraldry may not relate to the house in which it is found. There are also many modern, and usually inferior, imitations.

Heraldic artefacts have been embellished with coloured enamels since at least the thirteenth century and include such items as horse trappings, weapons, scabbards, goblets, ciboria, jewel boxes, fibulae and lamps. Memorials (notably monumental brasses – see Chapter Five) were also enriched by the addition of coloured enamels, and in the Gothic Revival of the nineteenth century the technique was widely used on memorial and commemorative plaques and in architectural decoration.

Enamel is a vitreous glaze, or combination of glazes, fused on a metalic surface. The base substance of enamel is a clear, colourless vitreous compound called flux, containing silica, red lead and potash. The material is coloured by the addition of metallic oxides while in a liquid state, so that the flux is stained through its entirety. The material is fired at varying temperatures into solid lumps: the higher the temperature, the harder the enamel. The brilliance of the enamel depends on the materials which are added to the flux, and their proportions, while the colour is affected by the constituents of the flux and the added oxides. Turquoise blue, for example, is obtained from the black oxide of copper by using a large proportion of sodium carbonate in the flux.

The process begins by pulverizing the lumps of prepared enamel, the resultant powder being washed in distilled water to remove contaminants. The pulverized enamel is then spread over the metal surface of the artefact which has been cleaned with acid and dried. The piece is then gently warmed before being introduced to the furnace which is then raised to the necessary temperature for vitrification – a process which takes only a few minutes. When the enamel is seen to have obtained an even sheen it is removed and allowed to cool. There are, of course, several methods of enamelling, each using different techniques. Raised metal ridges may separate different elements of a design, for example, or the work may be overlayed with a transparent enamel glaze.

Gold and Silverware

There are two types of heraldic gold and silverware: that which has been bought from stock and subsequently engraved with a customer's crest or coat of arms, and that which was designed and made for a particular patron and identified by his arms which, from the outset, were integral to the overall design. Contemporaneous literature may describe the circumstances in which such pieces were commissioned and approval sketches may still exist.

The scratched surfaces of this brass shield (at Chinnor, Oxfordshire) would have facilitated the application of coloured enamels

An inventory of Sir John Fastolf (d. 1459) records that he possessed 13,000 ounces of domestic silverware, with a further 1,200 ounces in his private chapel. Items associated with the Euchrist are not usually embellished with personal devices, though the occasional armorial chalice or paten may be found. Such decoration is usually indicative of a bequest of church plate or may depict the arms of a rector and is, to modern tastes, singularly pretentious. Of course, many church vessels and plate were originally intended for domestic purposes. The Boleyn Cup at Cirencester church, Gloucestershire, for example, belonged to Anne Boleyn and was later given to the church as a chalice. Regrettably, vast quantities of medieval silverware were melted down following the Dissolution of the Monasteries (1536–9) and, later, during the Civil War (1642–9). But that which has survived demonstrates both the medieval craftsman's mastery of heraldic motifs in cast forms of decoration and of the enthusiasm of royal, magnatial and ecclesiastical patrons for heraldic display in plate and table silver.

Complete coats of arms, cast in solid silver, were embodied as the centrepieces of magnificent 'sideboard' pieces such as the silver-gilt, 79 cm (31 in) diameter charger made by Paul de Lamerie (1688–1751), the acknowledged master of British goldsmiths, for the Worshipful Company of Goldsmiths in 1741. A crest may also be cast in silver and incorporated into the design, as in many of the heraldic items made by Paul Storr and his contemporaries during the Regency period. At Chatsworth, Derbyshire, silver vessels have handles of Cavendish snakes (from the crest) and plate is 'supported' by Cavendish stags; while at Woburn in Bedfordshire, silver salt cellars take the form of goats, the crest of the Russell family. Enamelling was widely used further to embellish items of gold and silver: the Cressener Cup, for example, which was made in 1503 for John Cressener of Hinckford Hundred in Essex, is a font cup on which the arms of Cressener, quartering Mortimer and with Ferrers in pretence, are depicted in champlevé enamel.

An alternative but time-consuming method of decoration is by raising an armorial design in low relief by chasing a flat sheet of slender gauge silver from its lower surface by numerous small punches and hammers. Such a technique is most effective when applied to large expanses of metal such as the 63.5 cm (25 in) diameter alms dish made for Westminster Abbey in 1685.

There are many items on which heraldry has been engraved which, from the outset, were intended for ornamentation rather than domestic use, and the quality of workmanship in such cases is often exemplary. But the majority of 'crested silver' was intended for everyday purposes and is therefore particularly susceptible to wear as the result of polishing and constant handling. Hallmarks, which include a date letter, are not always a reliable guide when attempting to identify armorial devices on silver. At first sight, the

Silver-gilt charger by de Lamerie

hallmark date should enable the researcher to determine which member or branch of an armigerous family commissioned the piece. But heraldic engraving was not necessarily contemporaneous with hallmarking, and many items were 'personalized' long after they had been purchased. For example, it is not unknown for a piece of silver, hallmarked with one date, to be engraved with a shield that shows a marriage which did not take place until a decade or more later.

Of course, not all heraldry is authentic. The most frequently encountered armorial decoration on Georgian and Victorian silver spoons or forks is an engraved crest, but heraldic reference works such as Fairbairn's *Book of Crests* (1859) were sold in large numbers to jewellers and engravers for whom they provided a wealth of artistic motifs. Although some non-armigerous clients chose to have their silver marked with a monogram or cypher, many simply copied an illustration of a crest which was once used by someone of their own surname. This heraldic free-for-all resulted in a plethora of engraved 'armorial' silver on which the devices have no historical significance whatsoever. The historian should also beware of drawing genealogical conclusions from engraved devices on the 'family' silver, for pieces may have been obtained by a late relative as a job lot at a clearance sale!

Heraldic colours in silverware may usually be identified by reference to the scheme of engraved dots and hatching now known as the Petra Sancta system (see p. 189). As elsewhere, mottoes are singularly unreliable references, for they may be changed at will. However, the combination of a clearly hatched crest or shield, motto and date mark may provide a starting point for research.

The stylistic fashions followed by engravers changed regularly. Between 1650 and 1685 it was fashionable to depict a shield supported on a pair of vigorously engraved crossed plumes, and towards the end of the seventeenth century the mantling of a helm was draped around the shield. Armorial engraving from 1705 to 1740 followed the baroque fashion with a cartouche replacing the shield and the surrounding decoration following a symmetrical, architectural form. This was followed by a rococo style with rocaille or foliated decoration around an asymmetrical cartouche and, from about 1770, the neo-classical style of Robert Adam was fashionable. This was followed by deep-cut engraving in which the silver was heavily carved at an angle to reflect the light. There are many examples of early silverware engraved at a later date and in an entirely inappropriate style. Occasionally, examples may also be found of early silver which has subsequently been engraved in a style corresponding to its age and provenance. Wherever there is doubt, reference should be made to the ledger entries in which a silversmith recorded the manufacture of a commission for his client.

Encouraged by a tax on the possession of silver plate (1756–77), Old Sheffield Plate, the precursor of electro-plating, was introduced in the late eighteenth century. In this process a sheet of sterling silver, too thin to be engraved, was fused on a thicker sheet of copper and worked as if it were silver sheet. Armorial engraving was accommodated by inserting a disc of pure silver within a recess cut into the fused plate. This was then burnished and engraved. Such inserts may be detected by breathing on the engraving to reveal the disc which will have a whiter appearance than the area around it.

There are numerous smaller items of silverware which are often embellished with heraldic devices. Souvenir teaspoons, for example, may have enamelled shields depicting civic heraldry inserted at the end of the handle. Engraved mementoes for liverymen and their dinner guests include pomanders, salts and dishes. Wine labels (also known as bottle tickets) were much used in the eighteenth and nineteenth centuries and many were specially commissioned from silversmiths. They consist of a decorative silver 'label', held in place round the neck of a bottle by a chain, and may have the owner's crest, pierced and engraved in silhouette, or shown in high relief above a description of the bottle's contents. Livery buttons, worn by retainers in the late eighteenth and nineteenth centuries, are usually of fused plate with their employer's crest and sometimes coronet in relief.

Ceramics

Earthenware is inherently fragile and it is therefore unusual for everyday domestic pieces to have survived. Fortunately, most armorial porcelain was specially commissioned (often in great quantities) for households in which it would be treated with considerable care.

A notable exception is heraldic Delftware which was widely used for domestic purposes following the establishment of a pottery in the City of London in 1571. Delftware was executed in blue, or sometimes polychrome, on a white ground and has an attractive vigorous style of decoration which, because of the absorbent nature of the tin-glazed material, lacks detail. It became so popular that numerous examples have survived, notably in collections at the Museum of London.

Chinese armorial porcelain was an extraordinary phenomenon. It has been calculated that some 4,000 services, providing a total of perhaps 80,000 separate pieces, were made in China between 1695 and 1820 and exported, at the rate of one every six days, to British clients. Best known of these is the 600-piece Hannay service made either for Alexander Hannay, Adjutant General in India, or his brother, Ramsay, a merchant trading between India and China. Richly decorated and gilded, it passed into the collection of the Winn family at Nostell Priory in Yorkshire (where it may now be seen) during the early nineteenth century, a time when it was considered fashionable to possess antique items which were decorated with arms other than one's own. The trade, which lasted over a century, declined rapidly following the imposition of a prohibitive 150 per cent tax intended to protect the expanding English potteries of the early nineteenth century. The Chinese, of course, had little understanding of European armory and the naive exactitude with which the copyists transcribed their clients' arms from drawings into ceramic painting is legendary. One example often cited is of the painstaking reproduction, on an entire dinner service, of the written instructions on the original sketch: 'This is gules . . . This is azure . . .' Armorial bookplates were often sent to China for this purpose, and the similarities in style are often evident (see Chapter Three). Missing or broken pieces were often replaced by reproductions from the Samson factory in Paris and these were distinguished by a letter S marked on the bottom of each piece, although this was easily removed by an unscrupulous owner!

No longer constrained by Chinese competition, the great English manufacturers of the eighteenth century – Wedgwood, Spode, Minton and Davenport – developed their own finely decorated armorial porcelain, a tradition which has continued to the present day.

But not all heraldic ceramic work is of such exquisite quality. The royal arms of Charles II, sometimes accompanied by the Boscobel Oak, was a favourite motif on Staffordshire slipware from 1670 to 1690. Many large dishes, of up to 60 cm (2 ft) diameter, have survived from this period, the crude decoration produced by piping liquid paste-clay, like cake icing, on to the body of the dish. Sunderland lustreware includes jugs and punch-bowls decorated with the transfer-printed 'arms' (rarely authentic) of masonic and agricultural fraternities, or those of the Shipwrights Company which appear on items sold to travellers at seaports. Since the mid-nineteenth century, numerous mass produced souvenirs of royal and national occasions have incorporated the royal arms and other devices such as the so-called 'Prince of Wales' Feathers'. In 1833 Adolphus Goss joined his father's china manufacturing firm of W.H. Goss and developed a new line of miniatures of ancient artefacts associated with particular places. These were hand painted with the appropriate town arms and sold through selected retailers. Goss souvenirs became extraordinarily popular in the early decades of the twentieth century, a time when railway travel, day trips and annual holidays were enjoyed by a rapidly increasing number of people. A contemporary catalogue lists 7,000 different armorial items produced by the Goss factory, though heraldic propriety was often stretched to the limit in an effort to provide a suitable shield of arms for each piece. The craze for 'crested china' lasted until 1930 when the bankruptcy of H.T. Robinson, who had bought out Goss and several smaller manufacturers, brought to an end the production of his vast *Arcadian China* range.

Fabrics

Tapestries were both decorative and functional. They served to brighten the drab uniformity of large areas of stonework and

Tapestry cushion, decorated with the arms of Throckmorton, at Coughton Court, Warwickshire

reduced draughts by covering doorways and open fenestrations. Most surviving medieval tapestries were woven in the Low Countries, Flanders and France, there being no significant workshops in England until the sixteenth century. Tapestries were sometimes commissioned for particular rooms and designs often included coats of arms and other devices, either within the overall design or, more usually, in the border. Few have survived the ravages of time and not all of these have remained at their original locations. At Hardwick Hall in Derbyshire, completed in 1597, a number of rooms were designed to accommodate tapestries. Flemish tapestries bought by Bess of Hardwick from the family of Sir Christopher Hatton were overpainted with her arms, though the original Hatton arms are now visible again. Also in Derbyshire, at Haddon Hall, one of a series of fine fifteenth-century tapestries included five representations of the royal arms, and at Montacute in Somerset the famous Millefleurs tapestry depicts a mounted knight holding a guidon charged with a strange chimerical beast (an *alphyn*) and gold cyphers. This tapestry was probably commissioned by the town of Tournai in 1477–9 as a gift to the Governor of Dauphiné, Jean de Daillon, whose arms are woven into the top left-hand corner. Many tapestries originally carried some form of identification mark woven into the selvage and these were often devices taken from the arms of the workshop owner or the town of manufacture.

Small items such as bed hangings, table carpets and cushion covers were often embroidered by the ladies of a household who were attracted to heraldic devices, especially personal badges and cyphers, though it may be difficult to distinguish these from other decorative motifs. Many examples have survived from the sixteenth and seventeenth centuries, as have the embroidered fire-screens, footstools and other furnishings of later periods.

In the Middle Ages ecclesiastical vestments (such as copes, chasubles and maniples) were often embroidered with heraldry; bishops and abbots enjoying the right to have their arms embroidered on the orphreys of a cope or on the back of a chasuble. The Syon Cope, at the Victoria and Albert Museum, is a wonderful example of a late thirteenth-century vestment with heraldic embroidery on the orphreys. Altar frontals and other furnishings were also richly decorated, but today the few surviving examples are generally to be found in museums. By contrast, vernacular heraldry may be found in abundance in colourful embroidered kneelers, cushions and chair backs, favourite subjects including the arms of lords of the manor, past patrons of livings, benefactors and monastic or lay rectors, diocesan arms and the attributed arms of saints. At Wells Cathedral in Somerset the cushions of the prebendal stalls are embroidered with the arms of former bishops.

Many floor carpets and rugs (notably those of the Victorian period) incorporated armorial devices. At Berkeley Castle in Gloucestershire, for example, a magnificent red carpet is embellished with white *crosses paty* and mitres from the family arms, and Beaumont lions are woven into a carpet at Carlton Towers in Yorkshire. A carpet at Charlecote, near Stratford-on-Avon in Warwickshire, is decorated with the *luces* (pike-fish) of the Lucy family, one of whom (Sir Thomas Lucy) was caricatured by Shakespeare as 'the old pike' Justice Shallow in *Henry IV* and *The Merry Wives of Windsor*.

Furniture

Heraldic ornamentation does not appear to have been a feature of most medieval furniture which was essentially utilitarian. Examples of finely painted and gilded furniture of the period are rare but, in royal and magnatial households, such decoration undoubtedly included heraldic devices. There are good examples of seventeenth-century upholstered chairs with seats and backs embroidered with heraldic motifs, but most commonly found are eighteenth- and nineteenth-century seats made for the halls and corridors of large houses, there to provide temporary relief for visitors awaiting reception, and for footmen. It seems likely that many of these chairs were made in large batches, from a fairly limited set of designs, and that painted armorial panels were added to order. These were usually inserted within a recess of the chairback provided for the purpose and the heraldry may, therefore, have suffered less wear than the chair itself. Devices varied from simple crests to full coats of arms, often with coronet and supporters. Specially commissioned armorial hall chairs may also be found, the designs of which were intended to complement the

Nineteenth-century leather chair-back painted with the arms of Bankes of Kingston Lacy, Dorset

crest or arms which might be inlaid in coloured veneers or carved from the solid backplate. These chairs are of far better quality than the 'off the peg' variety and have survived in greater numbers. Upholstered saloon chairs are also to be found with embroidered armorial devices. The fine set of mid-eighteenth-century chairs at Audley End in Essex, for example, which were re-upholstered and embroidered with the Howard de Walden crest and baronial coronet in 1786 in anticipation of a visit by George III and Queen Charlotte. Towards the end of the nineteenth century a number of cabinet makers were producing pieces of furniture which incorporated a blank cartouche in large quantities so that purchasers could add their own heraldry if they so wished.

There are, of course, many superb individual pieces of furniture in which heraldic motifs are an important element of design. At the Victoria and Albert Museum in London, for example, is a side table, of carved and gilded pine, by Flitcroft (1730), its scaglio top inlaid with an oval panel of the arms of George Lee, Second Earl of Lichfield, impaling those of his wife Frances, daughter of Sir John Hales. Also at the museum is a gilded table attributed to James Moore, royal cabinet maker to Queen Anne (1702–14) and George I (1714–27). The apron of this table is carved with the crest and coronet of Richard Temple, Baron Cobham. The coronet is that of a baron, so the table must have been made between 1714, when Cobham was elevated to the peerage, and 1718, when he was created a viscount. Perhaps the finest heraldic furniture is that made as far as was practicable in solid silver for the Crown and nobility. One of the best examples is a silver table, now at Windsor Castle, which was presented to William III (1689–1702) by the City of London. A minimum of wood and iron was used in the table's construction and its top is magnificently engraved with the royal arms. Also at Windsor is a silver table made between 1709 and 1718 for Edward Harley, second Earl of Oxford, the top of which is engraved with the Earl's arms – incorporating all seventy-two quarterings!

Bottle Seals

From the mid-seventeenth century, wealthy wine drinkers embellished their specially made bottles with bottle seals. A bottle seal was a blob of glass, attached to the body of the bottle, in which was impressed the customer's seal: usually a crest, a shield of arms, cypher or other device. The Oxford colleges, for example, used their own sealed bottles from the mid-seventeenth century to *c.* 1730, as did many tavern keepers who personalized their bottles with initials, perhaps a tavern sign, and the date when the wine was bottled or laid down. From that time, the practice was continued by private individuals until the mid-nineteenth century when personal devices were superseded by wine merchants' marks and, eventually, by brand names.

Signs

Inn signs originated in the medieval practice by which tradespeople declared their function to an illiterate populace. The butcher, baker and candlestick-maker each had his own symbol as did the taverner and maltster. Other twentieth-century survivors are the bloody, bandaged pole of the barber-surgeon and the

Late seventeenth-century bottle
seal depicting the lozenges and
dragon's wings of Daubeney

pawnbrokers' gold discs which originated in the *bezants* or gold
coins of Byzantium. By the end of the fourteenth century the
provision of a prominent and distinctive sign outside taverns and
alehouses was a legal requirement, at least in London. In many
cases these must have been very much larger than they are today.
In 1419 the encroachment of signs above the highway was restricted to just over two metres (7 ft) by statute.

Many inn names are of considerable antiquity as are the symbols
by which they are recognized. Regrettably, there is an increasing
tendency to change the names of inns without regard to their
historical significance. At Lydlinch in Dorset, for example, the

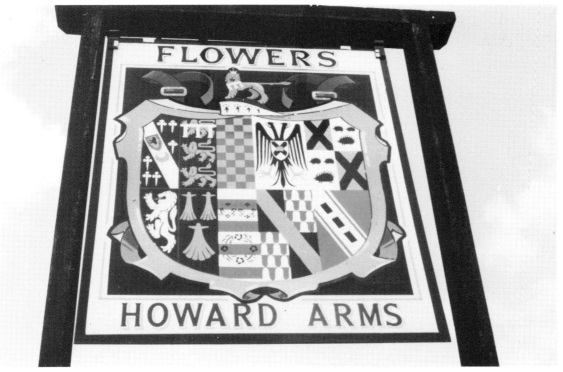

The Howard Arms at Ilmington, Warwickshire; an unexpected outpost of the ubiquitous Howard family

local inn was renamed The Deer Park in 1988, after the nearby deer park of Stock Gaylard. The owner's intention was to provide his establishment with a more 'relevant' name, and yet the original 'Three Boar's Heads' was a clear reference to the arms of the Lewys family, former lords of the manor of Lydlinch and Stock. In the past there were often sound political reasons for such changes. Following the Battle of Bosworth in 1485, for example, many White Boar taverns were hastily renamed and their signs modified to show the blue boar device of the victorious Earl of Oxford instead of the white boar of the ignominious Richard of Gloucester. Similarly, numerous King's Arms have been repainted, reflecting changing dynastic fortunes, often by artists whose understanding of heraldry was minimal. There are also instances of inn signs having been brought up to date. In 1955, for example, the Green Dragon at Downham in Lancashire was changed to The Assheton Arms to commemorate the elevation of a local landowner, Sir Ralph Assheton, to the peerage. At Long Burton in Dorset, the sign board of the Rose and Crown was repainted in the 1980s with the badge of York Herald on the one side and that of Lancaster Herald, who lives in the village, on the other.

The origins of inn names are often obscure. The Romans used the sign of a bush to advertise the sale of liquid refreshment. This symbol was often reduced to a garland of evergreens, and the hoop in names such as the Eagle and Hoop is probably derived from

The crowned white rose *en soleil* badge of York Herald and the crowned red rose of Lancaster Herald at the Rose and Crown Inn, Long Burton, Dorset

The sign of the Brownlow Arms Inn at Hough, Lincolnshire, displays the arms of Cust, Earls Brownlow

this. It seems likely that the expression 'a good wine needs no bush' has a Roman origin.

Many inn names have an obvious armorial origin: they are simply called the 'So-and-So' Arms, though all too often the heraldry of the signs is inaccurate or, perversely, has been replaced by lettering. Such names usually refer to the family arms of a past or present lord of the manor or to a guild or other institution which at one time was associated with the area – as rector or patron of a parish, for example (see plate 20).

Even more common are badges and crests taken from the arms of local families such as the Bear and Ragged Staff of the earls of Warwick, the Eagle and Child badge of the Stanley earls of Derby and the punning Talbot badge of the Talbot earls of Shrewsbury. Many of these inns are of medieval origin or occupy sites of former ancient hostelries provided by magnates for their retainers and manorial tenants. In such cases, a lord's badge (which was worn by his retainers) would have been a familiar symbol of corporate identity and affiliation – far more so than the coat of arms which was personal to the lord and his family.

Inns with 'So-and-So' Arms names are almost invariably more recent than those named after single devices, usually dating from

The sign of the Blue Boar at Chipping Norton, Oxfordshire. The blue boar was a badge of the victorious John de Vere, Earl of Oxford, who fought with Henry Tudor at Bosworth in 1485. Here, the earl's standard overlays that of the defeated Richard III

the eighteenth and nineteenth centuries. The Pembroke Arms and the Green Dragon at Wilton in Wiltshire, for example, both refer to the heraldry of the Herbert earls of Pembroke (of Wilton House), but while the former is of comparatively recent origin the latter name is derived from 'the dragon grene' badge used by the medieval earls of Pembroke and the site of the inn is probably of some antiquity even though the present building is not. Common signs such as the White Lion and the Chequers are almost certainly of armorial origin but are less distinctive and therefore more difficult to identify. The white lion may be that of the former Mowbray dukes of Norfolk or of the Mortimer earls of March, or indeed of several other families who used the same device, just as the chequers may be those of the de Warenne family whose arms were *Chequy Gold and Azure* or may have originated in the arms of an entirely different family. A further possibility, and an increasingly common one, is that the sign has been repainted incorrectly, by a sign-writer unaware of its heraldic derivation. To determine the correct armorial origin of an inn sign may require research into the heraldry of many local families and lords of the manor over several centuries and the name itself will often have survived long after the estate has changed hands or the family died out. The Hind's Head at Aldermaston in Berkshire, for example, is the crest of the Forster family, lords of the manor before 1711. Conversely, the name of a local inn may provide a clue to a former lordship of the manor.

Inn signs may not portray precisely the pub's name. The Prince of Wales may have a sign of three ostrich feathers (the badge of the Heir Apparent to the English throne), for example, while at Sonning in Berkshire the sign of The Bull shows the coat of arms of the Marquis of Abergavenny, the name of the inn being derived from the bull supporters and crest.

Inns called the King's Arms, Queen's Arms, Duke of York, Duke of Cambridge, etc. are ubiquitous. Most royal arms are those of the Tudors or the present queen though Stuart and Hanoverian examples are also to be found. At Winchester, the sign of the King's Arms has the earliest confirmed royal arms of England (*Gules three Lions passant guardant Or*) and the inn itself is believed to date from the reign of Henry III (1216–72). Royal heraldry should not be used to date the inn, however, for signs are regularly repainted and the owner or painter may choose to update the arms. It is much easier to paint the modern royal arms (from 1837), for example, than to repaint a complicated Hanoverian coat. Royal or dynastic allegiance is indicated in many signs by the use of royal badges such as the White Hart of Richard II and Edward IV, the Sun in Splendour of the Yorkist kings and the Antelope and White Swan of the Lancastrians which were inherited through marriage from the de Bohun earls of Hereford. In such cases, the antelope should not be represented as the natural but as the heraldic antelope: a deer-like creature with a horn on the nose and serrated antlers. It should be remembered, however, that badges were transferred both by inheritance and through the acquisition of seigniories and were frequently translated into crests and supporters (see Chapter Nine).

The sign of the White Lion at Tredington, Oxfordshire, depicts the White Lion of March holding a shield of the Yorkist livery colours, blue and murrey, charged with their badge, a white rose *en soleil*

Seven

BLAZON: THE TERMINOLOGY OF ARMORY

And like bright metal on a sullen ground,
My reformation, glittering o'er my fault,
Shall show more goodly, and attract more eyes,
Than that which hath no foil to set it off.

Shakespeare, *1 Henry IV*, I. ii

Correctly, the term coat of arms should be applied only to the shield of arms, the design of which was repeated on the surcoat or jupon of the medieval armiger: hence 'coat' of arms. However, it is now widely used to include all the component parts of an achievement – the shield, helm, crest, supporters and so on.

The Components of a Coat of Arms

The Shield

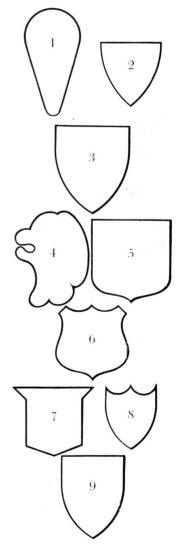

The shield is the essential element of a coat of arms and, with the banner, is the principal means of heraldic display. Effigies, monumental brasses, etc. may be dated with reasonable accuracy by reference to the type of shield held by a figure or depicted elsewhere on a monument. In the eleventh century, and at the beginning of the twelfth, shields were long, narrow and kite-shaped, covering most of the body. They had rounded tops and were made of wood covered with tough boiled leather (see illustration, 1). Such shields were in use at Hastings and during the first Crusade, where raised edges, studs and bosses were often picked out in colour. During the twelfth century the tops of shields became flatter, and decoration more personal. In the thirteenth century shields became shorter and were shaped like the base of a flat-iron, called a heater shield (2 and 3), and this style remained in use for heraldic purposes throughout most of the fourteenth century. But the increasing efficiency of the long bow and cross bow, and the rapid development of plate armour, reduced the effectiveness of the shield as a means of defence and by the fifteenth century it had been abandoned by mounted knights except for heraldic purposes, notably at tournaments. It was at this time that the *à bouche* shield was most in evidence. This took a

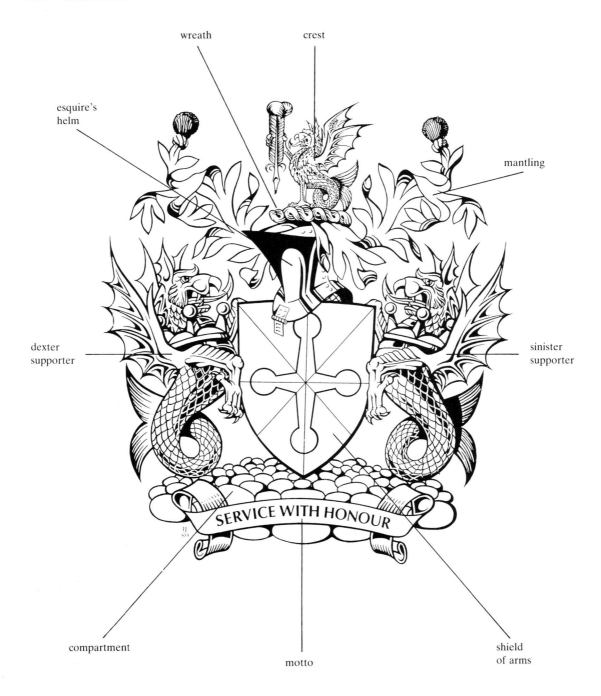

wreath

crest

esquire's
helm

mantling

dexter
supporter

sinister
supporter

compartment

shield
of arms

motto

The arms of West Dorset District Council

variety of forms but all had a small 'notch' cut in the side, apparently to allow for the free movement of a lance in the joust, though this may have been a stylistic affectation (4). The sixteenth century witnessed the decline of practical armory and a pre-occupation with heraldic display. In order to accommodate numerous acquired or assumed quarterings, shields of the period were almost invariably as broad as they were long (5 and 6). From the beginning of the seventeenth century many ornate shields found their way into armory, few of which could ever have been used on the battlefield. For the most part these reflect contemporary architectural styles, the most common being the eighteenth-century 'tablet' shield (7) and the popular nineteenth-century 'spade' shield (8). A beautifully proportioned 'heater' shield (9) is that which is most often used in the present century, though the *à bouche* style is also popular.

The 'shield' in a woman's arms is conventionally depicted in the shape of a lozenge, there being an assumption that women did not make war or participate in tournaments and, therefore, had no practical use for a shield. For the same reason, a lozenge is never accompanied by a helm and crest (see below), though there are exceptions – as in a hatchment at Marnhull church in Dorset where a lozenge of the arms of Beatrix Dive(?) is surmounted with a helm bearing the family crest. In such cases it is possible that a local craftsman was unaware of armorial convention. The lozenge is such an unattractive and inconvenient shape that considerable artistic licence, and not a little ingenuity, may have been required in order to accommodate the heraldry.

The Helmet

In the thirteenth and fourteenth centuries, when the helmet was an essential component of a knight's equipment, the cylindrical barrel or great helm, with a flat or rounded top, eye slits (sights) and ventilation holes (breathes) was invariably used in seals and other forms of armorial display (see illustration figures 1-2-3). From the end of the fourteenth century the great helm was superseded in England by the tilting helm (4). This had no visor and was permanently closed, with only a slit for the eyes. It was, therefore, effective only when leaning forward in the tilting position. Tilting helms carried the ornate tournament crests of the period and so were associated with chivalric superiority – both in the lists and in coats of arms. With the wholesale adoption of crests by the new gentility of the Tudor period (see below) the nobility perceived a need for further differentiation in their arms. An extraordinary variety of bizarre and impracticable headgear began to appear in achievements of arms towards the end of the sixteenth century and, by the early seventeenth century, these had been codified into a system in which different types of helm were assigned to

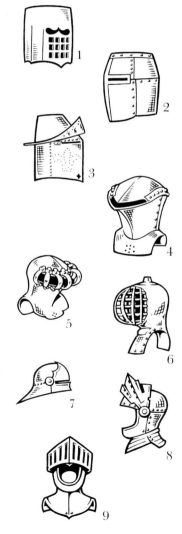

Hatchment for Beatrix Dive at
Marnhull in Dorset

armigers of different ranks (though, in Scotland, the great helm
continued in general use). These were also stylized forms of
tournament helms and, while they remain in use today, considerable artistic variations will be encountered, reflecting the heraldic
tastes of intervening centuries. The tilting helm (4) was retained in
the arms of gentlemen, esquires and corporations; the barriers
helm (9) was adopted for baronets and knights; and the mêlée
helm (5) for peers. The late fifteenth-century 'basket' helm (6),
armet (8) and sallet (or salade) (7) may also be encountered,
particularly in Scottish heraldry where the sallet is now used in
civic arms.

The Crest

A crest is a three-dimensional device affixed to a helmet and is so
depicted in the arms of male members of a family. Twelfth- and
thirteenth-century crests were simple fan-like projections (the

Crest depicting a freeminer of
the Forest of Dean in the brass
of Robert Greymdour at
Newland church, Gloucestershire

crista or cock's comb), the sides of which were painted with heraldic devices similar to those on the shield. These were succeeded by *panaches* of feathers which were often arranged in tiers. The ornate tournament crests of the high Middle Ages were moulded in light materials (pasteboard, cloth or boiled leather over a wooden or wire framework or basketwork) and these were fastened to the helm by means of laces or rivets, the unsightly join concealed by a wreath or coronet (see below) or by the material of the crest itself, the lower edge of which formed a mantling, often in the form of a beast's fur or feathers. It would appear that, up to the late fifteenth century, crests were considered to be the perquisites of the knightly class – those who possessed both the rank and the resources which enabled them to participate in

Crista or cock's comb

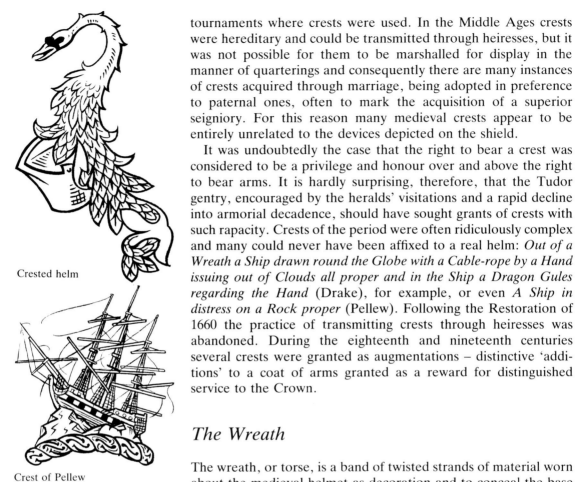

Crested helm

Crest of Pellew

Wreath

tournaments where crests were used. In the Middle Ages crests were hereditary and could be transmitted through heiresses, but it was not possible for them to be marshalled for display in the manner of quarterings and consequently there are many instances of crests acquired through marriage, being adopted in preference to paternal ones, often to mark the acquisition of a superior seigniory. For this reason many medieval crests appear to be entirely unrelated to the devices depicted on the shield.

It was undoubtedly the case that the right to bear a crest was considered to be a privilege and honour over and above the right to bear arms. It is hardly surprising, therefore, that the Tudor gentry, encouraged by the heralds' visitations and a rapid decline into armorial decadence, should have sought grants of crests with such rapacity. Crests of the period were often ridiculously complex and many could never have been affixed to a real helm: *Out of a Wreath a Ship drawn round the Globe with a Cable-rope by a Hand issuing out of Clouds all proper and in the Ship a Dragon Gules regarding the Hand* (Drake), for example, or even *A Ship in distress on a Rock proper* (Pellew). Following the Restoration of 1660 the practice of transmitting crests through heiresses was abandoned. During the eighteenth and nineteenth centuries several crests were granted as augmentations – distinctive 'additions' to a coat of arms granted as a reward for distinguished service to the Crown.

The Wreath

The wreath, or torse, is a band of twisted strands of material worn about the medieval helmet as decoration and to conceal the base of the crest where it was laced or bolted to the tournament helm. The wreath probably originated in the ceremonial torse of the Dark Age rulers of Western Europe and the colourful diadem of the Saracen. In armory, the wreath is conventionally depicted as having six visible twists of alternate tinctures, that to the left (the dexter) *always* being of a metal: *Or* (gold or yellow) or *Argent* (silver or white). On monuments in particular, the incorrect depiction of a wreath is invariably an indication that the heraldry has been repainted by someone who has no understanding of armory and the researcher should therefore be alert to the possibility of other errors in the painting of shield and crest. A crest and wreath are often depicted above a shield without helmet or mantling and, for peers, with a coronet of rank (see below).

Chapeaux and Coronets

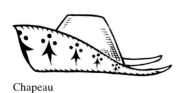

Chapeau

In some coats of arms a velvet cap (chapeau) is depicted affixed to the helmet instead of a wreath. In English armory, most chapeaux

Duke

Earl

Marquess

Viscount

Baron

Peers' coronets

are red and are lined with ermine which is turned up to form a brim ending in two 'tails' at the back. It is likely that medieval chapeaux were intended to indicate rank or preferment, as they do in Scottish armory today.

In a peer's letters patent of creation, the ceremonial insignia include 'a Cap of Honour' worn with 'a Coronet of Gold' on occasions of state, and these are clearly the lineal descendants of the combined medieval chapeau and gold circlet (coronet). In the fourteenth century, coronets as insignia of the higher nobility were restricted to dukes and marquesses and, after 1444, to earls. At that time they do not appear to have conformed to any particular pattern. Coronets were first granted to viscounts by James I and to barons by Charles II in 1661. In the coats of arms of peers, coronets indicative of rank are placed immediately above the shield and beneath, or instead of, the helmet.

The mitre of the bishops of Durham

Archbishops and bishops do not use crests, though they may now be granted for the benefit of their descendants, and their arms of office are depicted beneath a mitre, that of the Bishop of Durham being enclosed within a ducal coronet.

Not to be confused with coronets of rank, crest coronets are ornamental circlets, integral to the crest, and affixed to the helm in place of a wreath. (The recent practice of granting both wreath and crest coronet together is a nonsense for they perform the same function.) Confusingly, nearly all crest coronets are described as 'crowns', and they will also be encountered as charges. The most common are:

Ancient Crown   A recent addition to armory and usually indicative of armigers who have antiquarian interests.

Astral Crown   Associated with distinguished members of the Royal Air Force, eminent aviators and institutions associated with aviation.

Crown Vallary   From the Latin *vallare*, to fortify. Most commonly found in the arms of those associated with law and order, particularly police authorities.

Ducal Coronet   Composed of four strawberry leaves on a chased rim, the ducal coronet is sometimes described simply as a 'crest coronet'. Despite its name it has no nobiliary significance. When a beast is said to be *crowned* or *gorged* (collared) with a coronet, the ducal coronet is used unless another type is specified.

Eastern Crown   Associated with distinguished service in the Near or Far East.

Mural Crown   Widely used in civic heraldry and in the arms of distinguished soldiers where such a crown may be an augmentation.

Naval Crown   Usually reserved for distinguished sailors and local authorities which have naval traditions (such as Devon County Council).

Palisado Crown   The origin of this coronet is the defensive palisade and it is to be found in the arms of, for example, towns with Roman associations or those constructed within ancient fortifications.

Saxon Crown   Used to denote Saxon associations, particularly in civic arms.

In Scotland, the *Burghal Coronet* (a form of mural crown) was used by Scottish royal, parliamentary and police burghs prior to the reorganization of local government in 1974. Scottish counties also had their own type of crest coronet consisting of alternating projections and gold sheaves (*garbs*) set on a green rim.

Crest Coronets

Ancient Crown

Palisado Crown

Astral Crown

Mural Crown

Saxon Crown

Crown Vallary

Naval Crown

Scottish Burghal Coronet

Eastern Crown

Ducal Coronet

Former Scottish Counties

The Mantling

The mantling, or lambrequin, is a protective cloth affixed to the helmet and, in a coat of arms, is depicted as flowing from beneath the crest, sometimes terminating in tassels and scalloped or slashed in stylized form. Almost certainly, the mantling originated in the Holy Land where it was worn by crusading knights to absorb the sun's heat, thereby preventing the helmet from becoming unbearably hot. It is surprising, therefore, that the lighter colour (*Argent* or *Or*) is always depicted on the inside of the mantling.

A succession of English sumptuary laws from 1363 to 1532 sought to limit the wearing of 'sumptuous apparel' by forbidding 'the untitled commonality' to wear items such as gold chains and collars or cloth of gold, purple silks and crimson velvet. Interestingly, the use of ermine was reserved for the nobility and, as a token of royal favour, by concession to other magnates close to the Crown. It may be that the extensive use of ermine in the mantlings of many of the Garter knights of the period (together with crimson linings) was therefore intended to indicate their privileged position in medieval society.

The Motto or Slogan

A motto is an aphorism, the interpretation of which is often obscure but may allude to a charge in the arms, to the crest or to some event in a family's history: 'TOUCH NOT THE CAT BOT A GLOVE' (referring to the cat crest of The Mackintosh) and 'I SAVED THE KING' (Turnbull), for example. Mottoes, accompanying signatures, may be found in medieval documents and manuscripts and first appear in heraldry in the fourteenth century, though they were not in general use until the seventeenth century when coats of arms became stylized. It seems likely that some early mottoes were used, perhaps in abbreviated form, as *cris-de-guerre*, to rally troops in the field of battle: 'ESPÉRANCE' (Percy), for example. This appears to have been the practice in Scotland where the slogan (or slughorn) is the battle cry of the chief of a clan or house, as in 'I DAR' (Dalzell) and 'GANG WARILY' (Drummond). Significantly, mottoes also appear on standards, the great medieval flags at which military levies were mustered (see Chapter Nine). In Scotland, the slogan is depicted on a scroll above the crest and on the belt and buckle of a crest badge, while English practice is to depict it beneath the shield. In England, though not in Ireland and Scotland, mottoes may be changed at will and are therefore unreliable, and provide only a tentative starting point for research.

Crest badge of Drummond

Supporters

Supporters are figures, usually beasts, chimerical creatures or of human form, placed on either side of the shield to 'support' it. Unlike other elements in a coat of arms, supporters have no practical origin and cannot be traced with any certainty before the fifteenth century. Though similar devices may be found in early seals, where they occupy the space between the shield and the outer decorative border, their original purpose was almost certainly decorative. Others originated as personal devices which were also used in seals and later translated into badges and crests. In England supporters are granted to peers, knights of the Garter, and to knights of the first class of other British orders of chivalry including the Order of St John. In Scotland they are granted to peers, knights of the Thistle, knights of the first class of the orders of chivalry, chiefs of clans, and the heirs of minor barons who sat in parliament prior to 1587 as of right. In Scotland the heir apparent may use his father's supporters, but not so in England where, with the exception of hereditary peers, they are not transmitted. In both countries certain other families may claim an ancient right to include supporters in their arms and they may be granted to eminent corporations. In a coat of arms, the base on which the supporters are sometimes depicted is called a compartment.

Insignia

Insignia of office and of orders of knighthood may also be included in a coat of arms although they are not strictly a part of it. These include the episcopal crosses and croziers of ecclesiastics; the batons of field marshals and of similar offices; the collars, badges and circlets of members of the orders of chivalry; and decorations such as the Victoria Cross and Military Cross (but not campaign medals). Insignia are personal and should not appear in marital arms. For this reason, two shields may be used side by side (*accollé*); that to the dexter being the husband's coat (with insignia) and the other, the marital coat (without). A similar arrangement is used to display arms of office with marital arms.

Crossed batons of the Earl Marshal

Classification of Arms

There are, of course, different types of coats of arms other than personal and marital arms:

Arms of Adoption are those which have been assumed by someone who has no entitlement to them by descent. This may have been achieved by obtaining a royal licence, as the result of a Name and Arms clause in a will, for example, which enables a beneficiary to assume the name and arms of a testator.

Arms of Community, sometimes described as impersonal arms, are those of a corporate body such as a collegiate foundation or a civic authority.

Arms of Concession are those conceded as a reward or used in conjunction with existing arms as an augmentation 'by mere grace': Richard II's grant of the attributed arms of Edward the Confessor to Thomas Mowbray, Duke of Norfolk, for example.

Arms of Thomas Mowbray, Duke of Norfolk

Arms of Dominion (or *Arms of Sovereignty*) are those used by a sovereign within the territories over which he or she has dominion.

Arms of Office are those borne in addition to personal arms by holders of certain offices. Bishops, for example, impale their personal arms with those of their see which, as arms of office, are always placed to the dexter. Arms of office are never depicted in the same shield as marital arms.

Arms of Pretension are those borne to denote a claim to sovereignty, title, office or territory. In 1337 Edward III of England laid claim to the throne of France and quartered the arms of France with those of England to emphasize his claim.

Arms of office: George Law, Bishop of Bath and Wells

It was not until 1801 that the gold fleurs-de-lis of France were finally removed from the English royal arms.

Arms of Succession are those 'taken on inheritance to certain estates, manors or dignities to which insignia appertain' (Boutell). True arms of succession are rare and usually apply to certain feudal estates which have been vested in the Crown. Arms cannot normally be transferred with property unless there exists a corresponding right of armorial inheritance.

In a lighter vein, Arms of Expectation were a nineteenth-century conceit by which a single woman placed her paternal arms in the sinister half of her shield but left the dexter half void – as a sign that she was available to marry. It was suggested by Lower in *The Curiosities of Heraldry*, 1845 that maidens 'verging on the antique' might advertise for a husband in this way and that they be known thereby as 'ladies of the half blank shield'.

Banners

Banner of Trevithick: *Argent a Unicorn rampant Sable*

A banner is a square or oblong flag emblazoned with the arms (i.e. the devices which appear on the shield, though not the shield itself and never the crest and its appendages). This was the principal personal flag used throughout the Middle Ages by the nobility down to the knights banneret. It was, and is, indicative of the presence of an armiger and consequently, to 'raise one's banner in the field' of battle was a unequivocal indication of commitment to a particular cause. Similarly, to be deprived of it was considered a disgrace. Unlike the livery flags (the standard and guidon – see Chapter Nine) only one banner would be taken into battle and this would accompany the armiger wherever he went. In the Middle Ages the banner was also known as the lieutenant and was the responsibility of an officer of that name. Banners of member knights are hung above their stalls in the chapels of the orders of chivalry: at St George's Chapel, Windsor (the Most Noble Order of the Garter), and Henry VII's chapel at Westminster Abbey (the Most Honourable Order of the Bath), for example. On his death, a knight's banner is removed and by custom is conveyed to the king of arms of the order as his perquisite, though in practice it is often given to the family to be hung in their parish church. These ceremonial banners are easily recognized; they are usually $1\frac{1}{2}$ m square (5 ft), heavily embroidered and fringed (see plate 1).

Blazon

A blazon is a verbal or written description of armorial bearings using the conventions and terminology of armory (the corresponding verb is to blazon). Many terms are clearly derived from the

Top: the falcon and fetterlock badge of Richard, Duke of York (1411–60) in a misericord at Ludlow church, Shropshire. *Centre*: crampet badge of de la Warre and the Poynings key device in the gates of the de la Warre chantry at Boxgrove Priory, Sussex. A crampet (the metal tip of a sword scabbard), charged with a letter 'r' for *rex*, was adopted by Sir Roger de la Warre to commemorate his part in the capture of the French king at Poitiers in 1356. *Bottom*: ewer, bowl and soap-dish embellished with the arms of Bankes of Kingston Lacy, Dorset

The Crest

On a Helm   *with a wreath Argent Azure and Sable out of an Ancient Crown Or*

a male Griffin sejant erect Sable armed beaked and rayed Or

angued and holding a Key ward downwards and outwards Gules.   *Mantled Azure and Sable doubled Argent*

Quarterly 1 and 4 Argent on a Saltire dovetailed per gyronny Azure and Sable counterchanged a Lion's Face crowned with an Ancient Crown Or, 2 and 3 Gules a Lion rampant Argent within an Orle Or. On a Helm with a wreath Argent Azure and Sable out of an Ancient Crown Or a male Griffin sejant erect Sable armed beaked and rayed Or langued and holding a Key ward downwards and outwards Gules. Mantled Azure and Sable doubled Argent

19b

19d

Top left: rare example of the royal arms of Elizabeth I in the church of St Thomas, Salisbury. *Top right*: the Stuart royal arms (badly in need of gilding) at Abbey Dore, Herefordshire. *Bottom left*: pargeting, incorporating the royal arms of Charles II, on the magnificent Ancient House at Ipswich in Suffolk. *Bottom right*: the royal arms of George I, by Robert Bakewell, on a wrought-iron screen at Derby Cathedral

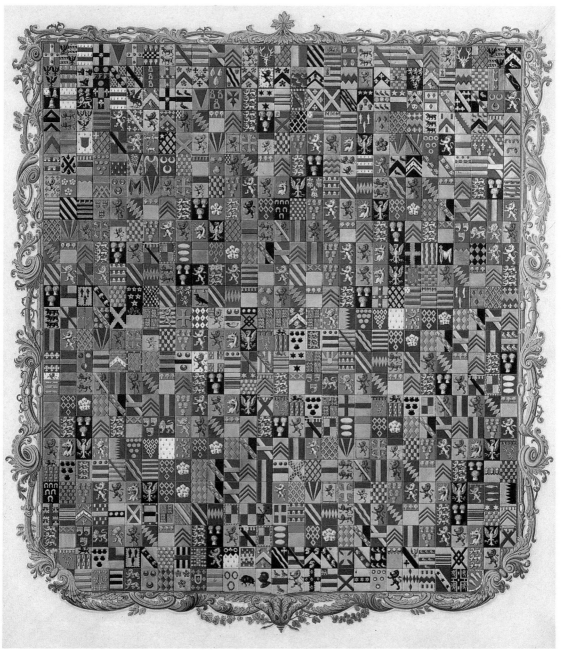

Opposite, top: the sign of the Swan Inn at Clare, Suffolk. *Left*: like many inns named after apparently mundane occupations, the Butchers' Arms at Sheepscombe, Gloucestershire, refers to the arms of a medieval livery company – in this case the Worshipful Company of Butchers of the City of London. *Right:* why should the arms of Darlington (County Durham) have found their way to the hamlet of Redhill near Bristol? Parish records reveal that the manor was once held by the Vane family who became Barons Barnard, Earls of Darlington and Dukes of Cleveland. The arms should, therefore, be those of Vane

This page: right-hand panel from a nineteenth-century diptych commissioned for Richard Plantagenet, Marquis of Chandos, son and heir of the first Duke of Buckingham and Chandos (ext. 1889). The diptych shows the 719 quarterings accumulated by the family of Temple-Nugent-Brydges-Chandos-Grenville, the only British family to have a five-part surname

corrupted French of thirteenth-century rolls of arms, but a large number of conventions were contrived by the 'Heralds of the Decadence' and, in the view of many modern armorists, are archaic and ineffectual. Nevertheless, they will be encountered during research and are therefore included here.

The ability to blazon accurately is an invaluable tool for the researcher. It enables him to record armorial devices quickly and accurately, to make effective use of reference works such as ordinaries (which list blazons alphabetically by the charges they contain), armories (dictionaries of blazons listed by surname), peerages, etc., and to communicate with armorists, of whom there is a growing number. The objectives of blazon are brevity and precision. An accurate blazon is unambiguous and from it a coat of arms which is correct in every detail may be painted (emblazoned) or researched. The conventions of blazon are well established and, for the most part, logical. Relatively few terms are met with regularly and it is recommended that the novice should concentrate on perfecting his understanding of basics before concerning himself with technicalities. Once the conventions are understood the terminology will come with practice and a few hours spent browsing through an illustrated peerage.

Letters patent are legal documents and blazons are therefore unpunctuated, except that the tinctures (colours) and charges begin with a capital letter. Adjectives, other than quantitative, follow the nouns they qualify, the tincture coming last; e.g. *a Dragon sejant reguardant Sable.*

A Dragon sejant reguardant

Common Terms and Conventions

In blazon, the left-hand side of a shield when viewed from the front is the *dexter* and the right is the *sinister*. Charges placed in the top portion of the shield are said to be *in chief* and those in the lower portion *in base*. There are three reference points in a shield: *fess point* at the centre (A) with *honour point* above (B) and *nombril point* below (C).

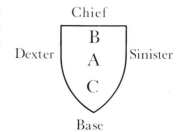

A charge is a pictorial representation or geometrical figure depicted in relief on a shield of arms. Something is 'charged' when it has a charge placed upon it. (Beware *diaper* which is a decorative pattern with no armorial significance.)

In a shield, a principal charge of bold rectilinear shape is called an ordinary (or honourable ordinary) and a smaller charge of geometrical shape, subordinate to the ordinary or other principal charge, is a sub-ordinary (see illustrations pp. 182–3).

The field (background) of a shield (or, indeed, of a charge) may be of a single tincture or comprise combinations of parted and varied fields (see illustrations pp. 183–4). The lines which separate these divisions (lines of partition), and those which delineate ordinaries and sub-ordinaries, may be straight or articulated in a

Sub-ordinaries

chief

orle

tressure

flaunches

inescutcheon

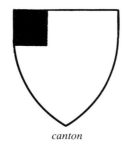

canton

quarter

bordure

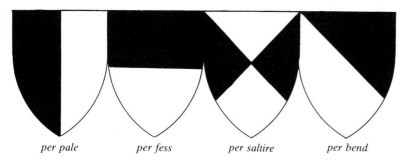

per pale   *per fess*   *per saltire*   *per bend*

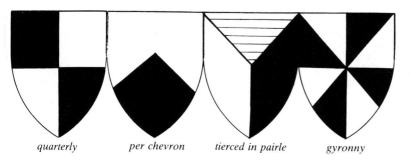

quarterly   *per chevron*   *tierced in pairle*   *gyronny*

Parted Fields

Varied Lines

arched or enarched

embattled grady

potenty

urdy

rayonné

dovetailed

raguly

embattled

wavy or undy

nebuly

dancetty

indented

engrailed

invected

variety of forms, each of which is possessed of its own term (see illustration p. 185).

Beasts and chimerical creatures (see below) are depicted in a variety of postures (attitudes), the most common of which are illustrated opposite. The inclination of a charge or the disposition of a number of charges are described by reference to the geometry of the ordinaries, e.g. *two Keys saltirewise* or *five Fleurs-de-lis in saltire* (see opposite).

Attributes are the properties and appendages associated with an armorial charge. Many are self-evident, e.g. *beaked, chained, collared*, etc. Other common attributes will be found in the Glossary and Index.

In blazon the attitudes of a charge always precede its attributes, e.g. *A Griffin segreant* (upright) *reguardant* (looking over its shoulder) *Sable beaked armed and langued Argent* (coloured black and having silver beak, claws and tongue).

A Griffin segreant reguardant

The metals, colours and furs used in armory are known as tinctures and are here listed together with the abbreviations most commonly used:

Metals:
Or	gold, often depicted as yellow
Argent (Arg)	silver, usually depicted as white

Colours:
Gules (Gu)	red
Azure (Az)	blue
Sable (Sa)	black
Vert (Vt)	green
Purpure (Purp)	purple
Murrey (Mu)	mulberry

Furs, each of which is possessed of several variations:
Ermine (Erm)	white with black 'tails'
Vair	white and blue 'pelts'

The so-called 'stains' are rare:
Sanguine	blood-red
Tenné	tawny

Sanguine and *Tenné* supposedly 'stain' the nobility of arms and are, therefore, associated with abatements of honour (see p. 214).

Where a charge is represented in its natural colours it is described as *proper*, e.g. *A Stag's Head erased proper attired Or* (having gold antlers).

Metals and colours, but not furs, are subject to the tincture convention, the fundamental rule of armory that metal shall not lie

Plate 17: Blazon

The Shield of Arms

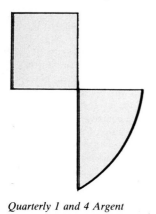

Quarterly 1 and 4 Argent

on a Saltire

dovetailed

per gyronny

Azure and Sable counterchanged

a Lion's Face crowned with an Ancient Crown Or

2 and 3 Gules

a Lion rampant Argent

within an Orle Or

18

Frontispiece to Smith's *Book of Sutes or Ordinaries* of 1599. William Smith (c. 1550–1618) was Rouge Dragon Pursuivan of Arms

20a

20b

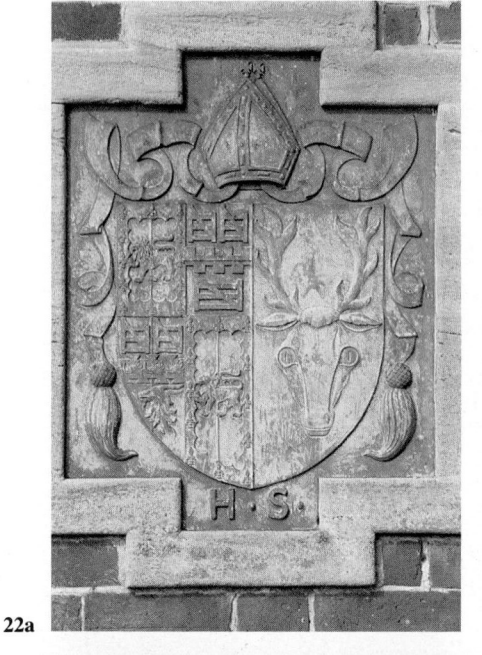

22a

22b

22c

22d

Top left: a lead plaque, bearing the arms of Bishop Yeatman-Biggs (d. 1922) impaling Legge, on a lodge at Stock Gaylard in Dorset. The gates ('yats') refer to the name Yeatman and the letters 'HS' are the initials of Bishop Henry Southwark. *Top right*: weather vane of the punning arms of Lucy (*Gules semy of Cross-crosslets three Luces* (pike fish) *haurient Argent*) at Charlecote, Warwickshire. *Bottom left*: the punning crest of the Lawson family, described as 'the sun supported by the arms of the Law', in the grounds of Isel Hall, Cumbria. *Bottom right*: a fountain, at Eastnor Castle in Herefordshire, erected for Isabel, eldest daughter and co-heiress of the third and last Earl Somers, who married (1872) Lord Henry Somerset, second son of the eighth Duke of Beaufort, and died in 1921. (The Beaufort *bordure* is depicted incorrectly)

Ordinaries and
their Diminutives

fess

bars

pale

pallets

bend

bendlets

bend sinister

bendlets sinister

chevron

chevronels

cross

saltire

pall

pile

Varied Fields

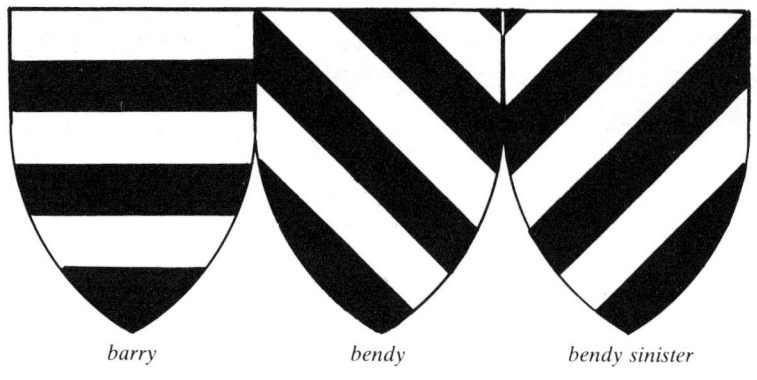

| *barry* | *bendy* | *bendy sinister* |

| *paly* | *chevrony* | *chequy* | *a bend compony* |

| *a bend counter-compony* | *lozengy* | *barry bendy* | *paly bendy* |

| *gyronny of twelve* | *pily* | *pily bendy* | *pily bendy sinister* |

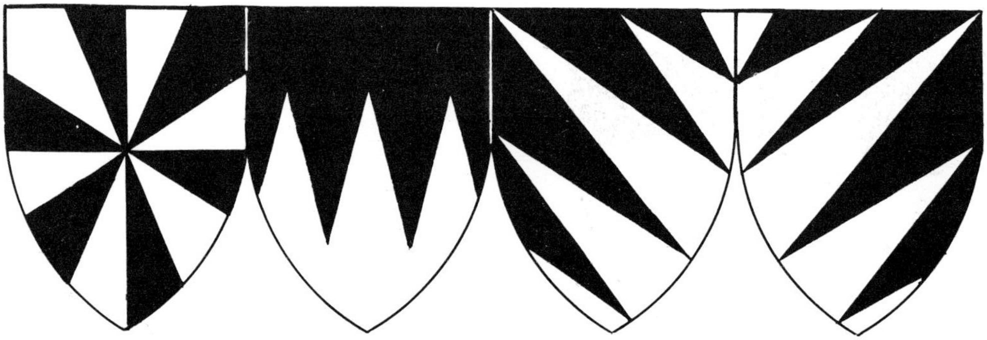

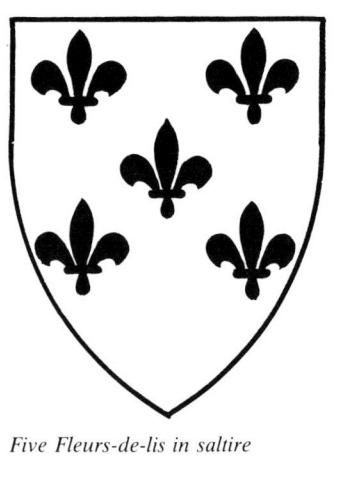

Two Keys saltirewise

Five Fleurs-de-lis in saltire

The attitudes of beasts and
creatures

couchant

salient

rampant

passant

sejant

dormant

statant

Arms of Codrington before (left) and after (right) augmentation

on metal, nor colour on colour. This convention seems to have been universally accepted from the earliest times and is clearly intended to facilitate the accurate identification of armorial devices; blue on silver is clearer than blue on black, for example. The convention applies only to charges that are placed *upon* a field or another charge. Adjacent divisions of a varied or parted field, for example, lie next to each other and do not break the 'rule'; neither do *bordures* (borders) or charges placed on varied or parted fields. Exceptions will be found and these are usually *brisures* (marks of cadency – see Chapter Eight) or augmentations of honour, intended to draw attention to an armiger whose service to his king was worthy of approbation. John Codrington, for example, banner-bearer to Henry V 'in battaile, watch and ward', bore in his arms a red *fess* (a broad horizontal band across the centre of the shield) between three red lions on silver. His loyalty to the House of Lancaster was eventually rewarded when he was granted an augmentation which deliberately broke the tincture convention by changing his red fess to *Sable fretty Gules* (black with a red trellis-like pattern).

The tinctures of uncoloured coats of arms, those engraved on silver or in bookplates, for example, may usually be determined by reference to the Petra Sancta system of hatching, or in documents by the presence of a trick, a line drawing in which abbreviations are substituted for tinctures and numbers or letters for charges (see illustration p. 189).

An indeterminate number of small charges, evenly distributed over a field to form a pattern, may be blazoned, e.g. *Azure semy of Garbs Or a Chevron Argent*. In this example, a blue field is *semy* (powdered) of gold wheatsheaves which are themselves defaced by the larger charge (the *chevron*) placed upon them. Certain forms of *semy* have their own terms, though these may be found with a variety of spellings, e.g. *bezanté* for *bezanty*:

bezanty (gold roundels)
platy (silver or white roundels)

20a

20b

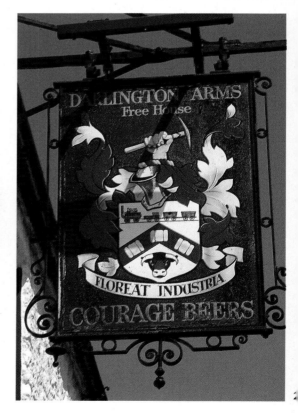

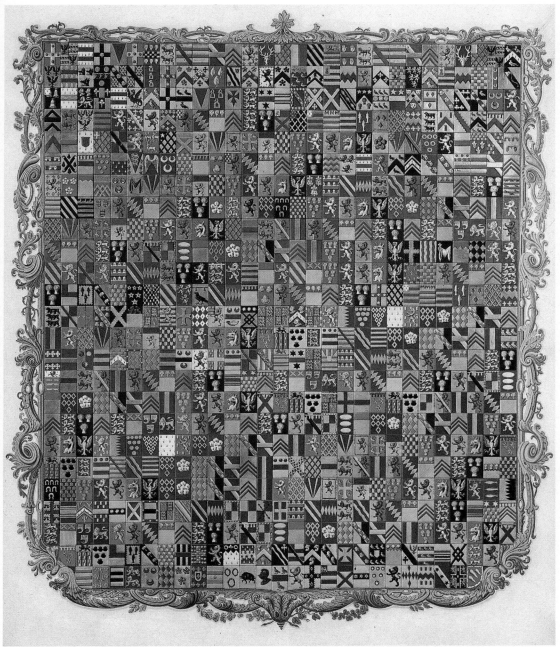

Opposite, top: the sign of the Swan Inn at Clare, Suffolk. *Left*: like many inns named after apparently mundane occupations, the Butchers' Arms at Sheepscombe, Gloucestershire, refers to the arms of a medieval livery company – in this case the Worshipful Company of Butchers of the City of London. *Right:* why should the arms of Darlington (County Durham) have found their way to the hamlet of Redhill near Bristol? Parish records reveal that the manor was once held by the Vane family who became Barons Barnard, Earls of Darlington and Dukes of Cleveland. The arms should, therefore, be those of Vane

This page: right-hand panel from a nineteenth-century diptych commissioned for Richard Plantagenet, Marquis of Chandos, son and heir of the first Duke of Buckingham and Chandos (ext. 1889). The diptych shows the 719 quarterings accumulated by the family of Temple-Nugent-Brydges-Chandos-Grenville, the only British family to have a five-part surname

Top left: a lead plaque, bearing the arms of Bishop Yeatman-Biggs (d. 1922) impaling Legge, on a lodge at Stock Gaylard in Dorset. The gates ('yats') refer to the name Yeatman and the letters 'HS' are the initials of Bishop Henry Southwark. *Top right*: weather vane of the punning arms of Lucy (*Gules semy of Cross-crosslets three Luces* (pike fish) *haurient Argent*) at Charlecote, Warwickshire. *Bottom left*: the punning crest of the Lawson family, described as 'the sun supported by the arms of the Law', in the grounds of Isel Hall, Cumbria. *Bottom right*: a fountain, at Eastnor Castle in Herefordshire, erected for Isabel, eldest daughter and co-heiress of the third and last Earl Somers, who married (1872) Lord Henry Somerset, second son of the eighth Duke of Beaufort, and died in 1921. (The Beaufort *bordure* is depicted incorrectly)

corrupted French of thirteenth-century rolls of arms, but a large number of conventions were contrived by the 'Heralds of the Decadence' and, in the view of many modern armorists, are archaic and ineffectual. Nevertheless, they will be encountered during research and are therefore included here.

The ability to blazon accurately is an invaluable tool for the researcher. It enables him to record armorial devices quickly and accurately, to make effective use of reference works such as ordinaries (which list blazons alphabetically by the charges they contain), armories (dictionaries of blazons listed by surname), peerages, etc., and to communicate with armorists, of whom there is a growing number. The objectives of blazon are brevity and precision. An accurate blazon is unambiguous and from it a coat of arms which is correct in every detail may be painted (emblazoned) or researched. The conventions of blazon are well established and, for the most part, logical. Relatively few terms are met with regularly and it is recommended that the novice should concentrate on perfecting his understanding of basics before concerning himself with technicalities. Once the conventions are understood the terminology will come with practice and a few hours spent browsing through an illustrated peerage.

Letters patent are legal documents and blazons are therefore unpunctuated, except that the tinctures (colours) and charges begin with a capital letter. Adjectives, other than quantitative, follow the nouns they qualify, the tincture coming last; e.g. *a Dragon sejant reguardant Sable.*

A Dragon sejant reguardant

Common Terms and Conventions

In blazon, the left-hand side of a shield when viewed from the front is the *dexter* and the right is the *sinister.* Charges placed in the top portion of the shield are said to be *in chief* and those in the lower portion *in base.* There are three reference points in a shield: *fess point* at the centre (A) with *honour point* above (B) and *nombril point* below (C).

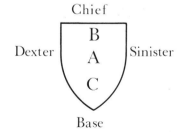

A charge is a pictorial representation or geometrical figure depicted in relief on a shield of arms. Something is 'charged' when it has a charge placed upon it. (Beware *diaper* which is a decorative pattern with no armorial significance.)

In a shield, a principal charge of bold rectilinear shape is called an ordinary (or honourable ordinary) and a smaller charge of geometrical shape, subordinate to the ordinary or other principal charge, is a sub-ordinary (see illustrations pp. 182–3).

The field (background) of a shield (or, indeed, of a charge) may be of a single tincture or comprise combinations of parted and varied fields (see illustrations pp. 183–4). The lines which separate these divisions (lines of partition), and those which delineate ordinaries and sub-ordinaries, may be straight or articulated in a

Ordinaries and their Diminutives

fess

bars

pale

pallets

bend

bendlets

bend sinister

bendlets sinister

chevron

chevronels

cross

saltire

pall

pile

Sub-ordinaries

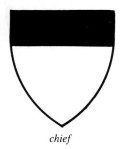

chief

orle

tressure

flaunches

inescutcheon

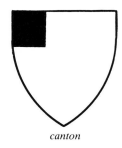

canton

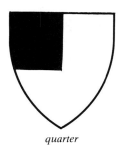

quarter

bordure

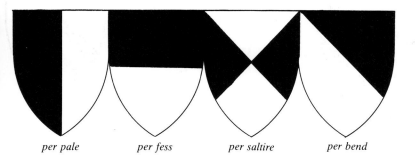

per pale   *per fess*   *per saltire*   *per bend*

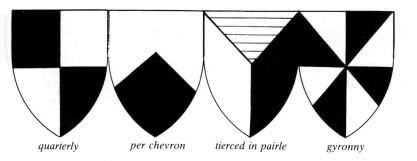

quarterly   *per chevron*   *tierced in pairle*   *gyronny*

Parted Fields

Varied Fields

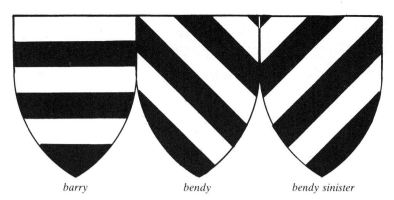

barry   bendy   bendy sinister

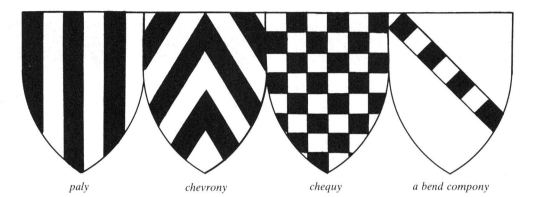

paly   chevrony   chequy   a bend compony

a bend counter-compony   lozengy   barry bendy   paly bendy

gyronny of twelve   pily   pily bendy   pily bendy sinister

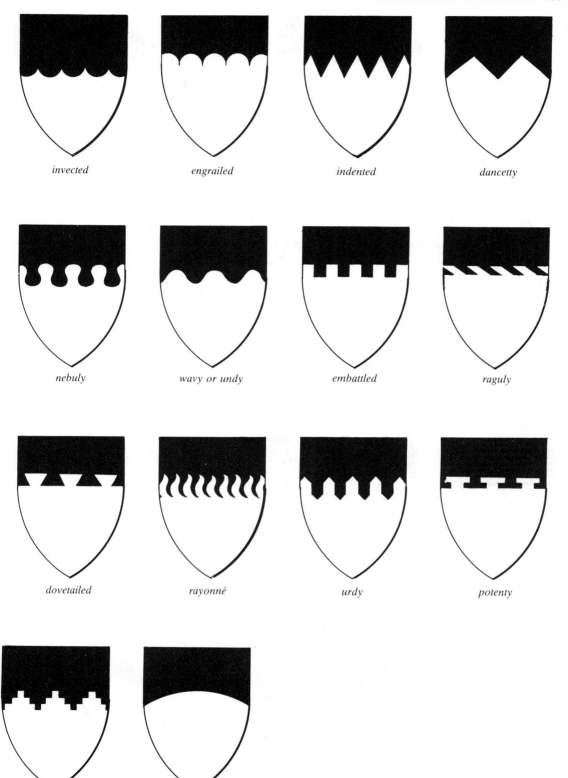

invected

engrailed

indented

dancetty

nebuly

wavy or undy

embattled

raguly

dovetailed

rayonné

urdy

potenty

embattled grady

arched or enarched

Varied Lines

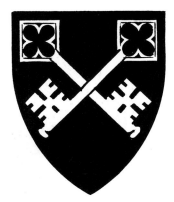

Two Keys saltirewise

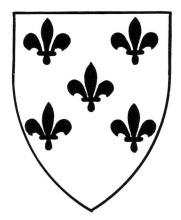

Five Fleurs-de-lis in saltire

The attitudes of beasts and creatures

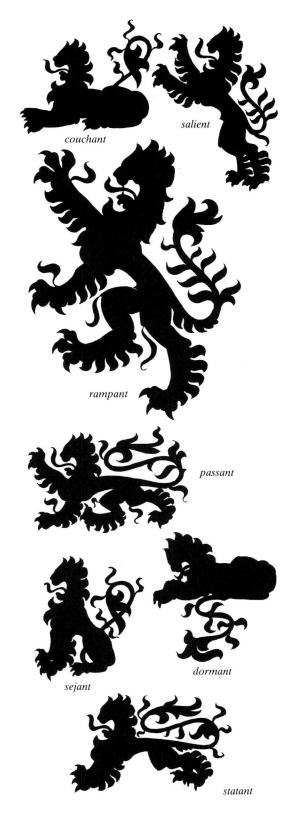

couchant

salient

rampant

passant

sejant

dormant

statant

variety of forms, each of which is possessed of its own term (see illustration p. 185).

Beasts and chimerical creatures (see below) are depicted in a variety of postures (attitudes), the most common of which are illustrated opposite. The inclination of a charge or the disposition of a number of charges are described by reference to the geometry of the ordinaries, e.g. *two Keys saltirewise* or *five Fleurs-de-lis in saltire* (see opposite).

Attributes are the properties and appendages associated with an armorial charge. Many are self-evident, e.g. *beaked, chained, collared,* etc. Other common attributes will be found in the Glossary and Index.

In blazon the attitudes of a charge always precede its attributes, e.g. *A Griffin segreant* (upright) *reguardant* (looking over its shoulder) *Sable beaked armed and langued Argent* (coloured black and having silver beak, claws and tongue).

A Griffin segreant reguardant

The metals, colours and furs used in armory are known as tinctures and are here listed together with the abbreviations most commonly used:

Metals:
Or	gold, often depicted as yellow
Argent (Arg)	silver, usually depicted as white

Colours:
Gules (Gu)	red
Azure (Az)	blue
Sable (Sa)	black
Vert (Vt)	green
Purpure (Purp)	purple
Murrey (Mu)	mulberry

Furs, each of which is possessed of several variations:
Ermine (Erm)	white with black 'tails'
Vair	white and blue 'pelts'

The so-called 'stains' are rare:
Sanguine	blood-red
Tenné	tawny

Sanguine and *Tenné* supposedly 'stain' the nobility of arms and are, therefore, associated with abatements of honour (see p. 214).

Where a charge is represented in its natural colours it is described as *proper*, e.g. *A Stag's Head erased proper attired Or* (having gold antlers).

Metals and colours, but not furs, are subject to the tincture convention, the fundamental rule of armory that metal shall not lie

Arms of Codrington before (left) and after (right) augmentation

on metal, nor colour on colour. This convention seems to have been universally accepted from the earliest times and is clearly intended to facilitate the accurate identification of armorial devices; blue on silver is clearer than blue on black, for example. The convention applies only to charges that are placed *upon* a field or another charge. Adjacent divisions of a varied or parted field, for example, lie next to each other and do not break the 'rule'; neither do *bordures* (borders) or charges placed on varied or parted fields. Exceptions will be found and these are usually *brisures* (marks of cadency – see Chapter Eight) or augmentations of honour, intended to draw attention to an armiger whose service to his king was worthy of approbation. John Codrington, for example, banner-bearer to Henry V 'in battaile, watch and ward', bore in his arms a red *fess* (a broad horizontal band across the centre of the shield) between three red lions on silver. His loyalty to the House of Lancaster was eventually rewarded when he was granted an augmentation which deliberately broke the tincture convention by changing his red fess to *Sable fretty Gules* (black with a red trellis-like pattern).

The tinctures of uncoloured coats of arms, those engraved on silver or in bookplates, for example, may usually be determined by reference to the Petra Sancta system of hatching, or in documents by the presence of a trick, a line drawing in which abbreviations are substituted for tinctures and numbers or letters for charges (see illustration p. 189).

An indeterminate number of small charges, evenly distributed over a field to form a pattern, may be blazoned, e.g. *Azure semy of Garbs Or a Chevron Argent*. In this example, a blue field is *semy* (powdered) of gold wheatsheaves which are themselves defaced by the larger charge (the *chevron*) placed upon them. Certain forms of *semy* have their own terms, though these may be found with a variety of spellings, e.g. *bezanté* for *bezanty*:

> *bezanty* (gold roundels)
> *platy* (silver or white roundels)

semy of torteaux (red roundels)
hurty (blue roundels)
pommety (green roundels)
pellety (black roundels)
goutty d'or (gold drops)
goutty d'eau (silver or white drops)
goutty de sang (red drops)
goutty des larmes (blue drops)
goutty d'huile (green drops)
goutty de poix (black drops)
annuletty (annulets)
billety (billets)
crusily (cross-crosslets)
estoily (estoils)
fleuretty or *semy-de-lis* (fleurs-de-lis)
fretty (frets)

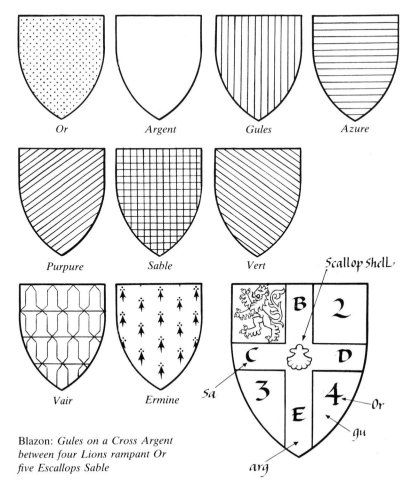

The Petra Sancta system of hatching and an example of tricking

Or · Argent · Gules · Azure

Purpure · Sable · Vert

Vair · Ermine

Blazon: *Gules on a Cross Argent between four Lions rampant Or five Escallops Sable*

The Order of Blazon in a Coat of Arms

(See colour plate 17.)

The Shield

This is the most important element in a coat of arms and may contain the impaled coats of a husband and wife (marital arms) or of an individual and those of his office (arms of office); a small central inescutcheon (indicative of marriage to an heraldic heiress), or several different coats (quarterings) obtained through the accumulated marriages of ancestors to heraldic heiresses (see Chapter Eight).

The senior dexter side is always blazoned before the sinister in impaled arms, and in quartered arms each coat should be described separately and in the correct order, starting with that in *dexter chief*, i.e. the top left corner, and working across and down, like reading lines of text. The first coat is invariably the principal (paternal) coat and may be repeated in the fourth quarter. When quarterings are themselves quartered they are described as grand-quarters, the individual coats being sub-quarters. In such cases, each grandquarter is blazoned sub-quarter by sub-quarter before moving on to the next quartering.

A shield containing several quarterings may also be surrounded by a *bordure* or overlaid by a charge such as a *label*, *baton* or *canton*. These should be blazoned last, together with any charges placed upon them, the terms '*within*' or '*over all*' being used to describe their relationship to the other devices on the shield.

A blazon should therefore open with a description of the layout of the shield: e.g. *per pale* (for two coats), *quarterly* (for four) or *quarterly of eight*, etc. (for more than four). Individual coats are then identified by number (e.g. *1st and 4th*) and blazoned.

The background (*field*) is first described: this may be a single tincture or comprise combinations of parted and varied fields. The description of the field is followed by the principal charge, which is often an ordinary or heraldic beast, together with its attitudes and attributes. Minor charges are then described, and finally any sub-ordinaries, cadency marks or marks of distinction (see Chapter Eight).

The Crest

This is that part of a coat of arms which is attached to the helmet above the shield. First described is the wreath, crest coronet or chapeau, followed by the crest itself. When two or more crests are shown they are blazoned and numbered in the following order: two crests 1-2, three crests 2-1-3, four crests 3-1-2-4 and so on. The mantling may also be described, e.g. *Gules lined Or* (red with the inner lining gold).

19b

19d

Top left: rare example of the royal arms of Elizabeth I in the church of St Thomas, Salisbury. *Top right*: the Stuart royal arms (badly in need of gilding) at Abbey Dore, Herefordshire. *Bottom left*: pargeting, incorporating the royal arms of Charles II, on the magnificent Ancient House at Ipswich in Suffolk. *Bottom right*: the royal arms of George I, by Robert Bakewell, on a wrought-iron screen at Derby Cathedral

Frontispiece to Smith's *Book of Sutes or Ordinaries* of 1599. William Smith (*c.* 1550–1618) was Rouge Dragon Pursuivant of Arms

The Crest

On a Helm   *with a wreath Argent Azure and Sable out of an Ancient Crown Or*

a male Griffin sejant erect Sable armed beaked and rayed Or

...angued and holding a Key ward downwards and outwards Gules.   *Mantled Azure and Sable doubled Argent*

Quarterly 1 and 4 Argent on a Saltire dovetailed per gyronny Azure and Sable counterchanged a Lion's Face crowned with an Ancient Crown Or, 2 and 3 Gules a Lion rampant Argent within an Orle Or. On a Helm with a wreath Argent Azure and Sable out of an Ancient Crown Or a male Griffin sejant erect Sable armed beaked and rayed Or langued and holding a Key ward downwards and outwards Gules. Mantled Azure and Sable doubled Argent

Plate 17: Blazon

The Shield of Arms

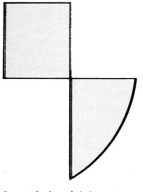

Quarterly 1 and 4 Argent

on a Saltire

dovetailed

per gyronny

Azure and Sable counterchanged

a Lion's Face crowned with an Ancient Crown Or

2 and 3 Gules

a Lion rampant Argent

within an Orle Or

Top: the falcon and fetterlock badge of Richard, Duke of York (1411–60) in a misericord at Ludlow church, Shropshire. *Centre*: crampet badge of de la Warre and the Poynings key device in the gates of the de la Warre chantry at Boxgrove Priory, Sussex. A crampet (the metal tip of a sword scabbard), charged with a letter 'r' for *rex*, was adopted by Sir Roger de la Warre to commemorate his part in the capture of the French king at Poitiers in 1356. *Bottom*: ewer, bowl and soap-dish embellished with the arms of Bankes of Kingston Lacy, Dorset

Supporters

Certain armigers are granted supporters which are depicted on each side of the shield, sometimes standing on a compartment. The dexter supporter is blazoned first followed by that to the sinister. If the two supporters are identical, only one need be described, the blazon beginning, *On either side . . .*

The Motto

Only the words should be recorded, there is no significance in the type of scroll on which the motto is depicted. In Scottish armory the motto is generally placed above the crest and some families possess more than one.

Pronunciation

The golden rule is to pronounce armorial terms as they are spelt, even the numerous words which are derived from the French; *Vert* rhymes with skirt, for example. Many words may correctly be pronounced in more than one way; *gules*, for example, rhymes with 'rules', and the initial g may be either soft or hard (though most armorists prefer the latter). *Saltire* begins as in 'salt and pepper' but the ending may rhyme with either 'tire' or 'tier', either is correct.

Reference Works

Shields of arms may be identified by using an ordinary of arms which lists blazons alphabetically by their principal charge. The best known is *Papworth's Ordinary of British Armorials* by J.W. Papworth, 1898 (reprinted Five Barrows, 1977). Unusual charges may be identified by reference to the illustrative index in C.N. Elvin's *A Dictionary of Heraldry* (1889), reprinted in 1977 by Heraldry Today.

Crests may be identified by reference to the illustrative index in *Fairbairn's Book of Crests of the Families of Great Britain and Ireland* by J. Fairbairn, 1905 (reprinted by The Heraldic Book Company, 1983). Fairbairn also lists mottoes, as does C.N. Elvin in his *Handbook of Mottoes* (1860), reprinted in 1986 by Heraldry Today.

Blazons of arms may be obtained from works such as *The General Armory of England, Scotland, Ireland and Wales* by Sir Bernard Burke (1842), reprinted in 1984 by Heraldry Today. This is essentially a list of armorial references, alphabetical by surname, with blazons of arms for each, together with crests, supporters and mottoes where known. It is generally acknowledged that Burke is not entirely reliable and, because they both include material from Burke, Papworth and Fairbairn are equally suspect, so that primary sources should be consulted wherever possible.

The Significance of Charges

The popular perception of heraldry is that all charges are possessed of some hidden significance or symbolism. While it is true that all arms are unique, charges may have been selected for purely aesthetic reasons and the significance of others is often immediately apparent. An open book is a universal symbol of learning, for example, and wavy blue divisions invariably represent water. Others demand some understanding of classical allusions; the Rod of Aesculapius, for example, (a serpent entwined about a rod) combines the attributes of Asclepius, the Greek god of medicine, and is generally associated with members of the medical profession. Historical references are also popular: the twentieth-century arms of Cooke of Athelhampton *(Quarterly Sable and Or four Hawk's heads in cross counterchanged)* are a direct reference to the arms of the de Pydele family *(Quarterly Argent and Sable four Hawk's heads counterchanged)* who were lords of the manor of Athelhampton, Dorset, in the late fourteenth century. Here, the significance of the hawk's heads remains a mystery but the historical rationale for the Cooke arms is obvious.

Arms of Cooke of Athelhampton

Arms often allude to the name, title, office or property of an armiger and these are correctly termed allusive arms or *armes parlantes*. The punning arms of Sir Thomas Harris of Shropshire, for example, are *Or three Herrisons* (hedgehogs) *Azure*, and his crest is a golden hedgehog (1622). Canting arms are a strict form of allusive arms in which the entire design of a shield is devoted to a pictorial pun on the name or title of the armiger. The arms of Sir Cecil Chubb, first Baronet of Stonehenge, *(Per fess Azure and Vert two Pales surmounted by a Chief Argent)* represent a pair of sarsen stones and a stone lintel on a background of sky and grass and refer to Chubb's gift of Stonehenge to the nation in 1918. Examples are numerous in early armory, indeed the frequency of allusive arms in the thirteenth and fourteenth centuries suggests that many examples exist which have yet to be identified, the allusion being obscure to the twentieth-century mind. Well-known early examples are those of de Ferres *(Argent six Horseshoes* (ferrs) *Sable)* and Tremain *(Gules three dexter Arms conjoined in triangle Or)*. In our own century, the arms of the Milk Marketing Board *(Vert issuant from the sinister base three Piles wavy bendwise conjoined at the dexter chief point Argent)* are a beautifully simple allusion to the Board's function.

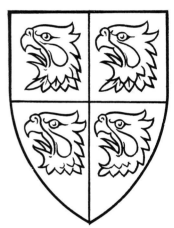

Arms of de Pydele of Athelhampton

Crests and, of course, mottoes may also be allusive. The arms of the Dymoke family, from 1377 hereditary Champions of England, include a punning motto *PRO REGE DIMICO* (I fight for the king) and a crest of two donkey's ears *(deux mokes)* which was later changed to those of a hare by disapproving members of the family.

Notable events may also be commemorated heraldically. The *Saracen's Head* crests in the arms of the Lygon, Stapleton, Warburton and Willoughby families recall crusading ancestors, though it should not be assumed that all *Saracen's Head* devices originated in this way and most were adopted several centuries after the event, often replacing earlier and simpler panache or

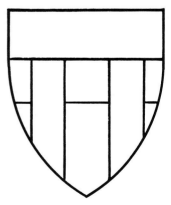

Arms of Sir Cecil Chubb, first Baronet of Stonehenge

Arms of Tremain

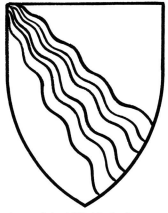

Arms of the Milk Marketing
Board

Urinal crest of Caerlyon

cockscomb crests. The almost identical *Moor's Head* crests of the Moore and Mordaunt families clearly allude to the names and have no further significance.

A recent grant of arms (1990) to the West Dorset District Council demonstrates how much historical information may be gleaned from an apparently simple design. The arms (which are illustrated at the beginning of this chapter, p. 170) are blazoned: *Gyronny Vert and Gules a Saxon Cross per gyronny Argent and Or. On a helm with a Wreath Argent Vert and Gules a Sea Wyvern sejant Argent winged Or grasping in the dexter paw an Ostrich Feather palewise also Argent penned Gold.* For supporters: *On either side a Sea Wyvern Argent winged and gorged with a Saxon Crown Or the Compartment composed of Graded Pebbles proper.* The shield is divided into eight pieces (*gyronny*) representing the four former urban districts (red) and the four former rural districts (green) which, following local government reorganization in 1972, were combined to create the new District Council. The Saxon Cross symbolizes the ancient kingdom of Wessex, a name which is synonymous with the novels of Thomas Hardy, and its four points represent the ancient monastic foundations of Abbotsbury, Cerne, Forde and Sherborne. The crest and supporters are *Sea Wyverns*, appropriate to a district which was once the centre of the kingdom of Wessex (whose kings used a golden wyvern as their device) and with traditional maritime associations. They are *gorged* (collared) with Saxon Crowns, as are the dragon supporters in the arms of Dorset County Council. The *Ostrich Feather* quill pen refers to Thomas Hardy and William Barnes and is an incidental allusion to the west Dorset estates of the Duchy of Cornwall, two such feathers occurring also in the arms of the Duchy. The compartment of graded pebbles is a representation of Chesil Beach.

Crosses, Beasts and Monsters

There are innumerable charges used in heraldry, ranging from the fleur-de-lis, a stylized form of the madonna lily (*Lilium candidum*), to the unique urinal crest of Dr Louys Caerlyon (1483). But by far the most common charge is the cross, a device which pre-dates Christianity by many centuries and became the universal symbol of the Christian church. The preponderance of crosses in armory, however, reflects both the influence of the Crusades and medieval man's preoccupation with his religion. According to various sources there are between three and five hundred different types of cross to be found in armory, though of these only about twenty or so are in regular use and are here illustrated on p. 196. There can be little doubt that the earliest armorial crosses were of the simplest kind and that the proliferation of variants resulted from casual embellishment and the desire of the post-medieval heralds to define forms which had been arrived at by artistic licence.

The vigorous late-medieval interpretation of beasts, birds, fish, reptiles and chimerical creatures is, for many, the quintessence of armory. Heraldic beasts and monsters are commonly found carved and painted in the tombs, monuments and architectural features of our medieval and Tudor churches. When not associated with a shield, they may be mistaken for allegorical or religious images or vernacular ornamentation.

In the Middle Ages the lion was considered to be the embodiment of courage, strength and nobleness, the King of Beasts and a fitting symbol of kings and kingdoms and of the great magnates. One of the earliest examples of hereditary arms is that of William Longespee, natural son of King Henry II, who bore six gold lions on a blue shield as did his grandfather, Geoffrey of Anjou. In early armory, what is now a *lion passant* was described as a leopard (hence 'the leopards of England' in the royal arms), indeed any lion that was not *rampant* was blazoned *leopardé*. The lions of mythology have magic in their tails – by sweeping them over their tracks they obliterate their paw-marks and make their ways unknown and by swinging them over their bodies they render themselves invisible. Thus, the longer the tail, the greater the magic. The lion is always alert and sleeps with his eyes open. He is of such a noble and compassionate nature that he will not attack a stricken man and is angered only when wounded. He fears nothing except a white cockerel and if he is sick he is cured by eating a monkey. According to the bestiaries, lion cubs were born dead and remained so for three days whereupon their father breathed into their faces and gave them life. For this reason, the lion is associated with Christ risen from the dead and is often depicted in church carvings as fighting with the devil in a dragon's form. Confusingly, the lion may also be found as a symbol of evil, trodden underfoot like the dragon and the serpent of the Psalms. The winged lion represents St Mark the Evangelist, being one of the four beasts 'round about the throne' which 'rested not day and night' (Revelation 4: 6–7).

The eagle was the standard of the Roman legion. In armory it is considered to be pre-eminent among the birds, and Charlemagne is said to have adopted an eagle as his device when he was crowned Holy Roman Emperor in AD 800. In the Christian church, the four beasts round the throne represent the four evangelists and of these the fourth, 'like a flying eagle', symbolizes St John. Until recently lecterns in the form of eagles were to be found in nearly every church, with wings open as in flight they carried forth the Word of the Gospel. The eagle's suitability for such a task is explained in the medieval *Book of Beasts*: 'When the eagle grows old and his wings become heavy and his eyes become darkened with a mist, then he goes in search of a fountain, and, over against

An Eagle displayed

Heraldic Crosses

1	*Cross-crosslet fitchy*	8	*Flory*	14
2	*Potent*	9	*Maltese*	15
3	*Patriarchal*	10	*Bottony*	16
4	*Tau (St. Anthony's)*	11	*Saxon*	17
5	*Recercely*	12	*Patonce*	18
6	*Fylfot or cramponned*	13	*Celtic*	19
7	*Formy or paty*			

1 *Cross-crosslet fitchy*
2 *Potent*
3 *Patriarchal*
4 *Tau (St. Anthony's)*
5 *Recercely*
6 *Fylfot or cramponned*
7 *Formy or paty*

8 *Flory*
9 *Maltese*
10 *Bottony*
11 *Saxon*
12 *Patonce*
13 *Celtic*

14 *Moline*
15 *Potent quadrate*
16 *Formy-fitchy at the foot*
17 *Fleuretty*
18 *Cross-crosslet*
19 *Formy-fitchy*

it, he flies up to the height of heaven, even into the circle of the sun [symbolizing Christ], and there he singes his wings and at the same time evaporates the fog of his eyes in a ray of the sun. Then at length, taking a header down into the fountain, he dips himself three times in it, and instantly he is renewed with a great vigour of plumage and splendour of vision.' (trans. T.H. White, London, 1954)

Medieval and Tudor magnates often possessed one or more distinctive creatures as personal emblems, culled from the pages of bestiaries or from the shadowy traditions of native art. Animal devices are found in early twelfth-century seals where they often alluded to their owners' names; the family of Swinford used a boar (swine), for example. But most of the chimerical creatures found in heraldry date from the fourteenth and fifteenth centuries when they were adopted as badges (see Chapter Nine) and were later translated into crests and supporters. Surprisingly few will be found on shields (see illustration p. 198).

Alphyn: a rare and curious creature, similar to the heraldic *tyger* but stockier and with tufts of hair on its body and a thick mane. It has a long thin tongue, long ears, and its tail is knotted in the middle. Sometimes its forefeet are like an eagle's claws and sometimes they are cloven. Occasionally, all four feet are those of a lion.

Antelope: usually described as the *heraldic antelope*, this creature has the face of an heraldic *tyger*, tusks, serrated horns, an antelope's body, a tufted spine and a lion's tail.

Centaur: a creature from Greek mythology, the centaur has the body and legs of a horse with a man's trunk, arms and head. When depicted holding a bow and arrow it is termed *sagittary* or *sagittarius* and may be found in churches where it represents Christ mounted on the horse of vengeance slaying evil or harrowing hell .

Cockatrice: a legendary monster, hatched on a dunghill from a cock's egg by a serpent. It is so venomous that its look or breath are said to be lethal to all other creatures, even from a distance, except for the weasel who will pursue it even to its den and kill it. At the age of nine years, the cockatrice will lay an egg on a dungheap and a toad will come to hatch it and produce, not another cockatrice, but a *basilisk* which is in every way as evil as its parent but also has a dragon's head at the end of its tail. So dreadful is its appearance that should it catch sight of its reflection it will instantly burst with horror and fear.

Dragon: originally, all scaly creatures with bat-like wings were 'dragons'. These were often depicted as serpents, without legs or sometimes with just two. With the arrival in the late medieval

bestiaries of a four-footed version, a distinction came to be made between the *wyvern* (with two legs) and the *dragon* (with four). The dragon probably entered British armory as the standard of the Roman cohort and remained in the symbolism of the post-Roman era and in the 'burning dragon' of Cadwallader from which the red dragon of Wales is derived. It is also associated with the ancient kingdom of Wessex and appears in the Bayeux Tapestry as Harold's personal device. The dragon was a symbol of sovereignty among the Celts. *Dragon* was the name for a chief and he who slew a chief slew a dragon. Unlike the dragon of the East, which is traditionally benevolent, the dragon of Western Europe is a malevolent and destructive power, symbolizing invincibility. It is often associated with water; the legendary *Gargouille*, a seventh-century river dragon who supposedly ravaged the city of Rouen, is commemorated in the water spouts of churches. The wyvern typifies viciousness and envy and became the symbol of pestilence and plague. Nevertheless, in armory it is used as a symbol for overthrowing the tyranny of a demonic enemy.

Griffin: the griffin is the most magnificent of heraldic beasts. It has the head, wings and talons of the eagle and the body, hindquarters and tail of the lion and therefore combines all the attributes of the king of beasts and the king of birds. The griffin was associated with the gods of the Minoan, Greek and other civilizations of the Near East. It was an animal of the sun and of justice and griffins are said to have guarded the gold mines of Scythia. In the Middle Ages its claws were endowed with medicinal properties (French *griff* – claw) and a griffin's feather could restore sight. It was sculpted in churches to denote the union of the divine and human natures. There is in armory a separate beast called the *male griffin* which dates from the post-medieval period. This has no wings but spikes protrude from its body like rays.

Martlet: in appearance, the martlet is similar to the house martin, swallow and swift, but it is always depicted without feet or claws. In the Middle Ages it was believed that these birds lived their entire lives in the air without ever having any need to touch the ground and consequently it has been suggested that they may be skylarks. Martlets are to be found in the early punning arms of the de Arundel family which are usually blazoned *Sable six Swallows Argent* (French *hirondelle* – swallow).

Panther: the heraldic panther is always termed *incensed* – having flames issuing from its ears and mouth. Although in appearance it is similar to the natural animal, it is depicted with various coloured spots on its body. In the medieval bestiaries it is described as being both beautiful and kind, and when it awakes from sleep 'a lofty sweet singing comes from his mouth and . . . a delightful stream of

OPPOSITE: heraldic beasts and monsters:

1 *Alphyn*
2 *Sagittarius*
3 *Cockatrice*
4 *Martlet*
5 *Male Griffin*
6 *Griffin*
7 *Dragon*
8 *Phoenix*
9 *Pegasus*
10 *Panther*
11 *Wyvern*
12 *Pelican*
13 *Salamander*
14 *Yale*
15 *Unicorn*
16 *Tyger*

sweet-smelling breath' that all other animals follow – excepting the dragon, who runs away and hides in fear.

Pegasus: the beautiful flying horse of Greek mythology has become the symbol of fame, eloquence and contemplation. A pegasus was the badge of the Knights Templar.

Pelican: the heraldic pelican is more graceful than the natural bird and is a symbol of charity, love and piety. Traditionally, the pelican is devoted to her young and is frequently depicted piercing her breast (*vulning herself*) in order that they should be revived by her blood. Thus the pelican became a mystic emblem of Christ, whose blood was shed for mankind. When depicted *vulning herself*, and nourishing her young while standing on the nest, the pelican is described as being *in her piety*.

Phoenix: the legendary Egyptian phoenix was believed to live until it was five hundred years old, when it became young again. When the time came for renewal, it would fly to Arabia and hide itself in a nest of rare, sweet-smelling spices which rose in flames when fanned by the bird's wings in the heat of the sun. The phoenix was burned to ashes but after three days a small worm appeared which gradually grew and became the new phoenix. Inevitably, it was adopted as a Christian symbol of resurrection and immortality and has been variously depicted – as a peacock, with a crest of feathers and long, sweeping tail, and an eagle – always rising from the flames.

Sagittarius: see *Centaur* above.

Salamander: the salamander is in reality a harmless little creature, possessed of none of the magical properties with which its heraldic cousin is endowed. It was believed that should a fire burn for seven years a salamander would be born. If frightened, it would exude a milky substance which moistened its skin and, so it was believed, could enable the salamander to extinguish fire. As an armorial device it is, therefore, always surrounded by flames and symbolizes enduring faith triumphing over the ardour of passion.

Tyger: the tyger of heraldry has the body of a wolf with a thick main and a lion's tail. He has massive, powerful jaws and a pointed snout. The tyger comes from Hyrcania where he was famed for his swiftness by the Persians who called their arrows *tygris* and who named their river after him. Females of the species were devoted mothers but could be tricked 'by those who rob the tygre of her young' who placed looking glasses in her way 'whereat she useth to long to gaze . . . and so they escape the swiftness of her pursuit.' Because of this fable, the tyger is often depicted looking into a mirror.

Unicorn: the unicorn appears in the traditions of many civilizations. The medieval unicorn of western Europe is depicted as an elegant and beautiful animal, like a horse but with cloven feet, a lion's tail, a goat's beard and a delicate spiralling horn on its forehead. It became a symbol of Christ because of its purity and virtue and to its horn were ascribed medicinal powers of healing and purification.

Wyvern: see *Dragon* above

Yale: in a twelfth-century bestiary the yale is described as being the size of a horse and having the tusks of a boar and extremely long horns that could be moved as required – either singly or together – to meet aggression from any direction. The yale of armory has retained the tusks and swivelling horns but its body is more that of an antelope than a horse.

During the post-medieval period (known as the Heraldry of the Decadence) many strange creatures were added to the heraldic zoo, often by the interbreeding of their medieval forebears to produce a singularly unattractive collection of armorial hybrids. Fortunately, most of these are confined to parchment, though a few may be discovered lurking in the ornamentation of Tudor houses.

Eight

MARSHALLING, CADENCY AND AUGMENTATIONS OF HONOUR

Yea, though I die, the scandal will survive,
And be an eyesore in my golden coat,
Some loathsome dash the herald will contrive,
To cipher me how fondly I did dote;
That my posterity, shamed with the note,
Shall curse my bones, and hold it for no sin
To wish that I their father had not been.

Shakespeare: *The Rape of Lucrece*

Marshalling is the correct ordering of armorial devices in a coat of arms to signify marriage, inheritance or office. Great care should be exercised when studying hatchments (see Chapter Five), the marshalling of which is often at variance with normal armorial conventions.

Hereditary Arms

By the late thirteenth century armory had assumed a significance additional to that of personal identification. Shields of arms were often arranged to denote marriage alliances, the acquisition or inheritance of lordships and the holding of an office to which arms appertained – that of bishop, for example. The most interesting of these was the practice of combining two or more shields to signify a union of lordships, though not all such arms were indicative of actual possession, some represent only a claim to possession.

An early form of marshalling is evident in several late twelfth-century seals in which a figure is depicted, sometimes in heraldic costume, between shields bearing arms of alliance. In others, a number of related shields were incorporated into a geometrical design, with that of the principal house at the centre.

Another early method of marshalling was by compounding charges from several different shields to form an entirely new one: the arms of John de Dreux, Duke of Brittany and Earl of Richmond, for example, whose mother was a daughter of Henry III. At Caerlaverock (1300) he bore a shield charged with the gold

Arms of John de Dreux

and blue chequers of de Dreux within a red border containing the gold lions of England and *over all a Canton Ermine* for Brittany.

From *c.* 1300 different coats were marshalled in the same shield of arms. At first this was achieved by means of dimidiation: the dexter half of a husband's arms being joined to the sinister half of his wife's to form a single shield (1). As may be imagined, this practice often resulted in somewhat alarming visual ambiguities and it was eventually abandoned in favour of impalement, by which two complete coats were placed side by side in the same shield, the husband's to the dexter and his wife's paternal arms to the sinister (2). (Presumably for reasons of clarity, *bordures*, *tressures* and *orles* continue to be dimidiated (3).) Impalement generally signifies a temporary or non-hereditary combination of arms, such as arms of office and those of a husband and a wife who is not an heraldic heiress but whose father is armigerous.

An armigerous woman who has no brothers living and no nephews or nieces from deceased brothers becomes her father's heraldic heiress upon his death. While he lives her arms are impaled with her husband's, but when her father dies they are

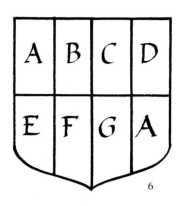

6

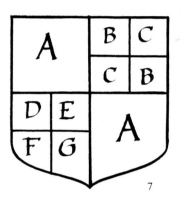

7

displayed on a small shield called an escutcheon of pretence in the centre of her husband's shield (4). After her death, her husband ceases to bear the escutcheon of pretence, and her children may quarter their arms by dividing the shield into four and placing the paternal arms in the first and fourth quarters and the maternal arms in the second and third (5). Thereafter, further inherited arms may be added in the correct sequence. When only three different coats are depicted, the principal coat is repeated in the fourth quarter. Once the number of coats exceeds four, further quartering is necessary and other coats are added in order of acquisition, with the principal coat in the first quartering and, if necessary, in the last also. Notice that the term 'quartering' is now used, and that there may be any number of these, not just four. Quarterings are numbered from left to right as you view the shield and from top to bottom (6).

It is important to remember that an heraldic heiress is one who inherits her deceased father's arms because she has no brothers or surviving issue of brothers by whom the arms may be transmitted. If she has sisters, each is a co-heiress, and each transmits her father's arms on equal terms. An heiress in her issue is one through whose issue arms descend when all male lines of her father have failed. It is possible, therefore, for descendants of the daughter of an armiger to inherit arms several generations after her death.

Quartered coats may themselves be quartered and in such cases the principal quarterings are called grand-quarters and the subsidiary ones sub-quarters (7). This method of marshalling, which is called counter-quartering or sub-quartering, continues in Scotland but not in England.

Of course, many armigers accumulated a large number of coats, sometimes adding ones which were already present in their arms through earlier marriages with heiresses of the same family. It is not necessary to retain all the coats that have been acquired in this way, indeed it is often impracticable to display more than four. Nevertheless, a nineteenth-century diptych, commissioned for Richard Plantagenet, Marquis of Chandos, shows no fewer than 719 quarterings accumulated by the family of Temple-Nugent-Brydges-Chandos-Grenville! (See plate 21.) But when a selection *is* made it is necessary to include those coats by which the selected ones were acquired. For example, were an armiger able to prove Nevill descent through a fairly humble ancestor called Brown, and thereby entitlement to the Nevill arms, it would be necessary to include the Brown coat in order to justify the use of the more illustrious arms of Nevill.

A widow continues to use her late husband's arms, but on a lozenge and without helm or crest, and with her own arms either impaled or in pretence as appropriate. If she is the widow of a peer she may continue to use supporters and the appropriate coronet of rank. In Scotland, a widow whose paternal family is not

Arms of the widow of a peer

armigerous may display her late husband's arms within a silver knotted cord or *cordelière*. If a widow remarries, she no longer uses the arms of her first husband.

A widower ceases to use his late wife's arms except on memorials and hatchments. If he remarries he may use the arms of *both* wives for commemorative purposes in the sinister half of his shield: either one above the other (with the arms of his first wife *in chief*) or side by side (with his first wife's arms to the dexter).

Unmarried women are entitled to bear their father's arms in a lozenge, but not his crest. A divorced woman reverts to her maiden arms which, again, are borne in a lozenge, and these are charged with a *mascle* (a voided diamond) to indicate that she is a divorcee.

Armorial badges, often in the form of chimerical and other creatures, were also acquired through inheritance and the transfer of seignioralties. These badges were often translated into crests and, from the fifteenth century, into supporters. Crests are hereditary and in the Middle Ages were transmitted through heiresses, though it may be that heritability was restricted to an heiress who transmitted also the headship of her house. Before the eighteenth century, only one crest was displayed in a coat of arms and it is likely, therefore, that a selection had to be made from a number of inherited crests. Presumably that of the most prestigious family was chosen and this would explain why so many ancient English arms have crests which appear to be unrelated to devices in the accompanying shield. It was not until the visitations of the Tudor period that crests became subject to systematic marshalling, probably as a result of the wholesale adoption of crests by the new gentility.

When, in post-eighteenth-century arms, two crests are depicted, the principal crest is placed in the dexter. When there are three, that in the centre is the principal crest, followed by that to the dexter. It may be that, where there is more than one crest, the principal crest has been granted as an augmentation (see below).

Supporters are hereditary only when granted to peers, other than life peers, and in effect they descend with the peerage. The sons of peers, even though they may use one of their father's junior titles, do not use his supporters, except in Scotland where the heir apparent is permitted to do so.

Occasional examples may be found of arms acquired through a Name and Arms clause in a will by which a beneficiary was required to assume the name and arms of a testator as a condition of inheritance. To comply, the beneficiary must apply for a Royal Licence within a year of the testator's death and the name and arms are then used instead of, or in addition to, his own.

Cadency

The first principle of armory is that every coat of arms should be unique – one man one coat. The requirement that different male members of a family and its cadet branches should amend their arms so that each might be identified is known as cadency. During the Middle Ages similar marks were also used to signify feudal tenure, elements of one coat being transferred to another for this purpose.

Since the fifteenth century, small charges (brisures), each appropriate to a particular male member of a family, have been used to denote cadency in English armory (see illustration). The three-pointed *label*, borne across the top of the shield by an eldest son, is discarded on the death of the head of the family, the heir using the undifferenced arms. Other brisures are usually placed centrally or at the top of the shield and may deliberately contravene the tincture convention in order do distinguish them from other charges.

In succeeding generations the brisure itself should theoretically be charged with a further cadency mark; for example, the third son

Eldest son   Second son   Third son

Fourth son   Fifth son   Sixth son

Seventh son   Eighth son   Ninth son

Brisures denoting cadency in English armory

of a second son would bear a star (*mullet*) on a *crescent*; the seventh son of a third son would bear a *rose* on a *mullet*, and so on. Such a system is clearly absurd and it is hardly surprising to discover that it has rarely survived the second generation. Brisures are hereditary to all legitimate descendants in the male line, though they may be dispensed with when arms are impaled or quarterings added, thereby making the arms distinctive from those of the senior branch. In blazon such charges are often described 'for difference'.

In Scottish armory there is no such thing as 'family arms'; undifferenced arms are borne only by Heads of Clans or Chiefs of a Family or Name. In Scotland it is an offence to bear arms unless

This late thirteenth-century Giffard effigy at Boyton, Wiltshire, illustrates the early use of the label as a mark of cadency

they have been matriculated with Lord Lyon King of Arms and entered into the Public Register of All Arms and Bearings in Scotland. But matriculation is not simply registration, the process requires the correct marshalling of the arms, together with the appropriate brisures indicating relationships within an armigerous family. Armorial bearings are succeeded to by the heir who may be an heir male, an heir female or an heir of tailzie (an heir nominated within the blood relationship) who uses a *label* which, as in England, is eventually discarded. Cadets, the younger sons of an armiger and progenitors of subsidiary branches of a family, are

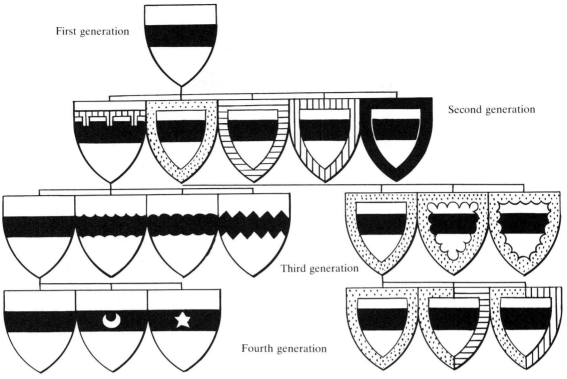

First generation

Second generation

Third generation

Fourth generation

Cadency: an example of the Scottish system

assigned amended versions of their paternal arms when they matriculate with Lord Lyon. These descend to their children on matriculation, again with appropriate differences. A system of *bordures* is used for this purpose by succeeding generations and this allows the degree of kinship to the main branch of the family to be shown (see illustration).

In England, with the exception of the royal family, women do not use brisures, for while arms may pass to a woman, this occurs only in the absence of male heirs, and since in theory it is always possible that a man may produce a son, even an heiress presumptive may not place a label on her arms.

In the Middle Ages a *label* of three or five points was usually the mark of an eldest son as it is today. But no system of brisures was then in common use and cadency was often indicated by the addition of minor charges or a sub-ordinary, for example. Care should be taken when interpreting early arms, for similar methods were also used as marks of distinction (see below).

Nevertheless, by the fourteenth century a distinction was made between marks of cadency and marks of difference which were used to avoid identity of arms between unrelated persons. In 1385 the Court of Chivalry attempted to determine which of two armigers, Sir Richard le Scrope or Sir Robert Grosvenor, was entitled to bear the arms *Azure a Bend Or*. In 1389 the Court pronounced that le Scrope should use *Azure a Bend Or* and that Grosvenor should use *Azure a Bend Or within a Bordure Argent*. But, on appeal, the king overturned this decision, stating that the plain *bordure* was a mark of cadency, intended to differentiate 'between cousin and cousin in blood' and 'not a sufficient difference in the arms between two strangers in blood in one kingdom'. He therefore annulled the sentence of the Court and Grosvenor thereupon adopted the arms *Azure a Garb* (wheatsheaf) *Or*.

A *bordure wavy*, to signify illegitimacy, in the arms of Wyndham at East Knoyle, Wiltshire. Notice also the *saltire wavy* by which the crest is 'differenced', the use of the *Petra Sancta* system of hatched lines to represent colours and the *crescent* cadency mark of a second son

Bastardy and Marks of Distinction

The historical concept of bastardy and the use of special armorial devices, marks of distinction, to signify illegitimacy continue to attract debate. Although in England such marks are theoretically 'abatements of honour' which 'debruise' a coat of arms, in the Middle Ages to be related, no matter how tenuously, to the Crown or to the nobility, was considered a privilege worth advertising. Neither did marks of distinction necessarily imply the illegitimacy of the armiger who bore them. Often they were intended to

Marks of distinction

indicate, not that he was personally illegitimate, but that he was not in legitimate line of succession,

Marks of distinction may be granted by virtue of a royal licence. If, for example, an illegitimate child can prove paternity, or if his natural father acknowledges paternity, he may petition for a royal warrant by which the arms of his father are granted, together with an appropriate mark of distinction. Subject to their obtaining a royal licence, adopted children may now use the arms of their adoptive parents which are differenced by a mark depicting two interlaced links of chain.

Contrary to popular belief it is not the *bend sinister* that denotes bastardy but the *bordure wavy* (2) which has been in use since the eighteenth century and which replaced the *bendlet sinister* for this purpose. Other charges have been used. The canton of Sir John de Warrene, natural son of the Earl of Surrey (1347), for example, which bore his maternal arms of Mowbray (1). In Scotland the *bordure compony* (4) is reserved to indicate illegitimacy. The *baton sinister* (5) (erroneously called a '*bar sinister*' by novelists) has almost invariably been used to denote illegitimacy in the English royal family, though there have been notable exceptions particularly during the Middle Ages when there were few established armorial conventions relating to bastardy. The Beauforts, for example, the illegitimate line of John of Gaunt and Katherine Swinford, following their legitimation in 1397, adopted the royal arms within a *bordure* of the silver and blue Lancastrian colours (3).

Augmentations of Honour

Augmentations of Honour are 'additions' or alterations to a coat of arms, usually awarded by a sovereign in recognition of signal service to the Crown. As such they are held in great esteem. They are of two kinds: the first, now rare, being granted 'by mere grace', the second being awarded in recognition of merit.

In the first category are augmentations such as those granted by Richard II to his kinsmen Surrey, Exeter and Norfolk, who were permitted to add the attributed arms of Edward the Confessor to their own. In our own century the grant of supporters to Captain Mark Phillips, on his marriage to the Princess Royal, may be regarded as an exceptional augmentation.

In the second category there are many instances, again down to the present century, of augmentations granted as rewards for acts of valour or service. Such augmentations seem to have existed since the earliest days of armory and may deliberately 'break the rules' in order to draw attention to the distinction.

Augmentations were particularly in evidence during the period of the English Civil War, and in 1645 Charles I empowered Garter King of Arms to award augmentations of honour to valiant

The Beaufort arms at Christ's College, Cambridge

royalists. One such grant was that to Dr Edward Lake who, for his services to the king, was given a quartering of honour which included sixteen *escutcheons* (small shields), said to represent the sixteen wounds the doctor received at the Battle of Edgehill. The arms of the city of Hereford (originally *Gules three Lions passant guardant Argent*) were augmented in 1645 with a blue border charged with ten silver saltires of St Andrew: '. . . for there hath not any city since this unnatural rebellion expressed greater fidelity and courage than the City of Hereford . . . the greatness of their loyalty, courage and undaunted resolution did most eminently appear when, being straitly besieged for a space of five weeks by a powerful army of rebellious Scots, and having no hopes of relief, they . . . defended themselves . . . with so great destruction of the besiegers that they became the wonder of the neighbouring garrisons . . . and therefore do justly deserve such characters of honour.' The augmentation clearly represents the city besieged by the 'army of rebellious Scots'.

Arms of the City of Hereford

There are numerous augmentations dating from the Restoration, made to royalists when 'the King enjoyed his own again' in 1660, and these record Charles's escapades as well as any historical novel. During the Stuart period the family of Churchill received two augmentations of honour. The first, *a Canton of St George*, was granted to Sir Winston Churchill for services to Charles I and the second to his son John, Duke of Marlborough, following his

Augmented arms of Churchill

victory at Blenheim, was *an escutcheon of St George charged with another of France* to be borne in the upper part of his shield.

Until the eighteenth century most augmentations were fairly restrained, but a general decline in armorial taste is reflected in several singularly ostentatious augmentations of the period. Perhaps the best known example is that of Horatio Nelson, who was first granted an augmentation of a red and gold *bend* charged with three exploding bombs. After the battle of the Nile he received a further augmentation of a broad wavy line (*a Chief undy*) at the top of his shield, to represent the sea, on which was depicted a landscape with palm tree, disabled ship and a battery in ruins! After Nelson's death a third augmentation was added comprising *a Fess wavy Azure charged with the word 'Trafalgar'*. Of course, all this almost obliterated the original and singularly beautiful arms of a black *cross patonce* on a gold field.

The converse of augmentations of honour, abatements of honour, probably never existed. Even so, they are to be found listed in several textbooks as a series of unusual minor charges (such as an *Escutcheon reversed Sanguine* (blood-red) signifying seduction or rape) which were placed over the other charges on a shield to show that a man had 'blotted his escutcheon'. J.P. Booke-Little, in

Augmented arms of Nelson

Boutell's *Heraldry* (London, 1983), confirms that '. . . there is no such thing as a mark of dishonour in English heraldry' while Fox-Davies (*A Complete Guide to Heraldry*, London, 1909), writing on the subject of 'stains', says that these strange tinctures were 'perhaps invented by the old heralds for the perpetuation of their preposterous system of abatements which will be found set out in full in old heraldry books, but which have yet to be found occurring in fact'. Characteristically, he describes them as 'pleasant little insanities'.

In practice, the granting of armigerous status could be revoked by means of a parliamentary declaration of attainder which was made after a judgment of death or outlawry on a capital charge. This resulted in the absolute forfeiture of all civil rights and privileges and was frequently applied in the Middle Ages in association with charges of treason. Attainder implied also 'Corruption of Blood' whereby the goods, lands, titles and arms of an attainted person could not pass to his heirs until revoked by parliament. Lands, and any rights in them, reverted to a superior lord subject to the Crown's rights of forfeiture. During the Wars of the Roses, acts of attainder were used by one side to liquidate the other, though it is interesting to note that during the period 1453 to 1504, of 397 acts of attainder no fewer than 256 were subsequently reversed.

Nine

LIVERIES, BADGES AND OTHER DEVICES

Might I but know thee by thy Household Badge . . .

Shakespeare, *2 Henry VI*, V. i

Livery and Maintenance

The term livery is derived through the French *livrée* from the Latin *liberare*, meaning to liberate or bestow, and originally implied the dispensing of food, provisions, clothing, etc. to retainers and domestic servants. In the Middle Ages the term was applied to the uniforms and other devices worn by those who accepted the privileges and obligations of 'embracery' or livery and maintenance.

Livery and maintenance, the practice of maintaining and protecting large numbers of retainers in return for domestic, administrative and military services, was common throughout medieval Europe and particularly so in England during the fourteenth and fifteenth centuries, when a magnate's influence was judged by the number of men wearing his badge and liveries and his ability to protect them when necessary in the courts of law. Some retinues were little better than brigands, terrorizing their lord's neighbours, seizing lands and bearing false witness against them in law suits, while others included the younger sons of the nobility, men of knightly and gentle rank and clerics who often possessed considerable administrative and scholastic ability.

The successful governance of the realm came to depend on the system which is now known as 'bastard feudalism'. Parliament was an occasional gathering and when not in session the sovereign needed to secure the cooperation of his subjects and, in particular, of the nobility through whom, in practice, he ruled the localities. This was achieved through the appointment of the lords and gentry to public office as (for example) stewards, constables, sheriffs and justices of the peace, and also through an informal system which relied on voluntary service and a sense of obligation and allegiance to a superior – often referred to as 'worship' in contemporary documents. The sovereign's principal subjects thereby enjoyed considerable political autonomy. Their power rested, not on lineage, but on wealth and the number and quality of the men at their command. They created retinues of indentured servants and others (often more numerous) whose support was based on patronage, who were employed to manage a lord's estates, to hold public office on his behalf and to settle his legal affairs. In time of war, or in their superior's defence, they could be summoned to array and many of the more senior members of magnatial households were themselves men of substance, capable of raising significant numbers of indentured retainers in their own right. Provincial political life revolved around these affinites and a magnate was expected to satisfy the aspirations of his followers. When he succeeded, his reputation (his 'worship') was enhanced and he thereby attracted more and better men to his service. Royal favour, and the ability to bestow offices, pensions and promotions on his followers, was, therefore, essential to the expansion of a magnate's influence.

With the parallel development of guilds and confraternities, following the granting of special privileges by Edward II, came a demand that every guild should have its own colours and uniforms, hence the rise of the livery companies, and as a result competition grew in both the bestowal and acceptance of liveries.

The ability of a magnate to summon to the field of battle large retinues of men whose allegiance was secured through the practice of livery and maintenance was a characteristic of the Middle Ages and a major factor during the civil wars of the period. This was recognized by successive sovereigns who attempted to legislate against abuses of the system, thereby reducing the effectiveness of the nobles' private armies: Richard II in 1392 and 1396 (at the same time increasing his own liveried retinue in Cheshire), Henry IV in 1399 and 1411, and Edward IV in 1468.

Ultimately, it was the Tudors who were successful, though by that time the practice of livery and maintenance encompassed several distinct offences and it is unlikely that any one act actually solved all the problems. Characteristically, the Tudors were also aware that, by judicious application of the law, the system could be exploited for pecuniary gain. By statutes of 3 Henry VII (which was intended primarily to suppress maintenance), 19 Henry VIII (which prescribed penalties for giving liveries to retainers) and 32 Henry VIII, the practice of bestowing a patron's liveries on retainers other than household servants was suppressed. But it was not until 1540 that the practice was finally abolished, and with it the private army, thereby bringing the Middle Ages to a close.

The widespread use of uniforms for domestic and military purposes is reflected in accounts of the medieval textile industry. In 1409, for example, the Castle Combe estate in Wiltshire passed to the medieval entrepreneur Sir John Fastolf whose patronage helped to establish an impressive textile industry along the banks of the local stream. From that time the community expanded into two vills: craftsmen with no agricultural holdings occupied the valleys of Nethercombe while those who were engaged in cultivation lived on the upper slopes of Overcombe. Fastolf succeeded in securing substantial orders for the local red and white cloth 'for the great livery of the lord beyond the sea' (the Duke of Clarence) and these continued from the invasion of France in 1415 until his retirement from military service in 1440. William of Worcester records, 'For the space of 22 years or more, Sir John bought every year to the value of more than £100 of red and white cloth of his tenants in Castle Combe. In this manner, he divided the rents and profits of his manors . . . among his tenants and clothiers of Castle Combe, and his doing so was one of the principal causes of the augmentation of the common wealth and store of the said town and of the new buildings raised in it.'

In the eighteenth and nineteenth centuries coachmen, footmen and other male household servants were often dressed in liveries – usually muted versions of the tinctures in a family's arms (grey for silver, oatmeal for gold, maroon for red etc.), with crested buttons and sometimes embroidered collars and cuffs.

In armory, the term 'of the liveries' (also 'of the colours') usually implies the principal metal and colour of the shield of arms and those first mentioned in a blazon. It is of these tinctures that the wreath and mantling are usually composed, though this was not invariably the medieval practice and today greater flexibility is allowed. The true livery colours (i.e. those used in the uniforms of retainers and troops) were very often at variance with the tinctures of the arms: Lord Hastings' liveries were purple and blue, for example, but his arms were *Argent a Maunch Sable* (a black stylized sleeve). Similarly, the liveries of John Mowbray, Duke of Norfolk (d. 1476) were 'dark blew and tawny' but his arms were *Gules a Lion rampant Argent*. The Lancastrian liveries were white and blue, the Yorkists' blue and mulberry (*murrey*) and the Tudors' white and green.

Badges

A badge is an armorial device but not part of a coat of arms. There are four types of badge, all of which may be found as decorative features in domestic and ecclesiastical buildings, monuments, fabrics, documents, artefacts etc.:

Livery Badges	(also known as *household badges*) which were issued in conjunction with liveries to retainers and armed retinues to be worn on uniforms and borne on livery flags (see below).
Personal Devices	for the adornment of clothing, jewellery, fabrics, furnishings and artefacts and for marking small personal possessions.
Insignia	issued to members of corporate bodies, such as

OPPOSITE: eagle badge of Thomas Bourchier, Archbishop of Canterbury (1454–86) and white hind of the Joan, Countess of Kent, 'the Fayre mayden of Kent'. From Fenn's *Book of Badges*

my lord *cantebery*

Thomas Bourchier
Archbishop of Canterbury
1454 — 1486.

as yt plese god

yͤ fayr *mayd of kent*

The. Fayr Mayd of Kent.

De Vere badges of the *cranket, mullet* and blue boar carved on the doors of Lavenham church, Suffolk

guilds and fraternities, and to members of orders of chivalry.

Badges of Office associated with specific household or corporate offices, including those of the Crown, government and judiciary.

Badges in the first two categories were essentially personal devices, often adopted for their hidden meaning (the enigmatic *cranket* of the de Vere earls of Oxford, for example) or in allusion to a name or title (a bottle with a blue cord was another de Vere badge, *de verre* being 'of glass'). Edward, the Black Prince, probably derived his nickname from the sable liveries of his retainers and his black tournament 'shield for peace' on which he bore the ostrich feather device adopted by his mother, Philippa of Hainault, as a punning allusion to Ostrevans which was held by the Counts of Hainault. Such devices were sometimes combinations of badges obtained through marriage and seigniorial alliances. An example of the former is the falcon and fetterlock badge of Richard Plantagenet, Duke of York. Political verses of the time suggested that this badge symbolized York's aspirations by showing the fetterlock (a manacle) open so that the falcon was no longer confined, as Edmund of Langley had borne it. The famous bear 'chained to the ragged staff' of Richard Nevill, Earl of Warwick, known as the Kingmaker, is an example of combined badges forming a single device. Two bears, each holding a ragged staff, appear as 'supporters' in the seal of Richard de Beauchamp, Fifth Earl of Warwick (d. 1439) and these passed, with the earldom of Warwick, to Nevill on his marriage to the heiress of the last Beauchamp earl.

Falcon and fetterlock

Personal devices were often adopted as livery badges which were worn on uniforms by domestic and military retainers. Muster rolls provide many examples and these are sometimes roughly sketched in the margins alongside details of the troops pledged by each magnate. The livery badge was particularly associated with those medieval magnates who were capable of sustaining military levies of several hundred men. Contingents from different estates would sometimes wear different badges, though on common liveries, and these would appear on the standards beneath which they mustered and the guidons which led them into battle (see below).

Tradition tells how Warwick the Kingmaker, in the mist-shrouded field of Barnet in 1471, mistook the Earl of Oxford's livery badge, a silver star, for the Yorkist white rose *en soleil* and ordered his men to charge at Oxford's contingent, believing them to be royal troops:

The envious mist so much deceived the sight,
That where eight hundred men, which valiant Oxford brought,
Wore comets on their coats, great Warwick's force, which
   thought
They had King Edward's been, which so with suns were drest,
First made their shot at them, who, by their friends distrest,
Constrained were to fly, being scatter'd here and there.

Drayton, *The Polyolbion*

As a consequence, Warwick was slain, Oxford fled the field 'and thereafter befell Tewkesbury, the murder of Henry VI, and the destruction of the House of Lancaster' (A.C. Fox-Davies).

Bear and ragged staff

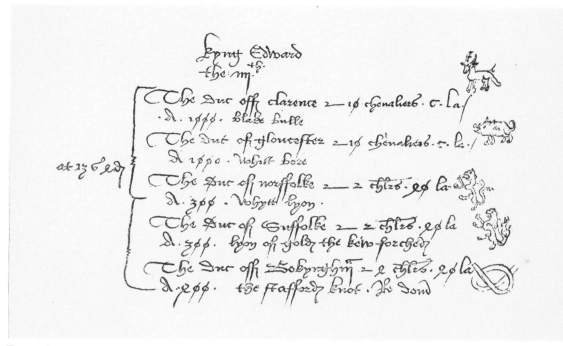

Extract from a muster roll of Edward IV's French campaign of 1475 with the magnates' badges sketched in the margin

The white boar of Richard of Gloucester in fifteenth-century glass at St Martin-cum-Gregory, York. Gloucester was patron of the church in 1476

Fox-Davies, in his book *Heraldic Badges* (John Lane, 1907), states, '. . . though [badges] were worn by retainers they were the property of the head of the family rather than the whole family. The likelihood is that cadets would render feudal service and wear the badge as retainers of the man whose standard they followed.' Typical are the mill-sail device of the lords Willoughby, the black bull's head of Boleyn, the fire beacon and chained panther of Baron Sudeley and the gold 'drag' or sledge of the Lords Stourton.

Perhaps the best known historical reference to household badges is in the prophetic rhyme imprudently circulated by William Collingbourn, sometime sheriff of Wiltshire and Dorset, prior to 1483:

> The Cat, the Rat, and Lovel our Dog
> Doe rule all England, under the Hog.
> The crooke backt boare the way hath found
> To root our roses from the ground;
> Both flower and bud will he confound,
> Till king of beasts the same be crown'd:
> And then the dog, the cat, and rat,
> Shall in his trough feed and be fat.

The hog was Richard of Gloucester, later Richard III, whose badge was a white boar (Gloucester's pursuivant was called *Blanc Sanglier*); the cat was Sir William Catesby whose badge was a white cat spotted with black and wearing a gold collar; the rat was

The fire beacon and chained panther badge of Lord Sudeley on a twentieth-century tombstone at Toddington, Gloucestershire

Sir Richard Ratcliff and the dog was Francis, Lord Lovel whose crest was a silver wolf-dog (*lupellus* – an allusion to his name) and his badge a gold padlock. The roses were, of course, the members of the royal house whom Gloucester was believed to have eliminated. Collingbourn was arrested and executed.

Many badges were translated into crests; Sir Walter de Hungerford, for example, combined his badge of a sickle with the *garb* (wheatsheaf) of the Peverels when he married the co-heiress of Thomas Peverel. Lord Hungerford's seal of 1432 shows both devices combined and borne as a crest: *A Garb between two Sickles* (see also plate 2).

Badges of Office were highly prized and were often incorporated into livery collars and other insignia. These are much in evidence in monumental brasses and effigies (see Chapter Five).

Crest of Hungerford

Livery Flags

In the early Middle Ages military command flags were simple lance pennons but, by the end of the twelfth century, senior commanders were using rectangular banners which were twice as high as they were wide. By the fourteenth century the banners of the nobility had become square, while the banneret (a small version of the banner) was used by knights banneret (who ranked between barons and knights bachelor) and the triangular or swallow-tailed pennon (which measured about one metre in length) remained the flag of the knight bachelor. It has been suggested that the tails of a pennon were cut off to form a banneret when a knight was promoted to the rank of banneret in the field of battle. Whether this was normal practice is uncertain but it is

Crown and hawthorn device of
Henry VI in the west front of
Bath Abbey, Avon

known that several knights, including Sir John Chandos (1367) and Sir Thomas Trivet (1380), were promoted in this way. Banners, bannerets and pennons were essentially the personal flags of nobility and knighthood, indicative of a man's presence in the field and of his hereditary superiority. They bore the devices peculiar to him and his family and these were repeated on his shield and surcoat and, in the tournament, on his horse caparison.

These personal flags accompanied armigerous commanders in battle, but mustering and rallying functions were performed by the livery flags; notably the standard and guidon which bore the liveries and badges familiar to retainers and soldiery (and of which their uniforms were composed) and national devices such as the cross of St George.

The medieval standard was usually about eight feet (2.4 m) long, but the Tudor heralds determined that flags of specific lengths should be prescribed to different ranks of the nobility. 'The Great Standard to be sette before the Kinges pavilion or tent – not to be borne in battel' was 33 ft long. A duke's standard was 21 ft in length, and that of a humble knight 12 ft. The shape of the fly was also specified according to degree, and crests and mottoes were sometimes depicted in addition to badges. Also known as the ancient, maintenance of the medieval standard was the responsibility of an officer of that name. Civic standards are sometimes hung in parish churches, as at Launceston in Cornwall.

The guidon was a small version of the standard, carried before a troop of retained men and essential as a rallying point in battle. It too was composed of the livery colours and bore a single badge but no motto. The modern cavalry standard is a direct descendant of the guidon and is often described as such.

Guidon (left) of Henry of Bolingbroke, with the white swan of Bohun (derived with the honour of Hereford from his first wife, co-heir of Humphrey de Bohun) on blue and white liveries of the house of Lancaster; and standard (right) of Richard of Gloucester with his white boar and Yorkist rose *en soleil* badge on liveries of blue and murrey

Heraldic knots:

1 *Harrington*
2 *Bourchier*
3 *Lacy*
4 *Cavendish*
5 *Stafford*
6 *Heneage*
7 *Hungerford*
8 *Bowen*

Knots

Intertwined cords in the form of slackened, symmetrical knots were particularly effective as badges. They are generally named after the families who adopted them and are often used in conjunction with other badges acquired through marriage or inheritance. Several have assumed somewhat spurious territorial designations as a result of their use as charges in the civic heraldry of a particular locality; the so-called 'Staffordshire Knot', for example, which was originally the badge of the earls of Stafford but is now ubiquitous as a charge in the heraldry of that county.

Rebuses

A rebus (*non verbis sed rebus*) is a pictorial pun on a name. Many early seals include simple rebuses and the concept therefore pre-dates armory. Rebuses were especially popular in medieval ecclesiastical circles and were widely used as personal devices and to decorate the fabric of buildings, chapels and tombs. At Milton Abbey in Dorset, for example, a stone corbel is carved and painted in the form of a windmill on top of a wine barrel (tun), the rebus of a former abbot of Mil-ton. At Canterbury, one Thomas Goldstone, Prior of Christchurch, used a gold flint stone ensigned with a mitre. Rebuses should not to be confused with armorial badges though many badges are effectively rebuses: the *talbot* (hound) of the Talbots, for example, and the *hirondelle* (swallow) of the Arundels. The term is also applied to the fanciful devices sometimes adopted by participants at a tournament who wished to disguise their identity, attributed arms being particularly suited to this purpose (see below).

Cyphers

A cypher is a monogram: two or more letters interwoven to form a symbol, sometimes ensigned with a coronet of rank and used as a personal or household device. Cyphers were particularly popular during the eighteenth and nineteenth centuries when the use of armorial badges was in decline and the new rich of the Industrial Revolution perceived a need for some means of personal identity.

Attributed Arms

The heralds of the medieval and post-medieval periods shared with artists and writers of the time a sense that the characters of 'history' were somehow familiar contemporaries. Just as King Arthur, Charlemagne, Prester John and King David would be depicted in medieval costume and leading medieval lives, so too

The cypher of a baron

Rebus of Baynton (a bay tree and a tun), on a late fifteenth-century tomb at Edington, Wiltshire

the heralds determined that, because all persons of consequence in their society were armigerous, so too were the characters of their religion and the heroes of legend and history.

Stephen Friar, *A New Dictionary of Heraldry*

Armorial bearings were devised and attributed to both persons and abstractions. The *Scutum Fidei* (the 'Arms of Faith'), for example, were devised as a symbol of the Trinity and consisted of

Scutum Fidei

a diagrammatic representation of the triune nature of the Holy Trinity in silver on a red field, this being the colour of rulers and princes. Religious concepts such as the Passion of Christ, the Precious Blood, and the Assumption of the Blessed Virgin Mary were provided with arms, as were the saints and martyrs, the apostles and disciples and the Old Testament prophets and kings. The early heralds were reluctant to attribute arms to Christ, however, the Instruments of the Passion – the *Arma Christi* or *Scutum Salvationis* (Arms of Salvation) – were frequently depicted on shields and clearly these were considered to be His personal emblems: 'that gintilman Jhesus . . . Kyng of the londe of Jude and of Jues, gentilman by his Modre Mary, prynce of Cote amure' (*The Boke of St Albans*). The Archangel Michael bore a red cross on a silver field and, not to be outdone, Satan himself bore arms (as a former seraph he was assumed to be armigerous) and to him was attributed a red shield charged with a gold *fess* (horizontal band) between three frogs, a reference from the Book of Revelation: '. . . three unclean spirits like frogs come out of the mouth of the dragon . . . for they are the spirits of devils.' The post-medieval heralds were particularly systematic, beginning with Adam (a plain red shield) and Eve (plain silver). To King David they attributed a gold harp on blue and to Joseph, not a multi-coloured coat as one might expect, but a simple black and white chequered shield.

But we should not mock the medieval mind. The need for symbolism was symptomatic of a desperate search for salvation. Great banners of Christ's Passion, the Trinity and the Blessed Virgin Mary accompanied the medieval army into battle and many a warrior emblazoned the *inside* of his shield with religious emblems in order to justify his actions before God. Our churches provide abundant evidence in glass and decoration, not only of medieval symbolism, but also of the continued use of many of those devices today.

Devices from the attributed arms of historical and legendary characters and of ancient kingdoms are much in evidence in the heraldry of civic and corporate bodies. The three *seaxes* (notched swords) of the kingdoms of the East and Middle Saxons, for example, and the gold *martlets* (swallows) of the South Saxons may be found in numerous civic arms throughout south-east England.

Identification of attributed arms can be great sport – but beware! There are instances of medieval tombs on which the attributed arms of a patron saint or religious concept are emblazoned together with inherited quarterings.

Merchants' Marks

There are, of course, numerous quasi-heraldic symbols which may be found on artefacts and in the fabric of buildings, both ecclesi-

Merchants' marks

astical and secular. Merchants' marks, for example, are commonly found in association with heraldry.

In the broadly illiterate society of medieval England, the ownership of trade goods was ascertained by reference to identification marks which were stamped on bales, casks and other containers or on the goods themselves. For safety reasons a consignment of items for dispatch by sea was often dispersed among a number of vessels. In such circumstances it was essential that the cargo should be properly marked to avoid confusion, and within the Hanseatic League merchants' marks on trade items were regarded as proof of legal ownership. A merchant's mark had to be recognizable, unambiguous and capable of being drawn, painted or scratched quickly. The majority of marks were built on the foundation of a single vertical 'stem': some combined a merchant's initials in an elementary form of cypher while others were runic in appearance. Merchant marks came to be used by non-armigerous men in much the same way as coats of arms were used by gentlemen. Members of the same family could sometimes be distinguished one from another by the adoption of small but distinctive variations in the family merchant mark, just as the cadet branches of armigerous families may be identified by the cadency marks added to their arms.

With increasing prosperity, merchants proudly displayed their marks in the fabric and artefacts of their homes and in the window

The Canynge tomb at St Mary
Redcliffe, Bristol

glass, tombs and memorials of the churches which benefited from
their patronage. They were often displayed within a shield for this
purpose; indeed, there are several examples of non-armigerous
merchants who, having married heraldic heiresses, impaled their
merchant marks with their wives' arms. The merchants who
attained armigerous status invariably continued to use their familiar and respected merchant marks alongside their newly-acquired
and less familiar arms. On the magnificent Canynge tomb at
St Mary Redcliffe, Bristol, for example, the family arms are
flanked by their merchant marks.

Although there were related classes of marks, indicating places of origin and craftsmanship (such marks were made on furniture and pottery, for example) there is as yet no evidence to suggest that the marks of merchants from the same guild, town or trade contained any common elements or were subject to any form of systematic registration or control, unlike those used by goldsmiths, masons and armourers.

Ten

ROYAL HERALDRY

Awake, awake English nobility!
Let not sloth dim your honours, new begot:
Cropp'd are the flower-de-luces in your arms;
Of England's coat one half is cut away.

Shakespeare, *1 Henry VI*, I. i

Royal Arms and Badges

Royal arms and other armorial devices occur frequently, not only in the ornamentation of royal and magnatial tombs and memorials but also in seals, stained glass, carved stone and decorative iron-work, illuminated manuscripts, rolls of arms, royal warrants and coinage.

It was during the reign of Henry I (1100–35) that the first lion was seen in England at the king's menagerie at Woodstock and it is probable that the king of beasts was adopted by him as a device. All Henry's descendants through his illegitimate children bore lions in various attitudes and sometimes combined with other devices. The coat of *Gules two Lions passant guardant Gold* is generally attributed to the Norman kings (see illustration opposite, 1) and it was the first Angevin, Henry II (1154–89), who added a third lion, perhaps that of his wife Eleanor of Aquitaine who is known to have borne a single gold lion on red. A shield bearing three lions (2) later appears on the second great seal of Richard I (1195) and was used thereafter by succeeding monarchs until *c.* 1340 when Edward III adopted both the style and arms of the kings of France (*Azure semy of fleurs-de-lis Gold* – known as *France Ancient*) which he quartered with the lions of England (3) to emphasize his claim to the French throne. These arms were modified slightly (4) in 1405 when Henry IV, following the example of Charles V of France, reduced the number of fleurs-de-lis to three (*France Modern*). This shield of arms continued in use until 1603 when James VI of Scotland succeeded Elizabeth I as James I of England and the arms of Scotland and Ireland (see below) were added as quarterings to those of France and England (5). These arms were also used by Charles I, Charles II, James II and Anne. William of Orange and Mary II used the Stuart arms with the arms of Nassau

The Royal Arms
of England

1

2

3

4

5

6

7

8

9

10

(*Azure billety a Lion rampant Gold*) in pretence (at the centre of the shield) (6). In 1707 the arms of Queen Anne were changed so that the English and Scottish coats were impaled (placed side by side) in the first and fourth quarterings with those of France and Ireland occupying the second and third (7). From 1714 to 1801 the first three kings George placed the arms of Hanover in the fourth quarter (8). The arms of Hanover are blazoned: *Tierced in pairle reversed* (divided into three) *1 Gules two Lions passant guardant Gold* (for Brunswick) *2 Gold semy of Hearts Gules a Lion rampant Azure* (Lüneburg) *3 Gules a Horse courant Argent* (Hanover) and *on an inescutcheon Gules the Crown of Charlemagne* for the office of Arch Treasurer of the Holy Roman Empire. From 1801 the French quartering was at last omitted and the remaining coats re-arranged: *quarterly 1 and 4 England 2 Scotland 3 Ireland and in pretence Hanover ensigned with the Electoral Bonnet* (9). When Hanover became a kingdom in 1816 the bonnet was replaced by a crown and in 1837, because Salic Law prevented Victoria from succeeding to the throne of Hanover, the Hanoverian arms were removed entirely leaving the royal arms in their present form: *Quarterly 1 and 4 England 2 Scotland and 3 Ireland* (10).

In Scotland, the red lion was probably a device of William I (1165–1214) who was known as 'The Lion'. A lion rampant within a *bordure* of fleurs-de-lis first appears during the reign of his son, Alexander II (1214–49) and the arms *Gold a Lion rampant within a double Tressure flory counter flory Gules* were first used in the Great Seal of Alexander III in 1251.

Although there has never been a separate title for the King of Ireland, from the accession of James VI of Scotland as James I of England the royal arms have included a quartering for Ireland: *Azure a Harp Gold stringed Argent*. The Irish harp has occupied the third quartering since that time, even during the Commonwealth when the other quarterings were completely changed (see below). Since 1603 the royal arms of Scotland have been marshalled with England in the second quartering and Ireland in the third.

From the reign of Edward III (1327–77) English sovereigns have born as a crest a *Lion statant guardant* crowned Gold. At first this was depicted on a red and ermine cap (chapeau) but Edward IV encircled the chapeau with a coronet which was later changed to an arched crown by Henry VIII and has remained in that form ever since (14). The red lion crest of the kings of Scotland was introduced during the reign of David II (1329–70) and was first depicted *sejant* (seated) in 1502 (16).

Several beasts have been used as supporters, many of which originated in the dynastic badges of magnatial families (see below). Richard II used white harts, Henry VI silver heraldic antelopes and Edward IV silver lions rampant (for Mortimer), as well as the black bull of Clarence and the white boar, a Yorkist badge which is most closely associated with Richard III, both as

11

12

13

14

SEMPER EADEM

15

16

17

18

19

Duke of Gloucester and as king. Henry VII and Henry VIII used the red dragon of Cadwallader and the white greyhound of Richmond, or two greyhounds. Henry VIII also used *a Lion imperially crowned Gold* together with a red dragon. Mary I's arms were supported by *an Imperial Eagle Sable crowned Gold* for Spain and her father's English lion. Elizabeth I used Henry's lion and dragon supporters, though the dragon was often gold rather than red (14). In Scotland unicorn supporters were adopted in 1440 and since 1603 the lion and unicorn in the English arms have remained constant, though their positions are reversed in the royal arms of Scotland.

Numerous badges have been adopted or inherited by British sovereigns and these will be found in the glass and fabric of royal palaces and memorial chapels and in the houses of those who enjoyed, or anticipated, royal patronage.

Henry II used the broom plant (*Planta Genista*) (12), which is clearly a pun on the name Plantagenet, as did Richard I who also used the star and crescent device later adopted by King John. Both badges were used by Henry III and by Edward I who also inherited a golden rose device from Eleanor of Provence. Edward II adopted a golden castle, for Castile, and Edward III used many badges of which a sunburst, a tree stock, for Woodstock, a falcon and an ostrich feather were particularly favoured. Richard II also used these, but his favourite badge was the white hart *gorged with a gold coronet* (11) which he inherited from his mother, Joan of Kent. The Lancastrian Henry IV used a monogram SS, a fire-basket (*cresset*), a red rose and the silver swan of Bohun, together with numerous other badges on liveries of white and blue. Henry V used a silver ostrich feather, a chained antelope with the motto DIEU ET MON DROIT and a chained swan. Henry VI adopted the chained antelope and added a spotted panther to the royal bestiary. Edward IV's Yorkist badges included the falcon and fetterlock (19), the sun in splendour (17), the white rose and the white lion of March, with liveries of blue and mulberry (*murrey*). At various times he also used the black bull of Clarence and the black dragon of Ulster and, following his marriage to the Lancastrian Elizabeth Woodville, he adopted a red and white rose *en soleil* (surrounded by rays of the sun). Richard III used the Yorkist badges to which he added his legendary white boar (13). The Tudors, with their white and green liveries, introduced the portcullis of the Beauforts, the red dragon, the silver greyhound and the Tudor Rose, a political combination of the Lancastrian and Yorkist roses. Henry VII also used a crowned hawthorn bush, with the cypher HR, to commemorate his exploits at Bosworth Field. Henry VIII added a white cockerel and Mary I a pomegranate for Aragon which she sometimes combined with a Tudor rose. Elizabeth I used a crowned falcon with a sceptre for Boleyn (15), a phoenix, a golden harp for Ireland and a crowned Tudor

rose with the motto ROSA SINE SPINA. James I inevitably introduced the Scottish thistle and a device which combined the Tudor
Rose and thistle beneath the Royal Crown with the motto BEATI
PACIFICI. The two kings Charles also used these badges, though
Charles II introduced several non-armorial devices associated with
his flight from Worcester, such as the oak wreath and crowned oak
tree. Thereafter, successive sovereigns made use of former royal
badges, notably combinations of the rose, thistle and shamrock
and crowned cyphers.

Royal Arms in Churches

The royal arms will be often found painted, and sometimes
gilded, on boards affixed to the interior walls of churches. They
were erected as tokens of loyalty to the Crown and obedience to
the sovereign as head of the Church, and consequently all but a
very small number date from after 1534 when Henry VIII
assumed the title of 'Supreme Head on Earth of the Church of
England'. Royal devices from earlier periods will also be found in
glass, furnishings, memorials etc., but their function is mainly
commemorative.

Church wardens' accounts suggest that, during the reigns of
Henry VIII and Edward VI, in many churches the royal arms were
erected on top of the chancel screen in place of the rood, or above
the chancel arch. But there is no known statute relating to the
practice and in one instance (during the reign of Edward VI) the
zealous curate and wardens of St Martin's in Ironmonger Lane,
London, were instructed to restore the rood and take down the
royal arms they had erected. Following the succession of the
Catholic Mary I, most royal arms were removed from churches,
notable exceptions being those at Westerham in Kent and Rush-
brooke in Suffolk. But the practice was again reversed by her
successor, Elizabeth I, for whom several examples are to be found
including a faded mural on the nave wall at Puddletown church in
Dorset. The practice continued through the early Stuart period
and in 1614 the Archbishop of Canterbury instructed a painter-
stainer to 'survey and paynte in all the churches and chappells
within the Realme of England, the Kinges Majesties Armes in due
form, with helmet, crest, mantell, and supporters as they ought to
be, together with the nobel young princes.' This directive, and its
reference to the future Charles I, may have encouraged the
appearance of boards bearing the 'Prince of Wales' Feathers',
though that in Sherborne Abbey, Dorset is dated 1611 and
suggests that the practice existed before the directive was issued.
(It should be noted that the so-called 'Prince of Wales' Feathers'
device is the badge of the heir apparent to the English throne, not
all of whom have been invested as princes of Wales.) In 1631 the
Archbishop again issued instructions that the royal arms should be

The impaled arms of Henry VIII
and Jane Seymour supported by
one of the King's Beasts at
Hampton Court Palace

painted or repaired, together with the ten Commandments and
'. . . other Holy sentences.'

During the Commonwealth (1649–60) many examples of the
royal arms were destroyed or defaced while others were taken
down and hidden or turned round and the Commonwealth arms
painted on the reverse. It seems that Protector Cromwell either
shared Julius Caesar's monarchal aspirations or that he acknowledged the transitory nature of the republic and recognized that he
held the monarchy in trust. Having refused the Crown, he
nevertheless incorporated the symbols of sovereignty in the arms
of the Commonwealth. The royal helm, crown, crest and supporter of a crowned lion were all retained, while the shield (*Quarterly
1 and 4 Argent a Cross Gules* (for England) *2 Azure a Saltire
Argent* (for Scotland) *and 3 Azure a Harp Or stringed Argent* (for
Ireland)) also included an inescutcheon of the Cromwell arms
(*Sable a Lion rampant Argent*). Significantly, the Scottish unicorn
supporter, with its Stuart associations, was replaced by the Welsh
dragon. According to Sir Bernard Burke, when Cromwell's coffin
was opened it was found to contain a copper plate engraved with
the royal arms of England impaling his own.

Following the restoration of Charles II in 1660, a statute
requiring that the royal arms should be displayed in all churches
resulted in many old boards being brought out of hiding and
repainted or new ones made. Wherever the Commonwealth arms
were displayed they were to '. . . be forthwith taken down; and
that the King's Majesty's Arms be set up instead thereof.'

Arms of the Commonwealth

The royal arms of Charles II at Milborne Port, Somerset. Erected in 1662, just two years after the Restoration, the legend is singularly apt

Although the composition of the royal arms was to change several times after 1660 (see above), royal arms in churches were affected only once more by changing dynastic fortunes. So concerned were the early Hanoverians with the claims of Stuart Pretenders that many Stuart arms in churches were repainted with those of Hanover. But the work was not always accurate, with only the fourth quartering being changed, and in some cases a painted canvas of the Hanoverian arms was hastily stuck over the board, as at Cirencester church in Gloucestershire.

The royal arms were usually painted on square or oblong boards or canvas, not to be confused with hatchments, though there are also examples in cast plaster, carved wood and cast iron and in a variety of other shapes. Most surviving examples date from the Hanoverian period, though all reigns from from James I to Victoria are well represented. There are very few from the twentieth century: those to Elizabeth II at Remenham, Berkshire and Shepton Montague in Somerset, are the exceptions. Many were moved from their original positions by Victorian restorers and dating is often difficult. Many have neither dates nor initials and dating by reference to the marshalling of the various quarter-

The Stuart royal arms of Queen Anne (d. 1714), superscribed 'G.R. 1715' for George I, whose arms should include those of Hanover in the fourth quarter

ings is not always conclusive. One combination was used by Queen Anne for only seven years and yet, following her death in 1714, the Hanoverian royal arms remained unchanged for eighty-seven years. Even examples with initials or dates must be treated with caution as they may have been altered; J (James) or C (Charles) were often changed to G (George) but their Stuart origins may still be evident in the floreated form of the initials. Similarly, dates may commemorate an alteration rather than the original painting and with careful examination the old date may be found painted out beneath the new. Churchwardens' accounts often provide invaluable information concerning the construction, repair and re-painting of royal arms in churches. Boards dating from the early nineteenth century are almost invariably characterized by the emasculation of the lion and unicorn supporters which, unlike their virile predecessors, are rarely *sexed*, *pizzled* or *coded*.

Royal Warrant Holders

A warrant is a written authorization to receive or supply money, goods or services or to carry out a course of action such as an arrest or search. The most familiar warrant is that which is issued in respect of personal services or the provision of goods to the sovereign or to members of the royal family. Henry II is believed to have initiated such a system and from the mid-twelfth century royal warrants were granted collectively to trade guilds such as the weavers, drapers and mercers. Although the practice was well-established by the reign of Elizabeth I, it is unlikely that warrant-holders were at that time permitted to display the royal arms as an indication of patronage as they are today. By the eighteenth century the majority of warrant-holders were in the cities of London and Westminster and in towns where there were royal residences such as Edinburgh and Windsor. The *Royal Kalendar* included such worthies as the Royal Rat-Catcher and the Royal Mole-Taker though, in 1775, a disgruntled Andrew Cooke complained that he had been omitted as Royal Bug-Taker, even though he had 'cured' some 16,000 beds 'with great applause'. In the late eighteenth century warrant-holders were permitted to use the royal arms (or the Ostrich Feathers device of the Heir Apparent) for promotional purposes; by means of discreet advertisements in newspapers, in books and on trade cards, for example. As the nineteenth century progressed, warrants were granted for specific products as well as general services to the sovereign and his family. Such warrants were granted under oath and by the Board of the Green Cloth, but the system was revised in Victoria's reign when responsibility passed to the Lord Chamberlain's office and the Royal Household Tradesmen's Warrants Committee. By the early nineteenth century a standard form of the royal arms, often fashioned in Coade stone, was to be found, not only above the shop fronts of warrant-holders, but also in many churches. A royal warrant lapses at the death of the member of the royal family in whose name it was granted, though the grantee may continue to use the phrase 'By appointment to His [or Her] Late Majesty', but, since 1978, not the coat of arms. The Royal Warrant Holders' Association received a royal charter in 1907 and today about one thousand firms enjoy the privilege of displaying the royal arms. They are listed in Debrett's *Alphabetical List of Royal Warrant Holders*.

Coinage

In 1344 Edward III (1327–77) introduced three gold coins, the florin (30p), the half-florin and quarter-florin, and these were the first coins to incorporate truly armorial designs. The obverse of the florin or double leopard, which was based on a Florentine gold coin, depicted the king enthroned beneath a canopy (the majesty), flanked by two leopards, on a field of fleurs-de-lis. The half-florin or leopard has a rather strange crowned *lion passant*, wearing as a cloak the banner of the quartered arms of England and, on the reverse, a cross within a *quatrefoil*, in the angles of which are further leopards. (A lion which was considered to behave in the

manner of a leopard was described by the early heralds as
leopardé.) The quarter-florin or helm depicted a helmet, chapeau
and royal crest of a crowned *lion statant*, all on a field of
fleurs-de-lis. Also in 1344 the Royal Mint issued further gold coins:
the noble (33.3p), half-noble and quarter-noble. The noble, which
replaced the short-lived leopard, was a fine coin with, on the
obverse, the king standing crowned and armed in the midst of a
ship and with a biblical text inscribed on the edge to discourage
clipping (the removal and melting down of small quantities of
precious metals). The design included, for the first time, the
quartered shield of arms of an English sovereign (here, held by the
figure of the king) and this continued to appear exclusively on the
gold coinage.

The noble was replaced in 1464 by a gold coin known as the
angel (33.3p) which had the Archangel Michael depicted on its
obverse. (The angel was pierced by a hole and was widely used as a
'touch-piece' to induce good health.) There was also a half-angel,
called an angelet, and further gold coins, the ryal (50p) and
half-ryal, were introduced by Edward IV (1461–83) in 1464. The
royal shield of arms appears in all these coins: in the noble and ryal
it is held by the king, and in the angel and half angel it is suspended
from the side of a ship. During the reign of Edward IV personal
and ecclesiastical devices (such as the Bourchier knot and the
pallium) appear for the first time, on coins minted at the metropo-
litan furnaces at Canterbury, as a gesture to Archbishop Bourchier
who had been such a staunch supporter of his king.

Gold coins continued to be minted until the Great War
(1914–18) and one of the most splendid of these was the sovereign
of Henry VII (1485–1509). It weighed 240 grains, was valued at
twenty shillings and was a large thin coin with a majesty on the
obverse and a Tudor rose and royal arms on the reverse. Type III
sovereigns show the king on a highly ornamented high-backed
throne, with his greyhound and dragon supporters on flanking
pillars. Some coins of the period had the Beaufort portcullis badge
at the king's feet, and the royal arms now appeared on silver
coinage. The Renaissance clearly influenced the design of coins
from that time, the portrait of Henry VII on the famous testoon
(5p) coin of 1504 (later called the shilling), designed by a German
die-sinker called Alexander Bruchsal, being one of the finest royal
portraits ever to appear on British coinage. The obverse of the
1489 penny was redesigned to show the enthroned king holding the
orb and sceptre, and a long cross quartered the royal arms on the
reverse. The posthumous coinage of Henry VIII incorporated a
crown above the shield and royal lion and dragon supporters.
Some of Henry VIII's coins were minted of inferior alloy of silver
and copper and the silver on the tip of the nose on the king's
portrait wore thin so that he thereby acquired the appellation 'Old
Coppernose'. Gold crowns (22.5p) and half-crowns were issued
from 1526 and those of Henry's son, Edward VI (1547–53), show

English gold coins:
1 Henry III halfpenny
2 Edward III noble
3 Henry VI half-angel
4 Henry VII sovereign
5 Charles II guinea

him mounted on horseback, a rarity in British coins. Four new denominations of silver coin were added during Edward's short reign – the crown, half-crown, sixpence and threepence – each of which had a similar reverse to the silver coins of previous Tudors. The shillings of Edward VI were inscribed with the date of minting, but in Roman numerals (MDXLIX), the dates beneath his equestrian portrait on the crowns and half-crowns of 1551 being in Arabic numerals. Mint marks were often depicted on English coins, at the termination of the legend, to identify where a particular coin was minted. As medieval coins were not dated, a mint mark may help to confirm a period of manufacture. Other marks may indicate the workshop in which a coin was made or even a particular craftsman.

Edward VI's half-sister, Mary (1553–58), married Philip of Spain and their heads appeared in profile facing one another on the obverse of shillings, thus – 'Still amorous and fond of billing / Like Philip and Mary on a shilling'. The silver coins of Philip and Mary had an oval shield of the impaled arms of England and Spain on the reverse. The coins of Elizabeth I (1558–1603) reverted to the former quarterings of French fleurs-de-lis and English lions, but the sovereign, which, by this time was valued at thirty shillings, was discontinued by James I in favour of the unite which now included the Scottish lion and Irish harp. Various royal badges appeared on silver coinage: a portcullis on the obverse of the silver halfpenny and a crowned rose on the halfgroat with a crowned thistle on the reverse, for example.

Charles I (1625–49) continued to use the royal arms, now within a cartouche, notably on the gold unite and crown, and a ship with the Stuart arms on the sail on the reverse of the angel. A particularly fine coin was the silver crown, on the obverse of which was an equestrian figure of the king, his sword raised and the horse caparisoned, with the royal arms within a cartouche on the reverse. The so-called 'Prince of Wales Feathers' device appears on several coins of this reign, as an adjunct to the royal arms or equestrian figure or, as on the silver penny and halfpenny, by itself.

During the Civil War coins were struck at a number of towns to supply those areas of the country which remained under royal control. At the mint at Combe Martin, for example, a half-crown of 1645 depicts a crowned shield encircled by the Garter and motto *HONI SOIT QUI MAL Y PENSE*, with lion and unicorn supporters.

In 1649, after the execution of Charles I, Parliament ordered gold and silver coins to be struck with English inscriptions instead of Latin, and no portraits. On the obverse of larger coins was a shield of the cross of St George within a laurel wreath and the legend THE COMMONWEALTH AND ENGLAND. On the reverse, the shields of St George and the harp of Ireland were depicted side by side, with the words GOD WITH US. On the halfpenny, the shield of St George was on the obverse and that of Ireland on the reverse, this being the only example of a coat of arms on a copper coin. Protector Cromwell intended to mint a very fine set of new coins but few seem to have been circulated. Significantly, these incorporated the royal crown together with Cromwell's personal arms which were depicted at the centre of a shield comprising the crosses of St George and St Andrew and the Irish harp.

A number of new coins were introduced following the Restoration in 1660 and, from the introduction of milled coinage in 1662, the quarterings of the Stuart arms were depicted on four separate shields (England, Scotland, France and Ireland) in a cruciform shape with the Garter Star at the centre. Variations of this design were to appear on common coinage down to the 1931 florin, and even later on special issues. Among these new coins was the guinea, valued at that time at twenty shillings and named after the Guinea Coast of west Africa from where the Africa Company imported gold for the new coinage. There were also five and four guinea pieces and a half-guinea. It became fashionable for professional fees to be reckoned in guineas which later were valued at twenty-one shillings (105p). Silver fourpence, threepence and twopence coins were also issued for general circulation and these, with the penny, became the traditional coins of the Maundy ceremonies. Those of Charles II's reign (1660–85) had crowned cyphers composed of interlaced letters C.

The cruciform pattern of four shields was continued on the larger gold and silver coins of successive reigns from James II (1685–8) through to George I (1714–27), and on the silver sixpence of George II (1726–60) and the shilling of George III (1760–1820). During this period, several versions of the royal arms were also used, notably on the half-crown of William and Mary (1688–94) and on gold coins of George II and George III.

A change to a gold standard and regular 'token' silver in 1816 resulted in coins which were made with an intrinsic value lower than their face value. A complete recoinage took place and beautiful versions of the Hanoverian arms appeared on the gold half-sovereign, the silver half-crown and shilling, the shield on the 1816 half-crown being surrounded by a fine representation of the collar of the Order of the Garter. The silver half-crown of 1824–6 (George IV, 1820–30) is surmounted by a barred, forward-facing helm with the royal crown and mantling and the motto *DIEU ET MON DROIT* on a scroll beneath the shield and, in common with several earlier proof coins, the silver half-crown of William IV (1830–7) has the royal arms depicted on a mantle, or ceremonial cloak.

On the first day of January 1877, Queen Victoria (1837–1901) was proclaimed Empress of India and the letters *IND IMP (Indiae Imperatrix)* added to her other titles on coinage. These remained (as *Indiae Imperator*) until 1947 when India and Pakistan gained their independence. Various designs from previous reigns were reintroduced on 'Jubilee' coinage. The florin and double florin, for example, had four crowned shields between four sceptres, surmounted by *crosses formy*, harp and thistle and with the Garter Star at the centre. The shield of the sovereign of the 'Young Head' series was ensigned by a royal crown, the whole within a laurel wreath, and the same design was used on the crown piece. The beautiful 'Gothic' crown of 1847 incorporated the badges of England, Scotland and Ireland (the rose, thistle and shamrock respectively) and, on the half-crown of the 'Veiled Head' series, the shield was spade-shaped, ensigned with the royal crown and encircled by the collar of the Order of the Garter.

APPENDIX I

Further Reading

See Chapter Three for medieval treatises and early printed books on heraldry.

The following works, several of which are concerned with related subjects, remain in print or are available through most public libraries.

Andrews, S., *Crested China, the History of Heraldic Souvenir Ware.* Ascot, 1980

Archer, M., *English Stained Glass.* Michael Joseph, 1985

Barber, R. and Barker, J., *Tournaments.* Woodbridge, Boydell and Brewer, 1989

Bernstein, D., *The Mystery of the Bayeux Tapestry*, Batsford, 1986

Billings, M., *The Cross and the Crescent.* BBC, 1987

Birch, W. de G., *Catalogue of Seals in the Department of Manuscripts in the British Museum.* 6 vols., London, 1887–1900

Bouquet, A.C., *Church Brasses.* Batsford, 1956

Boutell, C., *Boutell's Heraldry.* 1863 (revised J.P. Brooke-Little), Warne, 1983

Brault, G., *Early Blazon.* Oxford, Clarendon Press, 1972

Briggs, G., *Civic and Corporate Heraldry.* Marlborough, Heraldry Today, 1971

Brooke-Little, J., *Royal Heraldry: Beasts and Badges of Britain.* Macdonald, 1981

——, *An Heraldic Alphabet.* Robson Books, 1985

Burke, Sir B., *The General Armory of England, Ireland, Scotland and Wales.* 1842 (revised to 1884 and reprinted by Heraldry Today, Marlborough, 1984). A flawed but essential reference work – see Chapter 7

Burke's Family Index. Burke Publishing Co. Ltd. A comprehensive listing of the families which have appeared in the Burke's publications since 1826 and bibliography of all Burke's publications

Burman, E., *The Templars, Knights of God.* Wellingborough, Crucible, 1986

Campbell, L. and Steer, Dr F., *A Catalogue of Manuscripts in the College of Arms Collections.* Volumes 1 & 2, London, 1988

Chesshyre, H., *The Identification of Coats of Arms on British Silver.* Hawkslure Publications, 1978

Chesshyre, H., and Ailes, A. *Heralds of Today*. Gerrards Cross, Van Duren, 1986

Chesshyre, H., and Woodcock, T., *Dictionary of British Arms. Medieval Ordinary* Vol. 1 (1992)

Child, H., *Heraldic Design*. G. Bell & Sons Ltd, 1979

Coales, J., *The Earliest English Brasses 1270–1350*. Monumental Brass Society, 1987

Cokayne, G.E., *Complete Baronetage*. 1906 (reprinted Alan Sutton Publishing, Gloucester, 1982)

Collinson, H., *Country Monuments, Their Families and Houses*. Newton Abbot, David and Charles, 1975

Contamine, P., *War in the Middle Ages*. Oxford, OUP, 1984

Cowan, P., *A Guide to Stained Glass in Britain*. Cassell, 1985

Debrett's Peerage and Baronetage, Debrett's, 1985

Denholm-Young, N., *History and Heraldry 1254–1310: A Study of the Historical Value of Rolls of Arms*. Oxford, Clarendon Press, 1965

Dennys, R., *The Heraldic Imagination*. Barrie and Jenkins, 1975. Includes excellent chapters on the early heralds, attributed arms, chimerical creatures and medieval treatises

——, *Heraldry and the Heralds*. Cape, 1982

Dirsztay, P., *Church Furnishings*. Routledge & Kegan Paul, 1978

Eames, E.S., *Medieval Tiles: A Handbook*. Faber & Faber, 1976

Ellis, R., *Catalogue of Seals in the Public Record Office*. HMSO, 1978

Elmhurst, E., *Merchants' Marks*. The Harleian Society, 1959

Elvin, C.N., *A Dictionary of Heraldry*. 1889 (reprinted Heraldry Today, Marlborough, 1969). An invaluable illustrated dictionary of heraldic charges – see Chapter Seven

——, *Handbook of Mottoes*. 1860 (reprinted Heraldry Today, 1971)

Eve, G.W., *Decorative Heraldry*. Batsford, 1897

——, *Heraldry as Art*. Bell, 1908

Fairbairn, J., *Fairbairn's Book of Crests of the Families of Britain and Ireland*. 1904 (reprinted, Heraldry Today, Marlborough, 1983). An indispensable means of identifying crests by reference to illustrations

Foster, J., *Some Feudal Coats of Arms*. Harleian Society, 1901 (available through Heraldry Today, 1984

Fox-Davies, A.C., *The Art of Heraldry*. 1904 (reprinted Bloomsbury Books, 1986)

——, *Heraldic Badges*. John Lane, 1907. Still the best work on the subject

——, *A Complete Guide to Heraldry*. 1909 (revised J.P. Brooke-Little, Orbis, 1985)

——, *Armorial Families*. (*A Directory of Gentlemen of Coat Armour*) London, 1902

Franklin, C., *The Bearing of Coat Armour by Ladies*. John Murray, 1923

Franklyn, J., *Shield and Crest*. Macgibbon & Kee, 1961

Friar, S., *A New Dictionary of Heraldry*. Alphabooks/A&C Black, 1987. A modern A to Z companion to armory, heraldry and related subjects

——, *The Batsford Companion to Local History*. Batsford, 1991

Galloway, P., *The Most Illustrious Order of St Patrick*. Black, 1983

Gayre, R., *Heraldic Standards and Other Ensigns*. Harlow Oliver and Boyd, 1959. Includes an excellent chapter on heraldic weather vanes

——, *The Nature of Arms*. Harlow Oliver and Boyd, 1961

Girling, F., *English Merchants' Marks*. Batsford, 1964

Given Wilson, C., *English Nobility*. Routledge, 1987

Given Wilson, C. and Curtels, A., *The Royal Bastards of Medieval England*. Routledge, 1984

Greenhill, F., *Incised Effigial Slabs*. 2 vols, London, 1976

Griffiths, R. and Sherborne, J., *Kings and Nobles in the Later Middle Ages*. Gloucester, Alan Sutton, 1986

Gyngell, D., *Armourers' Marks*. Batsford, 1959

Haines, H. *A Manual of Monumental Brasses*. 1861 (reprinted Blandford, 1970)

Hallam, E., *Chronicles of the Crusades*. Weidenfeld & Nicolson, 1989

de Hamel, C., *A History of Illuminated Manuscripts*. Oxford, Phaidon, 1987

Harthan, J., *Books of Hours and their Owners*. Cassell, 1977

Hasler, C., *The Royal Arms*. Cassell, 1980

Heald, T., *By Appointment: 150 years of the Royal Warrant and its Holders*. Debrett, 1989

Heim, B., *Heraldry in the Catholic Church: its Origins, Customs and Laws*. Gerrards Cross, Van Duren, 1978

Hicks, M., *Who's Who in Late Medieval England*. Shepheard-Walwyn, 1991

Hieronymussen, P., *Orders, Medals and Decorations*. Blandford press, 1967

Hindle, P., *Maps for Local History*. Batsford, 1988

Homes, G., *The Order of the Garter: Its Knights and Stall Plates 1348 to 1984*. Windsor, 1984, reprinted Cassell, 1987

Hope, W.H. St. J., *Heraldry for Craftsmen and Designers*. J.Hogg, 1913

——, *A Grammar of English Heraldry*. Cambridge, CUP, 1953

Howard, D.S., *Chinese Armorial Porcelain*. Warne, 1974

Howard de Walden, T.E., *Some Feudal Lords and Their Seals 1301*. De Walden Library, 1903 (reprinted Crécy Books, Bristol, 1984)

Humphery-Smith, C., *Anglo-Norman Armory*. Family History, 1973

——, *Anglo-Norman Armory Two*. Canterbury, Institute of Heraldic and Genealogical Studies, 1984

Huxford, J.F., *Honour and Arms*. Orbis, Buckland, 1984

Innes of Learney, Sir T., *Scots Heraldry*. Harlow, Oliver and Boyd, 1956 (revised 1978)

Jones, E.J., *Medieval Heraldry*. William Lewis, 1943

Jones, M., (ed.) *Gentry and Lesser Nobility in Later Medieval England*. Gloucester, Alan Sutton, 1986

Keegan, T., *The Heavy Horse, its Harness and Harness Decoration*. Batsford, 1973

Keen, M., *Chivalry*. Yale University Press, 1984

Kemp, B., *English Church Monuments*. Thames and Hudson, 1980

Knight, S., *Historical Scripts: a Handbook for Calligraphers*. Black, 1984

Laird, M., *English Misericords*. Harmondsworth, Penguin, 1986

Larwood, J. and Hotten, J., *English Inn Signs*. Chatto and Windus, 1866 (reprinted Arco Publishing, New York, 1985)

Lee, B. North, *British Bookplates*. Newton Abbot, David & Charles, 1979

London, H.S., *Royal Beasts*. The Heraldry Society, 1956

London Survey Committee, *The College of Arms*. HMSO, 1963

Lynch-Robinson, Sir C. and A.L., *Intelligible Heraldry*. Macdonald, 1947

MacKinnon, C., *The Observer's Book of Heraldry*. Warne, 1986. An excellent and inexpensive pocket book

Macklin, H.W., *Monumental Brasses*. 1905 (revised J.P. Phillips, 1975)

Maclagan, M., Humphery-Smith, C. and Pereira, H., *The Colour of Heraldry*. The Heraldry Society, 1958. Medieval brasses and effigies in colour

Marks, R. and Payne, A., *British Heraldry from its Origins to* c. *1800*. British Museum Publications, 1978'

Martine, R., *Scottish Clan and Family Names: Their Arms, Origins and Tartans*. Blandford, 1988

Messenger, A., *The Heraldry of Canterbury Cathedral, Vol. 1 (The Great Cloister Vault)*. Canterbury, 1947

Metcham, J. and Dreisen, P., *Techniques of Glass Engraving*. Batsford, 1984

Moncreiffe, I. and Pottinger, D., *Simple Heraldry*. Walton on Thames, Nelson (reprinted 1987). This should be on every bookshelf!

Morgan, M., *A Survey of Manuscript Illumination in the British Isles*. Harvey Miller, 1988

Moule, T., *Bibliotheca Heraldica*. 1822 (reprinted Heraldry Today, Marlborough, 1966). An indispensable bibliography of British heraldry prior to 1821

Nisbet, A., *A System of Heraldry*. Edinburgh, 1722/1816 (reprinted, Heraldry Today, Marlborough, 1966)

Norris, M., *Monumental Brasses: The Craft*. Faber and Faber, 1978

——, *Monumental Brasses: The Memorials*. Philips and Page, 1978

——, *Monumental Brasses: The Portfolio Plates of the Monumental Brass Society 1891–1984*. Woodbridge, Boydell, 1988

Oman, C., *English Church Plate 597–1830*. Thames and Hudson, 1968

Pacht, O., *Book Illumination in the Middle Ages: an Introduction*. Harmondsworth, Penguin, 1986

Papworth, J.W., *Ordinary of British Armorials*. 1874 (reprinted 1977 and available from Heraldry Today). An indispensable reference work, but one which requires a facility in the use of blazon – see Chapter Seven

Pardoe, R., *Royal Arms in Churches: The Artists and Craftsmen*. 1988, The Heraldry Society

Parker, A.H., *A Glossary of Terms Used in British Heraldry*. 1894 (reprinted, Heraldry Today, Marlborough, 1970)

Payne, A., *Medieval Beasts*. British Library, 1991

Peal, C., *Old Pewter and Britannia Metal*. Batsford, 1971

Pinches, J. and R., *The Royal Heraldry of England*. Marlborough, Heraldry Today, 1974

Pine, L., *A Dictionary of Mottoes*. Newton Abbot, David & Charles, 1983

Pine, N., *The Concise Encyclopaedia and Price Guide to Goss China (Companion Vol 2: Guide to Crested China)*. Cassell, 1988

Platts, B., *Origins of Heraldry*. Procter Press, 1980

——, *Scottish Hazard*. Procter Press, 1985

Potter, J., *Antique Maps*. Octopus, 1988

Pugh, P.G.D., *Heraldic China Mementoes of the First World War*. Cassell, 1972

Riley-Smith, J., *The Knights of St. John of Jerusalem and Cyprus c. 105–1310*. Routledge, 1967

——, *The Crusades: Idea and Reality 1095–1274*. Routledge, 1981

Risk, J., *The History of the Order of the Bath and its Insignia*. Warne, 1972

Rogers, Col. H., *The Pageant of Heraldry*. Seeley Service, 1957

Ross, C., (ed.), *Patronage, Pedigree and Power in Later Medieval England*. Alan Sutton, Gloucester, 1979

Rothery, G., *Concise Encyclopedia of Heraldry*. Stanley Paul, 1915 (reprinted Bracken Books, 1985)

St. John Hope, W.H., *A Grammar of English Heraldry*. 1913 (revised A.R. Wagner, 1953)

Scott-Giles, C.W., *The Romance of Heraldry*. Dent, 1929 (revised 1965). A fascinating introduction to heraldry through history

——, *Civic Heraldry*. Dent, 1933 (revised 1955)

——, *Shakespeare's Heraldry*. Dent, 1950, reprinted Marlborough, Heraldry Today, 1971

Seaby, H.A., *The Story of British Coinage*. Seaby, 1985

Siddons, M.P., *The Development of Welsh Heraldry*, Vol. 1 (1991)

Smith, D., *Maps and Plans for the Local Historian and Collector.* Batsford, 1988

Smith, J., *A Guide to Church Wood Carving.* Newton Abbot, David & Charles, 1974

Squibb, G.D., *The High Court of Chivalry.* Oxford, Clarendon Press, 1959

——, *Visitation Pedigrees and the Genealogist.* Chichester, Phillimore, 1964

——, *The Law of Arms in England.* Heraldry Society, 1953 (revised 1967)

——, *Heraldic Cases in the High Court of Chivalry 1623–1732.* Harleian Society, 1956

Squire, G., *Buttons: A Guide for Collectors.* Batsford, 1972

Summers, P.G., *Hatchments in Britain.* 10 vols by county, Chichester, Phillimore

——, *How to read a Coat of Arms.* Sherborne, Alphabooks, 1986

Tymms, W., *The Art of Illumination.* Faber & Faber, 1988

Uden, G., *A Dictionary of Chivalry.* Batsford, 1968

Urquhart, R., *Scottish Burgh and County Heraldry.* Harlow, Oliver & Boyd, 1973

——, *Scottish Civic Heraldry.* Harlow, Oliver & Boyd, 1979

Verbatim Report of the Case in the High Court of Chivalry of the Lord Mayor, Aldermen and Citizens of Manchester versus the Manchester Palace of Varieties Limited on Tuesday, 21 December 1954. Heraldry Society, 1955

Wagner, Sir A., *Historic Heraldry of Britain.* Oxford, OUP, 1939

——, *Heraldry in England.* Harmondsworth, King Penguin, 1946

——, *The Records and Collections of the College of Arms.* Burke's Peerage, 1952

——, *Heralds of England.* HMSO, 1967 (re-issued 1985)

——, *Aspilogia I: A Catalogue of English Medieval Rolls of Arms.* Oxford, OUP/Society of Antiquaries, 1950

——, *Aspilogia II: Rolls of Arms, Henry III (Additions and Corrections).* Oxford, OUP/Society of Antiquaries, 1967

——, *Heralds and Ancestors.* Colonnade Books, 1978

——, English Genealogy, Phillimore (republished 1983)

Wilkinson, F., *Arms and Armour.* Black, 1978

Williams, D., *Welsh History Through Seals.* PRO, 1982

Woodcock, T. and Martin Robinson, J., *The Oxford Guide to Heraldry.* Oxford, OUP, 1988

Wright, C.E., *English Heraldic Manuscripts in the British Museum.* British Library Board, 1973

APPENDIX II

Addresses

Details of provincial and regional heraldry societies may be obtained from the national societies whose addresses are given below.

The addresses asterisked house notable collections of heraldic, genealogical or related archival material.

Ancient Monuments Society, St Andrew-by-the-Wardrobe, Queen Victoria Street, London, EC4
Antiquarian Booksellers Association, 31 Great Ormond Street, London, WC1
Arms and Armour Society, 30 Alderney Street, London, SW1
* Bodleian Library, Oxford, OX1 3BG
Bookplate Society, 20a Delorme Street, London, W6 8DT
* Borthwick Institute of Historical Research, University of York, Peasholme Green, York, YO1 2PW
British Association for Local History, Shopwyke Hall, Chichester, West Sussex, PO20 6BQ
* British Library, Great Russell Street, London, WC1B 3DG
* British Museum, London, WC1B 3DG
British Record Society, Department of History, The University, Keele, Staffordshire, ST5 5BG
British Records Association, 18 Padbury Court, London, E2 7EH
Burke's Peerage, Eden Street, Kingston-upon-Thames, Surrey
* Burrell Collection, Pollock Park, Glasgow, G43 1AT
* Cambridge University Library, West Road, Cambridge, CB3 9DR
Central Chancery of the Orders of Knighthood, St James's Palace, London, SW1A 1BG
Chapel Society, c/o Council for British Archaeology (Northern Office), The King's Manor, York, YO1 2EP
* Chetham's Library, Long Millgate, Manchester, M13 1SB
* Chief Herald of Ireland's Office, Genealogical Office, 2 Kildare Street, Dublin
Church Monuments Society, c/o The Royal Armories, H.M. Tower of London, London, EC3N 4AB
Close Society (map studies) c/o The Map Library, British Library (see above)
* College of Arms, Queen Victoria Street, London, EC4 4BT (enquiries should be addressed to the Officer-in-Waiting who is available between the hours of 10.00 am and 4.00 pm, Monday to Friday)
* Corporation of London, Record Office, Guildhall, London, EC2P 2E
Council for the Care of Churches, 83 London, Wall, London, EC2
Court of Lord Lyon, see Lord Lyon King of Arms
Debrett's Peerage, 56 Walton Street, London, W3
Early English Text Society, c/o Lady Margaret Hall, Oxford
Federation of Family History Societies, The Benson Room, Birmingham and Midland Institute, Margaret Street, Birmingham, B3 3BS
* Fitzwilliam Museum, Trumpington Street, Cambridge, CB2 1RB

Friends of St George's Chapel, Curfew Tower, Windsor Castle, Berkshire, SL4 1NJ

Genealogical Office, Dublin, see Chief Herald of Ireland's Office

* Guildhall Library, Aldermanbury, London, EC2P 2EJ

* Harleian Society, c/o The College of Arms (see above)

Heraldry Society, 44/45 Museum Street, London, WC1A 1LY

Heraldry Society of Ireland, Castle Matrix, Rathkeale, Co. Limerick

Heraldry Society of Scotland, 25 Craigentinny Crescent, Edinburgh EH7 6QA

Heraldry Today, Parliament Piece, Ramsbury, Marlborough, Wiltshire, SN8 2QH

* Heralds' Museum, H.M. Tower of London, EC3N 4AB

Historic Buildings and Monuments Directorate, Scottish Development Department, 20 Brandon Street, Edinburgh, EH3 5RA

Historic Churches Preservation Trust, Fulham Palace, London, SW6

Historic Houses Association, 36 Ebury Street, London, SW1

Historical Association, 59a Kennington Park Rd, London, SE11

* House of Lords Record Office, Westminster, London, SW1A 0PW

Imperial Society of Knights Bachelor, 21 Old Buildings, Lincoln's Inn, London, WC2A 3UJ

* Inn Sign Society, 2 Mill House, Mill Lane, Counters Wear, Exeter

* Institute of Heraldic and Genealogical Studies, Northgate, Canterbury, Kent, CT1 1BA

Institute of Historical Research, University of London, Senate House, London, WC1E 7HU

Ireland: see Heraldry Society of Ireland and Chief Herald of Ireland's Office

Irish Genealogical Research Society, the Challoner Club, Pont Street, London, SW1

* John Rylands Library, University of Manchester, Deansgate, Manchester, M3 3EH

* Lambeth Palace Library, London, SE1 7JU

List and Index Society, c/o Public Record Office, Chancery Lane, London, WC2A 1LR

Lord Chamberlain's Office, St James's Palace, London, SW1A 1BG

* Lord Lyon King of Arms and the Court of Lord Lyon, HM New Registry House, Edinburgh, EH1 3YT

Manorial Society, 104 Kennington Road, London, SE11 6RE

Military Heraldry Society, 25 Davies Avenue, Roundhay, Leeds LS8 1JZ

* Mitchell Library, North Street, Glasgow, G3 7DN

Monumental Brass Society, c/o NADFAS, see National Association of Decorative and Fine Arts Societies

* Museum of London, London Wall, London, EC2Y 5HN

National Association of Decorative and Fine Arts Societies (NADFAS), Church Records Office: 131 Regency Street, London, SW1P 4AR

National Horse Brass Society, Orchard End, Farm Road, Sutton, Surrey, SM2 5HU

* National Library of Scotland, George VI Bridge, Edinburgh, EH1 1EW

* National Library of Wales, Aberystwyth, Dyfed, SY23 3BU

* National Monuments Record, Fortress House, Savile Row, London, W1X 1AB

* National Monuments Record of Scotland, Melville Street, Edinburgh, EH3 7HF

* National Monuments Record of Wales, Aberystwyth, Dyfed, SY23 3BU

* National Register of Archives, Quality Court, London, WC2A 1HP

Royal Historical Society, University College, Gower Street, London, WC1

Royal Society of St George, Dartmouth House, 37 Charles Street, London, W1X 8AB

* St George's Chapel, The Aerary, Windsor Castle, Berkshire, SL4 1NJ

* St John of Jerusalem, Order of, Library and Museum, St John's Gate, Clerkenwell, London, EC1M 4DA

Scotland: see Heraldry Society of Scotland and Lord Lyon King of Arms

* Scottish Record Office, Princes Street, Edinburgh, EH1 3YY

* Society of Antiquaries, Burlington House, Piccadilly, London, W1V 0HS

* Society of Archivists, South Yorkshire County Record Office, Ellin Street, Sheffield, S1 4PL

* Society of Genealogists, 14 Charterhouse Buildings, London, EC1M 7BA

* Société Guernesiaise, Batu Tegar, Delancey 1A, St Sampson, Guernsey

Society of Heraldic Arts, 46 Reigate Road, Reigate, Surrey, RH2 0QN

Society for the Protection of Ancient Buildings, c/o 55 Great Ormond Street, London, WC1

Society of Scribes and Illuminators, c/o British Craft Centre, London, WC2H 9LD

* Spalding Gentlemen's Society, The Museum, Broad Street, Spalding, Lincolnshire

* University College of North Wales, Bangor, Gwynedd, LL57 2DG

* University of London, Library, Senate House, Malet Street, London, WC1E 7HU

White Lion Society, c/o The College of Arms, London (see above)

* William Salt Library, Eastgate Street, Stafford, Staffordshire, ST16 2LY

GLOSSARY AND INDEX

Armorial terms, as well as non-English words, are shown in *italics*. Page numbers in *italics* refer to illustrations and those in ***bold italics*** to colour plates.

bar gemel

barnacle

beacon

billety

blackamoor's head

bouget

bretessed

Caduceus

caltrap

celestial crown

cinquefoil

clarion

cornucopia

cotised

couché

counterchanged

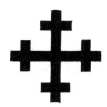

cross crosslet

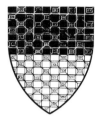

diapered

erased

displayed

dismembered

escarbuncle

estoil

fasces

fetterlock

fitchy or *fitched*

fleam

fleece

fountain

fret

fretty

gurges or *gorge*

in lure

in (his) splendour

jamb

jessant-de-lis

mascle

maunch or *manch*

mill rind or *fer-de-moline*

mullet or molet

pallium

panache

penner and inkhorn

pheon

planta genista

potent

rose en soleil

scaling ladder

Scotland, a bordure of

sea-wyvern

seax

shakefork

sunburst

trefoil

Tudor rose

vol

wool pack